MW01712125

STUDENT WORKBOOK AND STUDY GUIDE

Children with Exceptionalities in Canadian Classrooms

Sixth Edition

Margret Winzer
University of Lethbridge

Toronto

Prentice Hall

Copyright © 2002 Pearson Education Canada Inc., Toronto, Ontario

All Rights Reserved. This publication is protected by copyright, and permission should be obtained from the publisher prior to any prohibited reproduction, storage in a retrieval system, or transmission in any form or by any means, electronic, mechanical, photocopying, recording, or likewise. For information regarding permission, write to the Permissions Department.

ISBN 0-13-0915742

Acquisitions Editor: Andrew Wellner
Executive Developmental Editor: Marta Tomins
Production Editor: Susan Adlam
Production Coordinator: Kathrine Pummell
Cover Design: Amy Harnden

2 3 4 5 6 DPC 06 05 04 03

Printed and bound in Canada.

Prentice Hall

Table of Contents

How to Use This Book

Children with Exceptionalities in Canadian Classrooms deals with discrete categories of children with special needs and with special education. Each categorical chapter covers areas such as definitions and classification, prevalence, etiology and prevention, developmental consequences, and different forms of intervention. Inclusion in the general classroom is stressed both from philosophical and pragmatic stances.

This student workbook and study guide is designed to assist students to understand and learn a large body of knowledge. The workbook includes a summary of each chapter, a listing of key terms, examples of test questions in various formats, and applications and activities.

One way to learn about and appreciate disability is through a continuing portfolio. The theme of such a portfolio is not information as much as social and cultural perspectives on disability. Portfolios in this context are designed to challenge common assumptions and beliefs about disability through an analysis of the portrayal of disabilities joined to personal reflection. Tolerance and acceptance are the major aim. Each chapter of the workbook includes an item that may be included in a continuing portfolio that brings disability to the core of the study.

End tests at the close of each section draw previous information together. These end tests are cumulative—that is, although the focus is on the section just covered, material from other sections is also included. Answers are found in the appendix.

To use this book most effectively, students should:

- Review lecture notes and the relevant text chapters;
- Reread the main points as summarized in the workbook;
- Read the major learning outcomes for each chapter and reflect on whether these outcomes were achieved;
- Define or describe each new important term in the chapter;
- Complete the questions in the test at the close of each chapter;
- Undertake to complete one or more of the applications or activities found with each chapter;
- Complete a continuing portfolio on disability using the items that appear in each chapter;
- Complete the end-of-section test questions and score the test using the answer key;
- Review and reread if gaps in learning were found.

Section 1

Foundations of Special Education

Introduction and Overview

All children are special. However, **children with exceptionalities** have difficulty reaching their full potential. Their intellectual, emotional, physical, or social performance falls below or rises above that of other children. They have special needs related to physical, psychological, cognitive, emotional, or social factors, or a combination of these.

In the fields of medicine, technology, and psychology, recent decades have witnessed major gains in society's ability and willingness to assist persons with exceptionalities. For school-aged children, school districts have assumed responsibility for almost all educational services.

Special education is education **individualized** to the unique needs of a child with an exceptional condition. It is supported by related services, the services necessary for children with exceptionalities to benefit from special education.

Today's special education is a vital, exciting area, alive with the pulse of new ideas. However, many problems, issues, and movements remain prominent in current Canadian special education. Many of these revolve around the issue of inclusion or the location of schooling for students with special needs, how supports will be provided, and how teachers adapt or modify instruction.

As well as students with disabilities, contemporary teachers will meet many students who are **at risk**. These students have problems that make them vulnerable to a disability or to adverse effects on learning and behaviour. One way that teachers can assist children with disabilities or those at risk is through increased understanding of the conditions and associated factors. As the psychological, social, and educational factors related to a disability cannot easily be separated from the biomedical causes, teachers require an accurate and clear idea of the nature of the disability: its causes, developmental consequences, and prognosis. Teachers should have an understanding of developmental risk factors, the wide range of biological and environmental conditions that are associated with increased probability of cognitive, social, affective, and physical problems.

Chapter 1

Introduction to Children Who Are Exceptional

Learning outcomes

After reading this chapter, you should be able to:

- Understand and describe the difficulties found in definitions, classification systems, and prevalence figures in contemporary special education;
- Detail the pros and cons about the use of labels in special education;
- Explain the various modes of intervention with children who are exceptional;
- Recognize and explain the continuum of educational services and the service delivery models found in current special education;
- Explain the process and practice of Individual Education Plans (IEPs).

Introduction

All children differ from one another to varying degrees. However, in some students the learning difficulties are more serious, and the children deviate more significantly in one way or another. These are youngsters who are exceptional, those whose learning and behaviour deviates significantly from the norm. They may show differences in the physical, intellectual, communicative, social, or emotional domains, or in some combination of these.

The study of exceptionality

Because the child with an exceptionality is different from the average in some or many areas of functioning, the study of children with exceptionalities is the study of differences. However, children with exceptionalities do not differ in every way from their normally developing peers, and it would be quite wrong to focus the study of these children solely on differences.

Special education

One commonality found in children and youth with exceptionalities is the need for skilled **intervention** and special care from trained professionals. Intervention may take many forms: medical, technical, therapeutic, and educational.

Special education means instruction that is specially designed to meet the unique needs of children and youth who are exceptional. Special education requires a team effort. **Support services** refer to those services that permit a child who is exceptional to benefit from special education.

Definitions of persons who are exceptional

Although *children with exceptionalities* is the most encompassing term, children who have differences in the way they learn, respond, or behave are described in many ways.

Precise definitions and classification systems remain elusive. There is relatively little standardization in the field of special education; a single consistent and universally accepted method for describing the different kinds of children does not exist. Children with exceptionalities are constantly being reconceptualized, reconsidered, and renamed because:

- many disciplines contribute to research and intervention;
- each discipline tends to employ its own terminology and definitions;

- children with exceptionalities do not form a homogeneous population;
- a specific disability may produce quite different behaviour in different children. At the same time, children categorized as having different disabilities may manifest similar behaviours;
- there is considerable overlap among exceptional conditions;
- many children who are exceptional have more than one disabling condition.

Some important terminology

Exceptional is the most inclusive term, since it encompasses gifted and talented children as well as those who fall below the norm in some aspect of functioning. However, terms such as **handicaps**, **disabilities**, **impairments**, **atypical**, dysfunctional, **special needs**, and high-risk are often used synonymously with exceptional even though the meanings are slightly different. Children with significant disabilities may be referred to as **developmentally delayed**, **developmentally disabled**, having **special health management** needs, medically **fragile**, technology dependent, or severely handicapped.

Major categories of exceptionality

Considerable overlap occurs in the classification of disabling conditions. In this text, the special traits of children who are exceptional are grouped into the following categories:

- *children and youth with mild disabilities*, which includes communication disorders, learning disabilities, and mild mental retardation.
- *children and youth with behavioural disorders,* which includes conduct disorders, social maladjustment and delinquency, anxiety and withdrawal, and Attention Deficit/ Hyperactivity Disorder.
- *children and youth with sensory disabilities,* which includes hearing impairments and visual impairments.
- *children and youth with significant disabilities,* which includes a broad range from physical disabilities and impaired health to pervasive developmental disorders.

Additional qualifiers may be used to provide more specificity to these general classifications. Degrees of severity are the most commonly used qualifiers. Conditions are described as *mild, moderate, severe,* or *profound.* **Adaptive behaviour** is the ability to respond and function in the environment according to age and social standards.

Looking at labels

The use of labels for particular kinds of exceptional conditions is contentious in the field of special education and its related disciplines. While many researchers and practitioners see advantages to the **labelling** process, others hold that the practice offers few benefits to the labelled individual. Various arguments based on research findings and anecdotal reports have been advanced from both sides—those who wish to retain some labels and those who wish to eliminate labels altogether.

Some contend that labels serve as a necessary administrative arrangement for funding, for the provision of appropriate services, in simplifying information, in facilitating special treatment, and in promoting effective communication among those involved with exceptional youngsters. Others suggest that labels mean the presence of a permanent disorder. Labels often describe only an individual's deficits, overlooking the strengths and failing to reflect the educational and therapeutic needs. Moreover, people may base expectations on a label and view labelled individuals differently. In children, labels may deflate self-esteem and cause them to give up on learning.

Prevalence of exceptional conditions

It is extremely difficult to obtain accurate figures on the number of individuals who are exceptional in Canada. Figures are difficult to obtain because of definitional problems; changing diagnoses; the presence of multiple disabilities; the stigma of identification; and survey problems and sampling errors. **Incidence** refers to the number of new cases of a particular kind of condition identified over a give period of time. **Prevalence** applies to the total number of existing cases, old and new.

It is estimated that about 15.5 percent of school-aged students will require special education at some point during their school careers.

Intervention with children and youth who are exceptional

When professionals apply skills to maintain or improve an individual's functioning, the process is known as **intervention.** The establishment of educational and support services for young children and their families is referred to as **early intervention**. Intervention includes **habilitation**, **rehabilitation**, and **remediation.**

A variety of interventions are available for children with exceptional conditions. Generally, the greater the intensity of the disabling condition, the greater the number and variety of interventions required.

Medical intervention

Medical intervention includes surgery, treatment that is life saving, the controlled use of medication, and supportive therapy. Surgery includes a wide variety of procedures such as reconstructive surgery for cleft palates and orthopedic surgery for skeletal-system problems. Psychopharmacology, or drug therapy, is designed to manage problems of behaviour, activity, emotion, and epilepsy.

Therapy

The treatment of an illness or disabling condition is referred to as **therapy**. For children with exceptionalities, the major therapies are speech therapy, occupational therapy, and physical therapy.

Educational intervention

Education for children and youth who are exceptional is provided through a variety of arrangements and alternatives generically referred to as **service delivery models.**

Service delivery models

With a cascade of educational services, **educational settings** for children with exceptionalities ranges from the regular classroom to the residential school to homebound instruction. Placement in any setting is determined by the unique needs of a particular child at a certain point. But although a range of settings, as represented by the cascade or continuum of services, is still used, the inclusion of students with disabilities into general classrooms is becoming more prominent.

The major administrative arrangements and support personnel for children with special needs in Canada today are listed below.

- Homebound/hospital instruction designed for children unable to attend school, usually because of illness.
- Residential and special schools, which provide special education to specific groups of children. They may be day or residential facilities.
- Self-contained special classes, which are usually located within regular schools. Children with similar problems are grouped together and instructed by specially trained personnel.
- The regular classroom, which provides the **least restrictive environment** in that it allows the maximum integration of children with exceptionalities with their peers.
- Itinerant teachers, who provide individual assistance to children who are exceptional for specific periods during the normal school schedule.
- Consulting personnel, who fill many roles but generally do not provide direct services to children who are exceptional. Rather, they give assistance to regular classroom teachers and others involved with the child.
- Paraprofessionals, an integral part of the instructional team that shares responsibility in the area of learning facilitation.
- Speech/language, physical, and occupational therapists, who are important in special education services.
- Resource rooms, which allow children with exceptionalities to spend time with their peers in the regular classroom. Special help is obtained in the resource room.

Especially important is **collaboration** that forges a different relationship between teachers of special education and regular classes. Educational teams are a concrete manifestation of the collaborative process. School-based teams are designed to bring together all those who assist the student with an exceptionality in a collaborative and/or consultative relationship. One of the major duties of the team is to decide on both placement and program for a child assigned to special education.

Pre-referral interventions

In general, it is a classroom teacher who refers a student for special education, usually because of reading or behavioural problems. Before making such a referral, a teacher should attempt to change the environment and/or instructional practices in order to gather data on the student's learning and behaviour and to determine if special services are necessary, called a **pre-referral intervention**.

Individual Education Plans

The process of adapting or modifying the general curriculum and classroom environment often begins with an Individual Education Plan (IEP). Although formats differ considerably, most plans contain certain key elements. These are:

1. IEP data.
2. Placement.
3. A summary of the student's present level of performance across a range of domains.
4. The long-term or annual goals (a **goal** is a stated outcome desired as the result of some action).
5. Short-term objectives for each annual goal.
6. The specific educational and support services needed to attain each educational objective.
7. The personnel who will hold primary responsibility for specific long-range goals and short-term objectives.
8. The individuals responsible for specific elements, such as a speech therapist.
9. The anticipated duration of the services.
10. Specific evaluation procedures for each objective.
11. Procedures for re-evaluating the total IEP document.

Instructional practices

There exists no universal method or instructional approach that is successful for all students who are exceptional. A program should stress careful assessment, individualization of planning, modifications and adaptations of the curriculum and environment, and systematic monitoring of progress.

As just mentioned, the process of individualizing a program for a student begins with the development of an Individual Education Plan (IEP), which is generally drawn up by a team of educators. From a teacher's point of view, long-range goals and short-term objectives are the core of an IEP.

Social intervention

Child welfare covers a variety of services designed to stabilize noneducational aspects of children's lives, such as the family environment and the court system. Professionals involved include social workers, family counsellors, foster parents, **child advocates**, and many others.

Child advocacy

Advocates plead the cause of exceptional individuals. A major goal of **child advocacy** is to stimulate public and professional responses to identified needs and abuses.

Key Terms

adaptive behaviour
at risk
atypical child
child advocacy
child advocate
children with exceptionalities
collaboration
developmentally disabled
developmentally delayed
disabilities
early intervention
educational settings
goal
habilitation
handicaps
impairments
incidence
individualization
intervention
labelling
least restrictive environment
medically fragile children
pre-referral interventions
prevalence
rehabilitation
remediation
service delivery model
special education
special health management needs
special needs
support services
therapy

Practice Questions

Multiple-choice questions

1. Within the categorizations presented in the text, blindness and hearing impairments are classified as
   a. physical disabilities.
   b. health disorders.
   c. language disorders.
   d. sensory disabilities.
   e. pervasive developmental disorders.

2. Eight-year-old Sean has cerebral palsy, epilepsy, and is severely intellectually disabled. He has not yet developed speech and is in a wheelchair. Sean can be categorized as
   a. developmentally disabled.
   b. medically fragile.
   c. developmentally delayed.
   d. multiply disabled.
   e. all of the above

3. Of the following, which are considered to be high-incidence conditions?
   a. infantile autism and childhood schizophrenia
   b. muscular dystrophy and cerebral palsy
   c. learning disabilities and mild mental disabilities
   d. pervasive developmental disorders
   e. multiple disabilities and blindness

4. The primary difference between children with exceptionalities and non-disabled children is that
   a. children who are exceptional are unable to participate in most normal play activities.
   b. children who are exceptional develop more slowly than other children across all domains.
   c. children who are exceptional require skilled intervention in order to reach their full potential.
   d. children who are exceptional will always be dependent on society for their needs.
   e. all of the above

5. Mrs. Brown, a grade-four teacher, is working with Alan to help him learn to read through an alternative method. A general term for this procedure is
   a. remediation.
   b. rehabilitation.
   c. related services.
   d. therapy.
   e. diagnosis.

6. Major changes and reforms occurred in special education throughout the 1960s because of
   a. the normalization movement.
   b. a critical examination of placement in institutions, special classes, and special schools.
   c. questioning of the value of special education.
   d. a series of efficacy studies on just what special education was achieving.
   e. all of the above

7. The major reason that special education exists is to
   a. remediate learning problems.
   b. allow children who are exceptional to avoid competition with their peers.
   c. enable individuals who are exceptional to reach their full capacity.
   d. provide services not available in general classrooms.
   e. provide a "safety valve" for general classroom teachers.

8. In educational terms, children are considered exceptional only when
   a. they require all their education in the resource room.
   b. they require a full- or part-time teacher's aide.
   c. their educational programs must be altered to meet their needs.
   d. they suffer from a low-incidence handicap.
   e. all of the above are present.

9. Individuals who are developmentally disabled are best described as those who
   a. are slow or unable to reach many developmental milestones.
   b. suffer from chronic disabilities.
   c. have disabilities that are attributed to mental or physical impairments.
   d. suffer from disabilities that result in functional limitations for many activities.
   e. all of the above

10. In special education, intervention efforts are driven chiefly by the
   a. label assigned to a particular child.
   b. special needs of a child.

c. support services available.
d. structure of the general classroom.
e. availability of a paraprofessional.

11. The terms *incidence* and *prevalence* are often used interchangeably. Correctly, however, prevalence refers to the
    a. number of new cases of a particular condition over a period of time.
    b. total number of existing cases.
    c. prediction of the number of new cases.
    d. number of cases within a specified geographic area.
    e. distribution and determinants of diseases and disabilities within a population.

12. The author describes definitional systems in special education as characterized by "conceptual chaos." This results from
    a. the broad range of disciplines providing information and input.
    b. various classification systems.
    c. ongoing changes in terminology.
    d. new etiological discoveries.
    e. all of the above

13. According to the text, writing the first IEP for a child with special needs
    a. is largely guesswork.
    b. is precise, based on assessment results.
    c. can clearly detail the goals and objectives that the child will reach.
    d. is all that the child needs for success in the general classroom.
    e. is generally undertaken by the general classroom teacher.

14. On an IEP, present levels of functioning refer to
    a. the child's tested IQ.
    b. the child's performance in relation to other class members.
    c. the discrepancy between a child's IQ score and his or her score on standardized achievement tests.
    d. a child's score on standardized tests.
    e. none of the above

15. On an IEP, goals and objectives differ. We can say that
    a. goals are broad general statements; objectives are more specific.
    b. goals are always written for five years; objectives are written for one year.
    c. goals include all areas of functioning; objectives typically focus on language arts and math.
    d. goals are written in behavioural terms; objectives are task analyzed.
    e. goals are usually prepared by a school-based team; objectives by the classroom teacher.

16. Match the word to the definition.
    a. impairments
    b. handicaps
    c. atypical
    d. developmental delay
    e. medically fragile

___ significant pervasive delays in development
___ abnormalities of body structure and system function
___ children who fail to meet some prespecified norm
___ environmental or functional demands that a person who is disabled cannot meet
___ requires technology and additional medical intervention

Recall questions

1. Specially designed instruction for students who are exceptional is referred to as ________.

2. Two high-incidence disabling conditions are ________ and ________; two low-incidence conditions are ________ and ________.

3. Of low-incidence or high-incidence, ________-incidence disabilities are more likely to be identified in the preschool years.

4. Someone who pleads the cause of another or who defends a particular cause is a(n) ________.

5. Mr. Brown and the school-based team must prepare an IEP for Joe, a child with a visual impairment; for Cathy, who has a mild behaviour disorder; and for Leo, who has a severe language impairment. The IEP that will be the most complex and time-consuming is the one prepared for ________.

6. An individual's ability to respond and function in his or her environment according to age and social standards is referred to as ___________.

7. The study of the distribution and determinants of diseases in a population is known as ________.

8. Let's say that in 1964 there were two million hearing-impaired persons in Canada. During 1964, the worst year of the rubella epidemic, the number of affected infants was 1400. From these numbers, the incidence of hearing impairment in that year was ________ and the prevalence was ________.

9. Services that support and complement special education are referred to as ________ services.

10. Procedures that try to restore the individual to optimal functioning are grouped under the generic designation of ________.

True–false questions

1. The terms *exceptional* and *handicapped* are synonymous. T F

2. The general classroom is the least restrictive environment for the great majority of children with special needs. T F

3. Special education is an expanding field in Canada. T F

4. Definitions and classifications of children who are exceptional are fairly static and have remained the same for the past three decades. T F

5. Once a child is diagnosed with a particular condition, the diagnosis does not change. T F

6. A disability automatically limits all areas of an individual's functioning. T F

7. All a student needs for a successful experience within special education is a well-designed IEP. T F

8. Canadian figures on the prevalence of exceptional conditions are generally very accurate. T F

9. Youngsters with severe visual impairments make up one of the highest-incidence groups among children who are exceptional in Canada. T F

10. *Rehabilitation* refers to helping to remediate a child's learning problems. T F

Short-answer questions

1. List the components usually found in an Individual Education Plan (IEP).

2. An itinerant teacher may fill a variety of roles. List five of these roles.

3. A range of personnel are involved in community intervention with youngsters who are exceptional. List five of these types of personnel.

4. Child advocacy involves a range of activities. List five such activities.

5. List ten disciplines that contribute to the philosophy and practise of special education.

Applications

1. In the educational journals, find three articles relating to
   - the development and use of resource rooms in special education, or
   - the use of labels for persons with disabilities.

   Present a report consisting of a description, comparison, and evaluation of the three journal articles. Use the following format:
   a. Begin with a brief abstract of each article, including the name of the author, the journal, and publication details.
   b. Note the specific questions and problems discussed in the articles.

c. Discuss whether the authors' reviews of previous research are comprehensive and yet precise.
d. If the articles include research designs and procedures, note whether these are described adequately and appropriately.
e. Discuss whether the authors present their conclusions in a clear, unbiased, and impartial fashion.
f. Compare and discuss the findings of the three articles. Include a clear evaluation, outlining positive and negative findings, and the way that findings either confirm or refute each other.

2. Task analysis is an important aspect when preparing objectives within an IEP. In this procedure, the teacher breaks a skill down into its components and teaches in small building steps. Yet task analysis is something that we use every day in planning and executing various activities.
Break down each of the following tasks into the smallest, progressive components.
   a. Going from your own home to the university by public transport.
   b. You and three friends go to an expensive French restaurant for dinner. Analyze all the tasks from the time of confirming your reservation with the maitre d' at the door to ordering your meal.
   c. Your two-year-old throws a banana down the toilet. Analyze the progression of tasks needed to clear the toilet (do not call a plumber).

Activities

1. Interview at least three educators in your local school district. Discuss their perspectives concerning the provision of appropriate educational opportunities for children with special needs.

2. Sketch the continuum of educational services. In your own school district, find out how many of these services are available. How many children are educated in each option at the moment? What percentage of the school-aged population of children with exceptionalities is educated in each part of the continuum?

3. Interview a paraprofessional. Log all the activities that he or she undertakes in a normal day.

Portfolio item

Many novels and plays focus on persons with disabilities. Choose one novel or play. Begin your report with a brief overview of the story and theme. However, the core of the item is societal perceptions of disability as portrayed in the novel or play. Detail these thoroughly and add your own perceptions and reflections.

Chapter 2

Issues and Trends in Canadian Special Education

Learning outcomes

After reading this chapter, you should be able to:

- Understand the debates in contemporary special education in relation to reforms in general education;
- Recognize the changing paradigms in special education specifically as they relate to inclusive schooling;
- Understand the importance of legislation and litigation in both Canada and the United States;
- Detail and explain some major trends in contemporary special education;
- Relate the procedures of early intervention to the types of intervention discussed in Chapter 1;
- Understand the different stages of the assessment process and some of the procedures used, with particular reference to functional assessment.

Introduction

In recent decades, the prospects for individuals who are exceptional have altered dramatically. Together with a significant increase in public awareness and understanding, current social philosophy aims to provide such individuals with an education and a lifestyle that is as close to normal as possible.

A field as historically complex and diverse as special education is bound to reveal controversial issues and to reflect major trends and movements. Today's most hotly debated issue concerns inclusion, or inclusive schooling. A broad spectrum of other trends and movements, all related in some way to inclusion, are germane to contemporary special education as educators continue their efforts to reform, revamp, and generally improve services for students with special needs.

Changing views of exceptionality

Changing conceptions of exceptionality have come about because of increased public awareness and understanding of individuals who are exceptional. *Qualitative* conceptions of exceptionality, which view people with disabilities as deviant and different, are slowly being overtaken by *quantitative* conceptions in which the differences manifested by individuals who are exceptional are seen as a matter of degree, not of kind.

Real change can be traced to the 1960s; one major impetus was the normalization movement. **Normalization** is the philosophical belief that all individuals who are exceptional, no matter what their level and type of disability, should be provided with an education and living environment that is as close to normal as possible.

Reforms in education

In the past two decades, educational reform has become a major issue in North American education.

Reforms in special education

While reforms in special education are not new, contemporary special education is deeply involved in reform efforts and is being pressured to change by both internal and external forces. Inclusive schooling is one of the manifestations of current reform mandates.

Development of the inclusionary movement

Over the past four decades there has been a gradual increase in the numbers and proportions of children with disabilities who receive their special education while enrolled in general education classes and schools.

In the 1950s and 1960s, *integration* was the common term used to refer to the education of students with exceptionalities in regular classrooms. In the 1970s, *mainstreaming* emerged. Under mainstreaming principles, the instruction of children with learning, behavioural, physical, or other problems took place with normally developing peers to the greatest extent possible. The amount of integration depended upon the unique patterns of strengths and weaknesses in each child. In the 1980s, educators proposed the Regular Education Initiative (REI), which essentially sought to place more students with mild disabilities in regular classrooms and to create a merger of regular education and special education.

Defining inclusive schooling

The current stress is on inclusive schooling. Although there are many conceptions of the term, it basically means that all students are to be educated in the classrooms or schools they would attend if they were not exceptional. Schools should change to welcome all the types of diversity seen in students.

Inclusion is both evolving and changing. The current movement hosts a range of theoretical positions related to the underlying philosophy, the relationship of those targeted for inclusion, the nature of the general educational provision, and the manner in which supports are provided.

In this text, we define inclusion as "a system of equity for students with exceptionalities that expresses a commitment to educate each child to the maximum extent through placement, instruction, and support in the most heterogeneous and appropriate educational environment."

Examining inclusive schooling

There is not an area in special education more difficult than inclusion. At the root of the difficulties is the fact that inclusion is both a philosophy and a practice. While the philosophy is fairly well accepted, the major difficulties come with attempting to translate the principles into efficient school-based service delivery models.

Philosophy of inclusion

Philosophical strands supporting inclusive schooling include general school reform, civil rights, educational equity, and the difficulties of a dual system.

Implementation

Inclusive schooling is complex, involving not only the children with special needs but also teachers, evaluation, and attitudes; indeed, it means the restructuring of an entire school. Hence, successfully implementing inclusionary practices is a major challenge to school systems today. Diverse and complex threads must draw together if the most appropriate education is to be provided for every child who is exceptional.

It is not surprising that inclusive schooling remains the subject of often-contentious debate, most particularly in regard to students with serious behavioural disorders and those with significant disabilities.

The success of inclusive schooling depends on many factors, which include

- teacher expectations, attitudes, and acceptance of inclusive schooling;
- resources and personnel to support teachers and to assist children with special needs;
- curriculum matched to the needs of each student;
- accurate and ongoing assessment;
- social integration of students with special needs;
- collaboration and co-operation among regular classroom teachers, special education personnel, classroom paraprofessionals, and other support services;
- team approaches: in teaming, different people share information and expertise;
- administrators who support inclusion.

Typical services in Canada

All school districts in Canada appear to be moving toward inclusive models. However, many boards continue to approach inclusion on an individual basis.

Legislation

Law is the system of rules and regulations relating to the behaviour of individuals and society as a whole. **School law** defines the manner in which schools function. Legal issues that include both litigation and legislation have had a dramatic impact on special education in recent decades. Among other factors, parent pressure promoted and advanced litigation and legislation. Court rulings in favour of exceptional individuals prompted the passage of legislation that clearly spells out the responsibilities of the school system and the rights of children who are exceptional.

Legislation in the United States

The most significant and influential legislative enactment was the United States Education for All Handicapped Children Act, Public Law 94-142. PL 94-142 mandated that children with special needs must be educated in the least restrictive environment with an Individual Education Plan (IEP) developed, maintained, and evaluated for every child. States must assume non-discriminatory testing, confidentiality, and ensure due-process procedures for all children with disabilities and their parents or guardians.

Other important legislation complements PL 94-142. The Americans with Disabilities Act (ADA) of 1990 guarantees equal opportunity and access to all persons with disabilities, within and without the school system. Title V of the Rehabilitation Act, more commonly called Section 504 (1974), is a civil rights law that protects children and adults against discrimination. In the schools, it ensures that students can participate in educational programs. Students not included under other laws, such as those with Attention Deficit Hyperactivity Disorder, are served under

Section 504. Gifted and talented students were originally addressed in PL 95-561, the Gifted and Talented Children's Education Act of 1978.

Amendments

PL 94-142 has undergone a number of amendments and reauthorizations since its passage in 1975. In 1986, PL 99-457 included preschool children. In 1990 the Individuals with Disabilities Education Act (IDEA) added autism and Traumatic Brain Injury as categories of exceptionality and changed the terminology of the legislation to people-first language. IDEA was amended again in 1997.

Legislation in Canada

In Canada, the movement is toward the provision of mandatory special education legislation. Currently, all the provinces and the two territories have some form of legislated responsibility for the education of children who are exceptional, but the breadth of services varies.

Legislative activity has tended to focus on children with disabilities. Children identified as gifted have not fared as well in the legislative field.

Litigation

Legislation refers to laws or bills enacted by lawmakers. **Litigation** involves an individual or a small group filing a suit against another. The use of the court system to settle disputes, especially about educational placement, is widespread in the United States and on the increase in Canada. Cases in Canada have been settled under various modes; the *Charter of Rights* has been used in some recent decisions. Particularly important cases heard under the Charter are Elwood vs. Halifax County—Bedford School District (1986) and the case of Brant County Board of Education vs. Carol Eaton and Clayton Eaton (1997).

Trends and movements

Many trends and movements may be seen in today's special education. These include, but are not restricted to, the issues discussed below.

Expansion of services

Today's special education is reaching down to include preschoolers at-risk or with disabilities and reaching up to assist adolescents with transition into adult life.

Early intervention

Early identification and early intervention, both broader constructs of early childhood special education, are two of the most promising areas of contemporary special education. **Early identification** is used to identify children with established disabilities, those who are at risk for problems, and those experiencing lags and delays. **Early intervention** refers to the establishment of educational and support services for preschool children and infants who are at risk for disabilities, and their families.

Transition

Transition programs are designed to ease the movement of adolescents with disabilities into the adult world.

Parent involvement

Teachers should stress parental involvement if they wish to enhance the educational experience for all their students. When educators involve parents as partners in their children's education, parents appear to develop a sense of efficacy that communicates itself to children with positive academic consequences.

Technological advances

Huge advances in many areas of technology have brought major advances for people with disabilities. Computers are beneficial in education, and as communication and living aids.

Assessment practices

Assessment is designed to present a detailed picture of a child's unique pattern of strengths and weaknesses in a variety of areas. Recent years have witnessed major advances in assessment practices that include who administers measures, where they are administered, the procedures used, and the variety of tools.

Stages in assessment

There are different types of assessment, which employ different strategies and personnel. The major areas are screening, specific (psycho-educational) assessment, and intensive or medical diagnosis. Procedures overlap and complement each other, and each provides important information regarding a child's present and past functioning as well as potential.

Screening

Screening, a term used in both medicine and education, refers to the examination of large groups of children to find those performing above or below the norm. Screening is designed to separate at-risk children from those who are functioning within acceptable limits.

Educational screening devices include observations, interviews, past records, developmental checklists, behaviour-rating scales, skill inventories, teacher-made tests, criterion-referenced tests, curriculum-based assessment, and group achievement tests.

Criterion-referenced measures

Criterion-referenced tests do not measure a child's progress against a norm but against the child's individual progress. Criterion-referenced tests may be commercially produced; many are designed by classroom teachers to assess the progress of an individual child.

Curriculum-referenced measures

A special form of criterion-referenced test is referred to as curriculum-referenced testing or **curriculum-based assessment** (CBA). The stress is on assessing a child's progress within the curriculum taught. **Probes** are brief samples of academic behaviour and are a core method of CBA.

Portfolios

Portfolios are joint projects between the teacher and a student. They include information selected by the student under the guidance of the teacher as well as a series of statements that reflect a student's thoughts about the contents. Work samples, projects, and test results may also be included. A **rubric** is a generic scoring tool used to evaluate the quality of products and performance in a given area.

Functional assessment

Many of today's researchers speak to the overwhelming advantage of functional analysis over other approaches. Functional analysis—or functional assessment—is a broad approach useful for all children with disabilities but particularly relevant to those with behavioural disorders and students with severe or multiple disabilities. The major aims of functional assessment are to generate hypotheses about the possible causes of a student's behaviour and then develop intervention strategies that correlate with the hypotheses.

Overlapping and complementary components are included within functional assessment. Data are gathered through procedures that range from structured interviews with the parents and the target student to general observations, direct observations of naturally occurring behaviour, review of anecdotal records, and rating scales and checklists.

Parent interviews

Interviews are part of the assessment process; in fact, an assessment is incomplete without the careful collection of data from parent interviews. Parental insights about the child can complement information from other sources and paint a broader picture of a child's capabilities and educational needs.

Specific assessment

Psycho-educational assessment provides more information on children considered as high-risk in the screening phase. The diagnostic process should confirm or discount the existence of a problem and help in determining treatment and intervention for children identified.

Tests are controlled and structured procedures that attempt to elicit particular responses that a child might not demonstrate spontaneously. **Direct testing** refers to testing children across a variety of relevant domains. Many of the tests used in psycho-educational assessment are norm-referenced. Most cover a variety of developmental domains and include skills within each area.

IQ tests provide an **intelligence quotient**. The most critical notion underlying IQ tests is that of a normal distribution; that is, a continuum of scores that vary from the average by predictable amounts.

Developmental assessment

Developmental assessment compares a child's progress with the developmental milestones attained by most children at certain ages. It shows progress through the normal sequences of development.

Standards testing

Canadian jurisdictions are adopting province-wide testing for various grade levels. Accommodations are possible for students with special needs.

Cultural and linguistic differences

Recent demographic data suggest that public schools are faced with increasing linguistic and cultural diversity. One result of these demographic changes is that the special education system is increasingly serving students who are in the process of acquiring a second language or who come from home backgrounds that differ culturally or linguistically from the Canadian majority. One solution to the needs of students with cultural differences that simultaneously builds tolerance and understanding in other students is the process of multicultural education.

Key Terms

assessment
curriculum-based assessment
direct testing
early identification
early intervention
intelligence quotient
law
legislation
litigation
normalization
probes
rubric
school law
screening
tests

Practice Questions

Multiple-choice questions

1. According to the text, the critical decade for educational reform in special education was the
   a. 1940s—the foundation of special schools by parent groups.
   b. 1960s—the normalization movement.
   c. 1970s—the mainstreaming movement.
   d. 1980s—the Regular Education Initiative.
   e. 1990s—the inclusive schools movement.

2. The administrative model for special education that emerged in the early 19th century was
   a. the residential school.
   b. day classes.
   c. resource rooms.
   d. home training programs.
   e. clinic-based programs.

3. Many reforms that concern placement and the location of services have been implemented in contemporary special education. The reform movement that seeks to restructure and change the system (rather than the individual child) is known in Canada as
   a. mainstreaming.
   b. integration.
   c. inclusion.
   d. enlightenment.
   e. PL 94-142.

4. One way to view inclusive schooling is as a step in the progression of special education. Within this progression, the order of the steps is
   a. segregation, integration, mainstreaming, inclusion.
   b. integration, segregation, mainstreaming, inclusion.
   c. integration, mainstreaming, segregation, inclusion.
   d. inclusion, integration, mainstreaming, segregation.
   e. REI, segregation, mainstreaming, inclusion.

5. The author speaks to "inclusions" rather than to a single inclusion. This is because
   a. inclusion is implemented in different ways.
   b. the area is fluid and evolving.
   c. there are a variety of models and programs.
   d. the philosophy hosts a number of theoretical positions.
   e. all of the above

6. In an inclusive school, labels and categories for groups of children with exceptionalities
   a. should disappear as all children are accepted into general education.
   b. become more prevalent as teachers adopt more individual strategies.
   c. change in usage as we move from a medically oriented system to a school-based system of labels.
   d. stay about the same, as administrators and many practitioners wish to retain labels.
   e. become more prominent, as children need to be carefully identified before adaptations can be made.

7. Mark is a child with severe cognitive and multiple disabilities. However, his parents choose placement in a general classroom. If their hopes are consistent with the research, the reason for Mark's placement is chiefly for
   a. academic stimulation.
   b. positive effects in the social domain.
   c. enhanced achievement in core academic areas.
   d. vocational skills.
   e. general living skills.

8. Much technology is used with students with special needs, often divided into the categories of high technology, medium technology, and low technology. Among the following, the low-technology adaptations are
   a. computers and interactive multi-media systems.
   b. communication aids with speech output.
   c. adapted spoon handles and Velcro fasteners.
   d. videocassette players.
   e. computerized wheelchairs.

9. Early intervention can be described as
   a. the natural corollary of early identification.
   b. a process that includes early identification, infant programs, and early childhood special education.
   c. plans to assist young children and their families.
   d. a family-centred process.
   e. all of the above

10. Assessment is a cornerstone of contemporary special education. With regard to assessment, the one statement among the following that is true is
   a. only special education teachers are responsible for the assessment of special learners.
   b. the initial process should assign a label to a child.
   c. assessment in special education is quite different from the measurement and evaluation techniques used by all teachers to assess student learning.
   d. there is no such thing as a flawless diagnostic system in special education.
   e. a relatively narrow range of tools and procedures are used.

11. Mrs. Arms has given her grade-seven class a short test to investigate their note-taking skills. Within the context of curriculum-based measurement, this test would be referred to as
   a. functional skills assessment.
   b. a rubric.
   c. a probe.
   d. content assessment.
   e. developmental domain assessment.

12. Developmental scales are used to
    a. predict future school achievement.
    b. indicate whether a child is reaching developmental milestones.
    c. indicate a child's IQ level.
    d. determine educational placement.
    e. find where a child is functioning within a curriculum.

13. The functional approach to assessment stresses chiefly
    a. a child's attainment of developmental milestones.
    b. the match between a child's progress and the curriculum.
    c. a test-teach-retest format.
    d. the use of norm-referenced standardized tests.
    e. the behaviours and skills a child needs in present and future environments.

14. Medical screening is used to
    a. select from a large group those with suspected exceptional conditions.
    b. identify individuals with known exceptionalities.
    c. increase public awareness of services.
    d. establish specific strengths and weaknesses in a child's functioning.
    e. establish a child's mental ability.

15. Of the following, the *screening procedure* is
    a. a classroom teacher using a rating scale.
    b. a medical doctor performing amniocentesis.
    c. a public health nurse using a sweep test to check hearing.
    d. a delivery room nurse assessing an infant's functioning.
    e. All of the above are screening measures.

16. A number of acronyms are introduced in Section 1 of the text. What does each acronym stand for?
    a. CEC
    b. LRE
    c. REI
    d. IEP
    e. WISC-III

Recall questions

1. Two popular measures of mental ability for children are the ________ and the ________.

2. The natural corollary of early identification is early ________.

3. Practitioners undertake ________ to arrive at an accurate determination of a child's problems and to devise appropriate programming.

4. When we speak of "people-first" terminology, we mean that we ______.

5. The seminal legislation for special education in the United States, signed into law by President Ford in 1975, was _______.

6. In 1986, PL 99-457 amended earlier legislation in the United States and extended services to more age groups. This legislative amendment included children of _______ age.

7. The assessment process that examines a child's mastery of the curriculum is known as _______.

8. One province that has special legislation for students who are gifted is ______.

9. For the classroom teacher, the most important components of an IEP are goals and ______.

10. One example of litigation in special education in Canada is the ______ case.

True–false questions

1. Classroom teachers are responsible for presenting and scoring IQ tests. T F

2. Most learning and behavioural problems can be handled in the general classroom with some modification of the program. T F

3. Prior to the passage of PL 94-142, many children with exceptionalities in the United States were inappropriately or inadequately served. T F

4. In a special or residential school, services are provided by specially trained teachers to specific groups of students who are exceptional. T F

5. The terms *integration, mainstreaming*, and *inclusion* mean the same thing and can be used synonymously. T F

6. In the United States, PL 94-142 is a state law. T F

7. Very few school boards implemented appropriate special education policies before legislation forced them to do so. T F

8. Culturally different children with disabilities are represented in all categories of exceptionality. T F

9. The grade-five class has just completed a unit on fractions. To assess how much the children attained in the unit, the teacher could use developmental assessment. T F

10. During the 1960s, studies that compared progress in segregated and regular classes demonstrated that children in segregated classes outperformed their agemates in regular classes. T F

Short-answer questions

1. List four major forms of intervention used with children with exceptionalities. Provide an example of each.

2. A psycho-educational assessment should provide information on major areas or domains of functioning. List the critical domains.

3. Litigation related to special education generally involves suits filed for two reasons. List and briefly explain the reasons.

4. Many supports may be provided in the general classroom to assist teachers and students with disabilities. List four supports. Provide examples of each.

5. The text explains four major pieces of legislation in the United States relating to persons with disabilities and their education. List the legislation.

Applications

1. In the educational journals, find three articles relating to
   - the implementation of inclusive schooling in Canada; or
   - the use of functional assessment with students with behavioural disorders.

   Present a report consisting of a description, comparison, and evaluation of the three articles. (See Application Question 1 in Chapter 1 of this study guide for report format.)

2. Find out what type of legislation exists in your province regarding the education of exceptional children. What recommendations have been made? What do you see as future movements and trends?

3. Research and report on one Canadian case where parents undertook legal action to obtain educational rights for their exceptional child.

Activities

1. Observation of a child is an appropriate method that forms part of the screening process. Choose a child of any age to observe in a natural setting: home, nursery school, playground, or classroom. Extend the observation over at least one morning or one afternoon. During the observation, make yourself as unobtrusive as possible; do not intervene with the child at any time. Before you begin the observation, choose the behavioural area on which you will focus. For example, with the very young child, you may listen for language and note all utterances. In a classroom situation you may focus on attention and out-of-seat behaviour. When the observation is complete, write out your major findings. Compare the observed child's behaviour with that of other children of the same age.

Portfolio item

Interview a teacher who is including a child with a disability. Prepare a list of questions concerning the child, the IEP, classroom supports, and the teacher's attitudes and perceptions. Present the findings in essay form.

Chapter 3

Risk Factors and Children at Risk

Learning outcomes

After reading this chapter, you should be able to:

- Understand the variety of risk factors and how they affect development;
- Distinguish between established, biological, and environmental risk;
- Understand the many familial and extra-familial factors that can place students at risk for learning and behavioural problems;
- Understand the potential difficulties associated with cultural and linguistic differences.

Introduction

Dozens and dozens of factors surround children as they grow up. Some of them are related to the classroom; many, many more are familial or extra-familial.
At risk is a term used to describe a number of different categories of children. At risk refers to infants and young children who are physically, medically, or psychologically in danger of failing to thrive and also includes children who are affected by diverse economic, environmental, and geographical factors.

Risk factors are the biological or environmental causes of potential disabilities. When children are considered to be high risk or at risk, they are seen to be more prone to developing some form of disabling condition or for adverse effects of school learning and behaviour.

Etiological considerations

Etiology is the process of finding causes to explain how a particular problem came into existence. A knowledge of the pathophysiology, symptomology, and treatment of exceptional conditions is important for educational professionals because:

- the causes of disabilities cannot easily be separated from the developmental consequences;
- effective treatment requires an appropriate theoretical understanding of a problem;
- recent genetic research provides dramatic evidence that students affected by different genetic conditions present quite different profiles;
- teachers' knowledge imparts confidence in their ability to cope;
- teachers' understanding of medical conditions aids them in becoming sensitized to the social, emotional, and educational problems resulting from a child's disabilities;
- medical management for health problems can be a significant part of a child's daily life;
- some children with disabilities require medication on a regular basis;
- some children with disabilities have difficulty participating in certain physical activities.

The new morbidity

While many of the traditional causes of disabling conditions, such as scarlet fever, have been eliminated, a new group of diseases and conditions are affecting children today. As they result from new etiologies, these conditions are referred to as the *new morbidity*. **Comorbidity** is a relatively new term denoting the simultaneous occurrence of two or more unrelated conditions.

Risk factors and disability

Risk connotes a given probability but does not imply certainty, and not all children who fall within these categories of increased vulnerability become disabled. The thousands upon thousands of risk factors can be slotted into three major categories: established risk, biological risk, and environmental risk.

Established risk

The **established risk** category refers to medical conditions and anomalies that invariably result in a disability or developmental delay. Established risk is most often related to genetic and chromosomal problems, and includes conditions such as Down syndrome, fragile X syndrome, and infantile autism. Problems may range from relatively minor through to major difficulties, called the **continuum of reproductive casualty**.

Genetic and chromosomal differences

All individuals are born with a unique combination of genes that are theirs alone from the moment of conception. The first twenty-two pairs of chromosomes are autosomal. Many genes interact in polygenic inheritance. Multi-factorial inheritance results from the interaction of many genes with other genes and/or environmental factors.

One tiny flaw in the genetic structure can have tragic results. A flaw may create abnormalities present at birth, called *hereditary anomalies*. Because hereditary anomalies are in the genes, they may be passed on to subsequent generations. Some disorders are linked to the genes on the twenty-third pair of chromosomes. In X-linked inheritance, the sons have a fifty–fifty chance of inheriting the condition through the mother. **Cytogenetics** is the study of the location and organization of genetic material.

Genetic disorders

There are about 2000 confirmed or suspected dominant genetic disorders that can result in mental retardation and other disabilities. There are about 1000 confirmed or suspected recessive disorders. **Congenital abnormalities**, or **hereditary abnormalities**, are present at birth.

Inborn errors of metabolism

Metabolic problems due to heredity are termed *inborn errors of metabolism*. Most inborn errors of metabolism are the result of the action of a single pair of genes. Many result in missing or defective enzymes. The absence of, or defect in, one of the enzymes means that the normal chemistry of a cell is altered by the inability to provide or dispose of a critical chemical or protein, which leads to unusual levels of particular chemicals in the body. **Tay-Sachs disease**, diabetes, **phenylketonuria**, and galactosemia are all caused by errors of metabolism.

Deletion syndromes

In these rare diseases, is it not a case of aberrant genes. Rather, there is too little genetic material or there is at least one gene missing.

Chromosomal factors

Chromosomal problems result from chromosomal dysjunction, a malfunction in cell division. Problems occur when there is an extra chromosome, or when pieces or parts of chromosomes attach themselves to other chromosomes.

Down syndrome

The most common chromosomal aberration is Down syndrome, which occurs in approximately 1 in every 1000 live births. There are three types of Down syndrome—trisomy 21, translocation, and mosaicism. In each type, the mental and physical problems of the affected child are caused by extra chromosomal material that somehow disturbs the orderly development of the body and brain.

In general, the chances of having a Down syndrome child increase dramatically with the age of the parents, particularly the mother. However, very young mothers as well as more mature women are more likely to have a baby with Down syndrome.

Fragile X syndrome

Fragile X syndrome is second only to Down syndrome among genetic abnormalities associated with intellectual disabilities. Children who are affected by fragile X syndrome have cognitive deficits ranging from learning disabilities to severe mental retardation.

Turner's syndrome

Turner's syndrome (TUS) is characterized by short stature, growth failure, or gonadal dysgenesis that inhibits spontaneous pubertal onset and fertility. Individuals with TUS have a characteristic pattern of cognitive abilities consisting of normal verbal IQ and relatively lower performance IQ due to difficulty with space forms and number concepts.

Biological risk

Children who are at **biological risk** have a history of developmental events, such as prematurity, that place them in the at-risk category.

Prenatal period

At the beginning of life, the individual is a single cell, a tiny drop of fluid made up mainly of non-living material surrounding a minuscule nucleus of living matter. By the time of birth, some thirty-eight weeks later, the individual weighs about 3.5 kilograms and contains 200 billion specialized cells.

From the moment of conception until delivery nine months later, the human being is more susceptible to the environment than at any other time. The opening third of pregnancy, the **first trimester**, is the most important to development. Potentially dangerous prenatal factors include infections and intoxications as well as chromosomal and genetic aberrations.

Infections and intoxicants

Many agents act deleteriously on the developing fetus. **Teratogens** are environmental agents that can cause damage.

Rubella

Rubella is a potential source of a variety of disabilities; when the mother contracts the virus in the first trimester of pregnancy, approximately 70 percent of fetuses are damaged. The fetal organs likely to be affected by rubella are those whose development is underway when the mother contracts the virus. The eye, ear, nervous system, and heart are especially vulnerable.

Syphilis

Syphilis affects the fetus after the sixteenth or eighteenth week of gestation. It does not affect the developing organs as does rubella but produces destructive lesions (abnormal changes in structure) on already developed organs.

Drugs

Drugs include over-the-counter drugs, prescription drugs, hard drugs, and alcohol and nicotine.

Prescription drugs

Prescription drugs have been shown to have an adverse effect on fetal development.

Cocaine

Some neurochemical studies on cocaine in utero suggest that if it is present during gestation it may affect developing fetal neuromotor systems, which could have a significant impact on the developing nervous system.

Heroin

Heroin passes the placenta so that infants of addicted women are born addicted. Withdrawal symptoms can prove fatal to the tiny infant. Survivors suffer a number of difficulties, but it is not known whether these extend beyond infancy.

Fetal alcohol syndrome

A **syndrome** is a constellation of findings similar from patient to patient. A proportion of children of drinking mothers are born with Fetal Alcohol Syndrome (FAS). In children affected by FAS, intellectual disability is a major characteristic.

FAS exists on a continuum ranging from the full-blown syndrome to minor developmental defects. Full-blown FAS affects the whole body system, causing malformations and anomalies in the nervous system, the musculoskeletal structure, and internal organs, especially the heart and urinogenital tracts.

Maternal smoking

Very heavy smoking in mothers may have a severe enough cumulative effect to contribute to spontaneous abortions, bleeding during pregnancy, premature rupture of the amniotic sac, fetal deaths, and deaths of newborns.

Maternal nutrition

Inadequate prenatal nutrition can affect the relationship between the body's biochemistry and the functioning of the brain. Severe malnutrition can stunt brain growth and produce a significant lowering of intellectual ability. Postnatal nutrition, especially during the first six months of an infant's life, is also a critical factor in brain development.

Unknown prenatal influence

There are a number of conditions present at or before birth for which there is no known cause. **Microcephaly** is a rare phenomenon in which brain development is impaired by an abnormally small cranium. **Macrocephaly** refers to an enlargement of the head, most frequently caused by **hydrocephalus**, a build-up of cerebrospinal fluid in the brain.

Birth and neonatal development

Birth can be dangerous for the child or the mother. Sometimes inadequate uterine environments pose additional risks. If the child is overly deprived of oxygen, the condition is called **anoxia.** Most birth injuries result in deprivation of oxygen to the immature brain, which then leads to abridgment of nervous system function. If supplies of oxygen to the nerve cells of the brain are too greatly reduced, brain damage or death can result.

Neurological impairments

Neurological impairments can occur pre-, peri-, or postnatally. The incidence of infant and preschool brain injury is increasing. Causes include household and auto accidents, meningitis and encephalitis, and anoxia caused by such events as near drowning, inhalation of toxic fumes, choking, and periventricular hemorrhage.

Pre-term and low-birth-weight infants

Prematurity occurs in ten or twelve births per hundred. Pre-term or **premature babies** are generally defined as those born before the completion of thirty-seven weeks, a full week short of the full thirty-eight-week term. Research has clearly established that pre-term infants have a higher incidence of developmental problems in childhood than do full-term infants.

An abnormal length of pregnancy can also be problematic. Infants born two weeks or more beyond the expected due date are said to be postmature. These children are somewhat more at risk than children born at the normal 266 to 270 days.

CMV and herpes

Two potentially harmful or fatal conditions transmitted to the baby at the time of delivery are cytomegalovirus (CMV) and herpes.

Pediatric AIDS

Some researchers predict that **pediatric AIDS**—AIDS contracted by children under thirteen years of age—is destined to become a major cause of developmental and physical disabilities and death among infants and children in North America.

The vast majority of children with pediatric AIDS obtain their infection during birth from the mother who used intravenous drugs or was sexually active with an infected partner. AIDS in children may also be the result of tainted blood transfusions. Rarely, it may be contracted through the mother's milk.

Postnatal development

In the postnatal period, infections such as meningitis and encephalitis can present dire sequelae. Child abuse and child battering are further potent causes of childhood handicapping conditions.

Environmental risk

Both heredity and environmental factors are crucial to child development. A child's growth factors will be seriously hampered by **environmental risks**. These are conditions that occur when a child is biologically normal but does not develop age-appropriate behaviour at the normal rate. In this grouping, *at risk* refers to students who have characteristics, live in an environment, or have experiences that make them more prone to developing some form of disabling condition and/or more likely to fail in school.

Family structures

Teachers must be aware that the child population of today is different from earlier generations. One factor is destabilization of the institution of the family shown in mounting divorce rates and increases in the number of single-parent families. As families change, new problems emerge.

Poverty

Lower socio-economic status (SES) negatively correlates with eight adverse socializing factors—harsh discipline, lack of maternal warmth, exposure to aggressive adult models, maternal aggressive values, family life stresses, mother's lack of social support, peer group instability, and lack of cognitive stimulation.

Cultural and linguistic differences

To live and develop in two culturally different systems is sufficiently challenging for students without exceptional conditions. The difficulties multiply for students who are culturally and linguistically diverse and also disabled.

Culturally different students with special needs

Culturally diverse students are represented in all categories of exceptionality and can experience any disability that is found in other children. Disability and cultural and linguistic concerns are not unrelated phenomena; rather, they play interconnected and complementary roles in children's development and progress. Programs must address the interacting influences of all student variables.

Prevention

The prevention of disabling and potentially disabling conditions is usually classified as *primary, secondary,* and *tertiary.*

Primary prevention is concerned with removing the factors that account for the occurrence of disorders as well as strengthening the well-being of individuals in the population. Genetic counselling and educational programs on conditions such as Down syndrome are part of primary prevention.

Secondary prevention refers to ascertaining, as early as possible, the evidence of disorders that may cause disabilities as well as allied attempts to reduce, remove, or reverse complex aspects of disabilities. Secondary prevention includes prenatal screening measures such as amniocentesis and chronic villi sampling.

Tertiary prevention consists of intervention strategies after a negative outcome has occurred. The object of tertiary prevention is to minimize residual disabling conditions and maximize future potential.

Key Terms

anoxia
biological risk
comorbidity
congenital abnormalities
continuum of reproductive casualty
cytogenetics
environmental risks
established risk
etiology
first trimester
hereditary anomalies
hydrocephalus
macrocephaly
microcephaly
pediatric AIDS
phenylketonuria
premature babies
primary prevention
risk factors
secondary prevention
syndrome
Tay-Sachs disease
teratogens
tertiary prevention

Practice Questions

Multiple-choice questions

1. Treatment for the medical causes of conditions and disabilities can be classified into five categories. Insulin for diabetes would be considered a treatment that is
   a. ameliorative and avoids secondary complications.
   b. necessary and lifesaving.
   c. adaptive and facilitates development.
   d. unproven but potentially useful.
   e. controversial but unproven.

2. Teachers should clearly understand the causes and developmental consequences of a child's disability because
   a. educational factors related to a disability cannot easily be separated from the biomedical causes.
   b. knowledge of the pathophysiology, symptomatology, and treatment of an exceptional condition leads to a better appreciation of its developmental and educational implications.
   c. effective intervention requires an appropriate theoretical understanding of the problem.
   d. understanding of a condition leads to greater acceptance and tolerance.
   e. all of the above

3. In special education, the concept of risk is important. When discussing risk, it is true that
   a. risk is basically a statistical concept.
   b. there exist thousands upon thousands of risk factors, all of which can be clearly identified.
   c. risk implies a certainty of later problems.
   d. all children who fall within the categories of increased vulnerability become disabled.
   e. all of the above

4. The first two weeks of pregnancy is described as the
   a. period of the embryo.
   b. perinatal period.
   c. prenatal period.
   d. third trimester.
   e. second trimester.

5. Jane was three weeks premature and born after a long and difficult labour. Most correctly, she will be referred to as
   a. developmentally delayed.
   b. high risk.
   c. mentally retarded.
   d. atypical.
   e. handicapped.

6. The most common postnatal cause of disabilities in children is
   a. accidents.
   b. cancer.
   c. meningitis.
   d. encephalitis.
   e. pediatric AIDS.

7. The term *teratology* refers to the
   a. process of finding causes to explain how a particular problem came into existence.
   b. overt reactions or manifestations of the body to a certain condition.
   c. study of symptoms and characteristics.
   d. study of the agents involved in diseases and conditions.
   e. process of counting the number of individuals affected by a particular condition.

8. Extrinsic risk factors refer to the
   a. physical, cultural, and social environment that elevates risk.
   b. study of the agents involved in major congenital malformations.
   c. causes of malformations.
   d. physiological outcomes of long-term importance in the medical and psychological functioning of a child.
   e. knowledge of the psychology, symptomatology, and treatment of exceptional conditions.

9. Some conditions affect development only during critical periods. Which of the following conditions provide examples of infections that cause problems only in a critical period in fetal development?
   a. herpes and toxemia
   b. meningitis and encephalitis
   c. rubella and syphilis
   d. Rh factor and phenylketonuria
   e. hydrocephalus and spina bifida

10. With hereditary anomalies, dominant conditions tend to show
   a. little variability.
   b. very similar symptoms.
   c. similar degrees of the condition.
   d. marked variability.
   e. Too little research has been undertaken to make definitive statements.

11. According to recent figures, approximately _____ percent of all students are seriously at risk.
   a. 10 to 15
   b. 25 to 35
   c. 50 to 60
   d. 70 to 75
   e. 90

12. Which of the following students would be considered to be at risk?
   a. young girls who become pregnant
   b. adolescents involved in drugs and crime
   c. school dropouts
   d. groups for whom English is not the first language
   e. all of the above

13. The best way to describe multicultural special education is to say that it is
   a. a way of teaching shaped by beliefs about how our society should function.

b. the use of culturally responsive instruction.
c. a means to celebrate cultural pluralism.
d. a way to provide knowledge about the majority culture and other cultures.
e. all of the above

14. Children with full-blown Fetal Alcohol Syndrome are likely to have anomalies in
    a. central nervous system functioning.
    b. musculoskeletal structure.
    c. craniofacial areas.
    d. internal organs.
    e. all of the above

15. In risk categories, the category that includes medical conditions and anomalies that invariably result in disability or delay is ________ risk.
    a. secondary
    b. established
    c. primary
    d. environmental
    e. low

16. Match the disorder to the type of transmission.
    a. X-linked
    b. dominant
    c. chromosomal dysfunction
    d. recessive
    e. multifactorial
    ___ muscular dystrophy
    ___ Huntington's disease
    ___ cystic fibrosis
    ___ Down syndrome
    ___ spina bifida

Recall questions

1. An example of a metabolic disorder that if left uncontrolled results in mental retardation is ________.

2. A genetically determined inborn error of metabolism involving the exocrine glands is ________.

3. When meningitis and encephalitis are compared, more children affected by ________ suffer subsequent mental retardation.

4. The study of the location and organization of genetic material from chromosomes is known as ________.

5. ________ risk factors refer to aspects of an individual's make-up; ________ risk factors refer to an environment that elevates risk.

6. When the prevalence of genetic defects and that of chromosomal aberrations in newborns are compared, ________ are the more common problem.

7. In humans, chromosome ________ is the smallest chromosome.

8. Anoxia can be simply defined as ________.

9. Of primary, secondary, or tertiary, genetic counselling is a component of ______ prevention.

10. The process of extracting amniotic fluid to check for chromosomal anomalies is known as ______.

True–false questions

1. Poor maternal nutrition can have seriously negative developmental effects on a fetus. T F

2. The prenatal period is from birth until two weeks of age. T F

3. Metabolic disorders are the result of too much of a particular enzyme. T F

4. Amniocentesis is a procedure considered to be part of the tertiary prevention of mental retardation and other anomalies. T F

5. Within the etiologies of childhood disabilities, rubella is considered to be an intoxication. T F

6. Women who drink during pregnancy are certain to have children affected by FAS. T F

7. The majority of children within the traditionally accepted categories of biological and environmental risk will develop normally. T F

8. Professionals intervening with children who are exceptional require an accurate and clear idea of the nature of the disability: its causes, developmental consequences, and prognosis. T F

9. Colour blindness is caused by an inborn error of metabolism. T F

10. The PKU infant test is an example of a screening procedure. T F

Short-answer questions

1. Teachers need basic information about medical problems encountered in the classroom. List five reasons why.

2. Chart and compare the physical characteristics of individuals with Down syndrome and those with fragile X syndrome.

3. List the physical anomalies that may be observed in a child with full-blown Fetal Alcohol Syndrome.

4. The prevention of disabling conditions is divided into three major areas. List these, define them, and provide some examples of strategies for each.

5. List five causes of central nervous system damage. Provide an example of a resulting disability with each cause.

Applications

1. In the educational journals, find three articles relating to one of the following topics:
   - pediatric AIDS;
   - Fetal Alcohol Syndrome; or
   - fragile X syndrome.

   Present a report consisting of a description, comparison, and evaluation of the three articles. (See Application Question 1 in Chapter 1 of this study guide for report format.)

Activities

1. Fetal Alcohol Syndrome is a major cause of mental retardation and developmental anomalies, yet the condition can be prevented. Prepare a series of five thirty-second television clips that could be used to warn the general public of the dangers of drinking by pregnant women.

Portfolio item

The Internet provides much information about disabilities. Undertake an Internet search for items written by (not about) people with disabilities. Choose a variety of sites. Present in report form. Provide brief explanations, the address of the site, and the date accessed.

End Test 1

1. There are varied service delivery models in special education because there
   a. is such a wide range of conditions that can affect students.
   b. are varying degrees of disability.
   c. are different types and degrees of assistance needed at various age levels.
   d. is differing availability of support services.
   e. all of the above

2. All of the following statements about labelling are true, except
   a. many people tend to view a labelled person differently from a non-labelled one.
   b. labels accentuate stereotyping.
   c. labels always guarantee better services and positive experiences for a child who is exceptional.
   d. expectations and views of an exceptional person can be biased by labelling.
   e. parents may appreciate labels.

3. Ms. Jones, a grade-three teacher, is attempting to describe Jimmy, a child in her classroom. Ms. Jones has a background in education. Given this, she is most likely to describe Jimmy's problems with reading in these words:
   a. He is functioning two standard deviations below the norm.
   b. The differences appear to be the result of familial genetic reading disorder.
   c. Jimmy is lagging about one year behind the rest of the class in reading.
   d. Jimmy shows signs of minimal brain dysfunction.
   e. none of the above

4. John was born in 1942 and diagnosed as having infantile autism. The most likely educational placement for John at that time would have been a
   a. regular classroom.
   b. resource room.
   c. clinic.
   d. residential school.
   e. day school.

5. When risk factors and at-risk status are considered, it is true that
   a. increased risk means higher vulnerability to disabilities and delays in functioning.
   b. almost all children designated as at-risk or high-risk develop conditions that eventually impair their behaviour or learning.
   c. less than 10 percent of children designated as at-risk actually develop problems.
   d. once a risk factor is present, the environment has little effect in ameliorating vulnerability.
   e. All of the above are true.

6. Parents are becoming more involved in their children's educational programs because
   a. teachers and schools are demanding more involvement.
   b. parents are crucial in facilitating developmental gains.
   c. the schools need parental volunteers.
   d. schools can no longer afford classroom aides.
   e. many parents are dissatisfied with the school system.

7. Psycho-educational diagnosis using IQ tests may be characterized by all of the following statements except
   a. the tests cover a spectrum of developmental domains.
   b. the tests include a variety of skills within each domain.
   c. the tests provide a profile of a child's pattern of strengths and weaknesses.
   d. the tests are open to use by a variety of educational personnel, including teachers.
   e. the diagnosis is one factor in determining eligibility for special education services.

8. The IDEA of 1990 brought some important changes to American special education legislation. Under IDEA,
   a. children with exceptionalities are guaranteed a free and appropriate education.
   b. children aged three to five years are provided full special education services.
   c. autism and Traumatic Brain Injury are categories of exceptionality.
   d. "people-first" terminology is used.
   e. all of the above

9. For students with mild disabilities, research on inclusive schooling suggests that there are significant gains in
   a. academic areas.
   b. graduation rates.
   c. involvement in community living.
   d. post-secondary schooling.
   e. none of the above

10. Ultrasound can detect the presence of
   a. neural tube defects.
   b. cystic fibrosis.
   c. muscular dystrophy.
   d. diabetes.
   e. Down syndrome.

11. The Education for All Handicapped Children Act (PL 94-142) is
   a. legislation in the United States guaranteeing rights to exceptional youngsters.
   b. a textbook on exceptional children.
   c. a recent CBC documentary.
   d. a bill recently passed in New Brunswick.
   e. Canadian federal special education legislation.

12. Inclusive schooling is best described as
    a. school restructuring.
    b. a new innovative program.
    c. a discretionary responsibility of school boards.
    d. a minor reform exclusive to special education.
    e. a parallel movement to the mainstreaming of the 1970s.

13. Within the large categories of exceptionality outlined in the text, which of these groups of children would not generally be considered exceptional in terms of special education?
    a. youngsters who are behaviourally disordered
    b. visually impaired children
    c. children who are lagging in reading
    d. gifted and talented children
    e. children with intellectual disabilities

14. In the instruction of children with exceptionalities, which of the following statements is true?
    a. The best instruction is provided by teachers certified in the area.
    b. Instruction for children with various mildly disabling conditions does not differ dramatically.
    c. General class teachers cannot provide appropriate services to children with exceptionalities.
    d. Students who are mildly intellectually disabled are the most challenging group to teach.
    e. all of the above

15. Current trends in definitions and labels assigned to children with exceptionalities
    a. tend to reflect the child's functional level.
    b. are becoming more flexible.
    c. emphasize the behavioural characteristics of a child.
    d. vary from province to province.
    e. all of the above

16. Match the terms to the meaning.
    a. etiology
    b. symptoms
    c. developmental risk factors
    d. symptomology
    e. teratology
    ___ the process of finding causes to explain how a particular condition came into existence
    ___ the overt reaction or manifestations of the body to a certain condition
    ___ the study of symptoms and characteristics
    ___ the study of the agents involved in major congenital malformations
    ___ conditions associated with increased probability for cognitive, social, or physical problems (5 x 1)

17. Match the description to the condition.
    a. oxygen deprivation

b. maternal infection
c. maternal intoxication
d. child infection
e. genetic defect
___ anoxia
___ Tay-Sachs disease
___ meningitis
___ rubella
___ FAS (5 x 1)

18. Match the condition to its type.
a. Down syndrome
b. colour blindness
c. Prader-Willi
d. Tay-Sachs disease
e. spina bifida
___ X-linked
___ multifactorial inheritance
___ inborn error of metabolism
___ deletion syndrome
___ chromosomal problem (5 x 1)

19. Match the description to the condition.
a. cystic fibrosis
b. Down syndrome
c. Fetal Alcohol Syndrome
d. muscular dystrophy
e. PKU
___ multifactorial hereditary anomaly
___ genetically transmitted autosomal metabolic disorder
___ chromosomal difference
___ X-linked genetic anomaly
___ maternal intoxication (5 x 1)

20. In Canada, special education is an important and expanding field. T F

21. Severe intellectual disability is a high-incidence exceptionality. T F

22. *Adaptive behaviour* refers to how well a person is able to adapt to environmental demands and differs according to the individual's age group and particular situation. T F

23. By labelling a child who is exceptional, we guarantee an increase in positive experiences for that child. T F

24. Of intrinsic or extrinsic risk factors, intrinsic refers to the environment that elevates risk: physical, cultural, and social. T F

25. Risk status is best conceptualized as a complete catalogue of risk factors. T F

26. Public Law 94-142 was signed into United States law by President Kennedy in 1961. T F

27. Under PL 94-142 and its amendments, such as IDEA of 1990, children with exceptional conditions from six to eighteen years of age only are served. T F

28. *Assessment* is simply the process of attempting to discover if a child has a problem. T F

29. For the general classroom teacher, the most important components of an IEP are long-term goals and short-term objectives. T F

30. The actual term *inclusion* as used in special education emerged in the 1960s. T F

31. The term *inclusion* is mentioned in all federal laws in the United States that deal with special education. T F

32. Jane has a severe cognitive disability. Her classroom teacher could use curriculum-based assessment to check her progress. T F

33. An IQ score of 70 would be considered to be within one standard deviation of the mean. T F

34. About 24 percent of Canadian school-aged students require special education at some point in their school careers. T F

Total /50

Section 2

Children and Youth with Mild Disabilities

Traditionally, the area of mild disabilities has included communication disorders, learning disabilities, mild mental retardation, and mild behavioural disorders. In this section, we examine children and youth with communication disorders, learning disabilities, and mental retardation.

Language is an important part of most human activity; it functions as a means of social interaction. Most small children develop communicative competence quite early in life. Some children, however, have *communication disorders*, impairments of the processes of speech and language. Speech and language problems not only constitute a field of exceptionality by themselves, but they cut across other categories of exceptionality.

Children with learning disabilities manifest a wide range of behavioural and learning characteristics. Learning disabilities is not a unitary concept and does not represent a homogeneous group of children. The only commonality is the existence of a learning problem that can threaten a child's entire educational experience.

Individuals who are described as intellectually disabled vary widely in almost every aspect of human behaviour, human personality, and human temperament. Students who are intellectually disabled will have difficulties with complex academic material; they are markedly slower than their agemates in using memory effectively, associating and classifying information, reasoning, and making judgments.

Chapter 4

Children with Speech and Language Differences

Learning outcomes

After reading this chapter, you should be able to:

- Understand the major elements of language and the stages and process of language acquisition in normally developing students;
- Differentiate between language delays and language disorders;
- Understand the major types of speech and language disorders, their developmental consequences, and the influence the various disorders have on children's behaviour and learning;
- Apply incidental techniques for speech and language improvement in the classroom.

Introduction

Of all the achievements of early childhood, the acquisition and development of speech and language is one of the most remarkable. The first three years is the crucial period for the development of speech and language. About twice as much language growth occurs between the first and third years as between the third and fourth years.

As the use of language is closely tied to cognitive development and self-concept, what happens in the early stages of acquisition of speech and language is critical for **communicative competence**, and is reflected in the child's performance in the classroom later on. Problems can impair a child's functioning in play and with peers resulting in the development of secondary behavioural problems, and can hinder a child's academic progress.

Overview of speech and language

Communication is the transmission of information; the process of exchanging ideas between participants. **Language** is a system of sound symbols organized into conventional patterns to communicate meaning. **Speech** is the mechanical output of language.

It is still not known exactly how children acquire language. However, children typically pass through certain stages in speech and language development. They show creativity in language and seem to acquire language in the same order.

Elements of language

There are a number of distinct elements of language—phonology, morphology, semantics, pragmatics, and syntax. **Syntax** is the network of organization principles underlying linguistic expression. **Semantics** is concerned with word meaning. **Morphology** refers to word building. *Morphemes* are groupings of phonemes into meaningful units; *bound morphemes* are not words but units of meaning when combined with words. **Phonology** is the sound system of the language; *phonemes* are the smallest sound units of a language. **Phonetics** describes the speech sounds of a language. **Pragmatics** relates to the ways in which language is used.

The speech mechanism

Structures involved in the oral production of language include the nervous system, the respiratory system, the oral portion of the digestive tract, and the auditory sense receptors.

Speech is produced when the airstream is shaped and resonated by the lips, tongue, teeth, jaw, nasal cavity, larynx, and pharynx. Vocalization, articulation, modulation, respiration, phonation, and resonance are major components of the speech process.

Speech and language development

Language learning begins in infancy and continues throughout life. In the early stages, the quality of adult–child interaction (sometimes referred to as **motherese**) is the single most important influence on a child's language development.

Infants attend to language from a very early age and learn from those around them. They also practise language, moving through distinct stages that include **cooing**, **babbling**, **echolalic speech**, and single words. In normal children, first words emerge between nine and nineteen months. Children in this developmental stage use single words, or **holophrasic speech**, to express ideas. Between eighteen and twenty-four months children begin to combine words, first in presentences and then in sentences, the first of which are referred to as **telegraphic speech**.

The sentence is a landmark in language acquisition. Once children reach this milestone, language competence develops rapidly. School-aged children are sophisticated language users; they use more complex linguistic structures, such as embedded and subordinate clauses. They understand personal pronouns and passive voice and they develop **metalinguistic** skills.

Speech and language differences

Communication disorders include a range of difficulties associated with speech, language, and hearing, or a combination of these. Language and speech problems may exist as sole disabilities, although in many cases they cut across many areas of exceptionality.

Problems may be both the result of and the cause of delayed development. For example, children with intellectual disabilities often have language levels below those expected for their mental ages. Because of auditory dysfunction, deaf children confront severe problems in the acquisition of speech and language. Many learning-disabled children have difficulties with language. Problems may occur in the comprehension of meaning, use of complex syntactic structures, use of vocabulary, and reading.

Definitions of language problems

Language problems are problems in the recognition and understanding of language, or in the ability to generate well-organized and grammatical sentences. **Language delays** are lags in the acquisition and development of language. **Language disorders** are impairments in, or deviant development of, the language system.

Children who are language-disordered are described by a number of terms that include *aphasic, dysphasic, communicatively impaired*, or *language learning disabled.*

Prevalence of language problems

As many as 15 percent of school-aged children may have some type of communication problem. Of these, perhaps 5 percent have speech and language disorders.

Classification of language problems

Receptive language disorders interfere with the comprehension of spoken language. **Expressive disorders** affect the formulation of grammatical utterances.

Delayed language development

A child with delayed language development learns language in an orderly progression but more slowly and less proficiently than normal-age peers. Many young children who show minor delays catch up with their peers by the time they are five or six. Other children with language delays may not close the gap in functioning.

Language disorders

Children who are language impaired or disordered show a developmental language disorder in the absence of other potentially contributing conditions. Some of these children show such difficulties in developing language in a normal progression that they may never attain adult levels. Others with language disorders may demonstrate bizarre language behaviour.

Aphasia

Children with **aphasia** lack the ability to communicate effectively with verbal language. *Developmental aphasia* means that the condition was present before a child had fully acquired language. *Acquired aphasia* refers to conditions that occurred after the development of language.

Mutism

The condition where there is no voice is known as **aphonia**. This is different from **mutism**, the total absence of speech. Mutism is a rare condition, related to severe emotional, neurological, or sensory deficit. Elective or selective mutism describes the condition of individuals who do not speak voluntarily or speak only in certain situations.

Etiology of language problems

Many causes contribute to language delays and language disorders. These include neurological dysfunction, accidents, and other disabilities such as hearing impairment. Severe language deficits can result from social deprivation and isolation. Early studies of feral children emphasize the importance of language stimulation.

Definitions of speech disorders

Speech disorders are problems encountered in the oral production of language. There may be deficits or deviance in articulation, voice quality, and dysfluency of speech. Speech disorders should not be confused with the speech errors that all young children make when learning to talk. Mispronunciations and dysfluencies become disorders only when they persist as characteristics in the speech of children who should have acquired certain sounds.

Prevalence of speech disorders

Speech disorders are one of the most prevalent childhood exceptionalities. Although criteria and definitions of communication disorders vary, it is estimated that five percent of the population between five and twenty-one years of age have speech disorders.

Classification of speech disorders

Children with speech defects are those whose speech interferes with communication. There are a number of ways to classify speech disorders.

Articulation disorders

When a child has a sound and pronounces it correctly in some contexts but not in others, the child has a **phonological problem**. Articulation problems are not related to use but to ability. With a phonological disorder, a child may have but not use a sound; with an **articulation disorder**, a child cannot actually make or produce a sound. Both phonological and articulatory disorders are characterized by omissions, substitutions, distortions, and additions of speech sounds.

Voice disorders

Voice disorders include deviations of pitch, quality, and intensity. Most voice disorders are related to poor learning of voice control.

Dysfluency

Stuttering, the most common speech **dysfluency**, is characterized by blocking, repetition, or prolongation of speech sounds, words, phrases, or syllables. Speech rate and rhythm are also involved.

Cluttering

Cluttered speech involves excessive speed of speech. This is combined with disorganized sentence structure and articulation problems.

Muscle control

Dysarthria refers to a partial or complete paralysis of the muscles associated with speech. It is caused by disturbances of motoric function brought about by damage to the nervous system.

Apraxia involves the inability to program, position, and sequence the muscle movements involved in speech. The child with apraxia can produce the movements involved in articulation but often fails to combine these movements with meaningful speech.

Orofacial defects

Orofacial defects are structural anomalies that include various types of clefts.

Etiology of speech disorders

Structural inadequacies are a major cause of speech disorders in children. Nervous system damage is a second prime cause. Clefts of the orofacial structures may produce delayed articulation in children.

Developmental consequences of speech and language problems

Because speech and language are so closely connected with every part of development, problems can create grave consequences for children.

Cognitive development

On tests of mental ability, children who are language disordered fall within normal limits on non-verbal measures. However, it is clear that many cognitive abilities, such as higher abstract thinking, are language dependent.

Academic achievement

Children with language disorders perform poorly in academic subjects where learning is dependent on language. Reading is especially affected.

Social and emotional development

Speech and language disturbances impact negatively on a child's social adjustment. Children who find communication difficult may become frustrated, withdrawn, and depressed. They may resort to compensatory measures such as gesture and body language.

Language disorders affect reciprocal family interactions. Parents may engage in fewer play and language activities with language-disordered children or may tend to assume greater responsibility in talking for their children.

Cultural and linguistic differences

Within special education, language-minority children are treated as a further differentiation of those with language problems. Limited English proficient (LEP) students make up an increasingly high proportion of special classes.

Assessment of speech and language problems

Assessment of articulatory, voice, and fluency disorders is usually performed by a speech/language clinician. Young children imitate the clinician's speech model; older children name objects or pictures, or read words and sentences aloud.

Assessing language problems

The assessment of language delays and disorders means a thorough and comprehensive study of a child's linguistic skills. Standardized tests are available for both screening and diagnosis. Language sampling is also used.

Assessing speech disorders

Assessment of articulatory, voice, and fluency disorders is undertaken by a speech/language therapist in the school or in a clinic setting. During the assessment, the clinician may test the child's production of phonemes in isolation and in the initial, medial, and final position in words. The clinician also tries to determine whether there is a consistency in the child's error patterns.

Intervention with children who have speech and language disorders

With the complex and varied nature of speech and language disorders, it is not surprising that many treatment modes are possible. Language specialists and educators have developed many new forms of treatment for children with speech and language disorders, both for the classroom and the clinic. Nevertheless, a guaranteed method to correct speech and language difficulties simply does not exist, and diversity in remediation programs characterizes the status quo.

Medical intervention

Early surgical intervention and plastic surgery are important in the treatment of structural defects associated with clefts of the lip and/or palate and other vocal parts. Lacking successful surgery, the child may encounter problems with feeding, speech, and respiration.

Therapy

Speech/language therapists or pathologists are concerned with all aspects of communication and its correction. In the treatment of articulation disorders, stress is placed on learning to listen, sound production, and retention. Treatment for voice disorders stresses listening training, articulatory adjustments, and breath control.

Many reasons are given to explain stuttering and various treatments have been developed. Therapy for stutterers includes psychotherapy, behaviour modification, and biofeedback.

Technical aids

For those unable to use speech, many augmentative communication techniques are available. These are discussed in Chapter 14.

Educational intervention

Minor speech and language disorders can be adequately helped by school speech/language clinicians. Children with significant deficits need intensive therapy, although education will almost always be in natural settings.

Service delivery models

The key word in recent language intervention trends is *natural*. Natural procedures take place in naturally occurring situations, pay attention to functional communication and conversational skills, and involve all those close to the child—parents, peers, and teachers. This means that the regular classroom is the most appropriate setting for almost all children with speech and language difficulties as their sole impairment.

Educational approaches

A variety of approaches and models are available to assist children with speech and language difficulties.

Grammatical approaches

These include specific approaches such as syntax-based programs.

Naturalistic approaches

The general classroom teacher can improve language performance with techniques such as rephrasing, imitating, and expanding children's utterances.

Curriculum

No special curriculum exists for children with speech and language disorders. Generally, language teaching for delayed children is based on normal language acquisition processes.

Key Terms

aphasia
aphonia
apraxia
articulation disorder
babbling
communicative competence
cooing
dysarthria
dysfluency
echolalic speech
expressive disorders
holophrasic speech
language
language delays
language disorders
language problems
metalinguistics
morphology
motherese
mutism
phonetics
phonological problem
phonology
pragmatics
receptive language disorders
semantics
speech
speech disorders
stuttering
syntax
telegraphic speech

Practice Questions

Multiple-choice questions

1. The most common disabilities that teachers at the preschool level will see are
   a. speech and language problems.
   b. intellectual disabilities, specifically Down syndrome.
   c. health disorders.
   d. learning disabilities.
   e. behavioural disorders.

2. Communicative competence refers to how children
   a. interact with others.
   b. communicate in various situations.
   c. make sense of what others say.
   d. form meaningful utterances.
   e. all of the above

3. Language is sometimes described as involving form, content, and function. Content refers to
   a. phonological elements.
   b. semantics.
   c. pragmatics.
   d. syntactical and morphological elements.
   e. phonetics.

4. Before young school children can be taught reading and writing, they require
   a. developing skills in syntax.
   b. a firm linguistic base.
   c. use of pragmatics.
   d. adequate phonological skills.
   e. all of the above

5. Between nine and eighteen months, the normal infant will produce
   a. non-reduplicated babbling and expressive jargon.
   b. reduplicated babbling.
   c. vocal play.
   d. cooing.
   e. reflexive crying.

6. Ten-year-old Jimmy can think about language, talk about language, and manipulate language. These skills are referred to as ________ skills.
   a. metalinguistic
   b. metacognitive
   c. meta-audition
   d. metaspeech
   e. meta-idiomatic

7. Sentence A is "The car hit the truck." Sentence B is "The car was hit by the truck." In terms of children's language development, we would expect
   a. three-year-old Jessie to understand B but not A.
   b. three-year-old Jessie to understand both A and B.
   c. eight-year-old Sean to understand A but not B.
   d. eight-year-old Sean to understand both A and B.
   e. five-year-old John to understand both A and B.

8. When speech impairments and language disorders are compared, it can be said that
   a. language disorders are more complex.
   b. speech impairments are more difficult to remediate.
   c. in the remediation process, articulation disorders are the most difficult to remediate.
   d. through a developmental approach, language disorders are relatively easy to remediate.
   e. all of the above

9. The characteristics of voice disorders relate most specifically to
   a. substitutions and omissions.
   b. distortions and dysfluencies.
   c. deviations in pitch, intensity, or quality.
   d. syntactic difficulties.
   e. semantic and pragmatic problems.

10. Fluency refers to the
   a. degree of vocabulary development in a particular language.
   b. eloquence with which a child can express himself or herself.
   c. smoothness with which words, sounds, and phrases flow together.
   d. degree of expression and animation in a child's speech.
   e. blocking, repetitions, or prolongations of sounds, words, or phrases.

11. Echolalia is best described as
   a. prolonged repetition of other people's words and phrases.
   b. made-up language constructed by a child with emotional disturbance.
   c. syntactic problems.
   d. difficulties in articulation.
   e. strings of consonant and vowel sounds.

12. A child says to the teacher, "Me sick today." The teacher responds with "You feel rather sick today." This is an example of
   a. imitation.

b. expansion.
c. cause and effect.
d. an open-ended question.
e. metalinguistics.

13. *Delayed language* is a term most closely related to the
    a. deviations heard in a child's language.
    b. lag behind normal language development.
    c. type of remediation program necessary.
    d. areas of the language hierarchy affected.
    e. dysfluency in a child's speech.

14. Holophrasic speech refers to
    a. single-word utterances.
    b. complex sentence structures.
    c. simple sentence structures.
    d. delayed speech.
    e. a form of babbling.

15. Among the many theories that account for language acquisition and development, imitation is an element of the ________ theory.
    a. social learning
    b. cognitive-developmental
    c. humanistic
    d. behavioural
    e. ecological

16. Match the term to the definition.
    a. communication
    b. communicative competence
    c. motherese
    d. language
    e. speech

    ___ the ability to use language in different interactions and situations
    ___ the process of exchanging information and ideas
    ___ a system of symbols that communicate meaning
    ___ the mechanical production of language
    ___ a simpler version of language used with infants and toddlers

Recall questions

1. Speech that is an immediate imitation of that of another speaker is known as ________.

2. Although there are many causes of speech disorders, the three major causes are ________, ________, and ________.

3. When young children use single words to express a more complex idea, this is referred to as ________ speech; when they use reduced speech that includes only the essential aspects of a message, this is referred to as ________ speech.

4. ________ is a speech disorder characterized by blocking, repetition, or prolongation of speech sounds, words, or syllables.

5. The use of language in its social context is referred to as ________.

6. Two major approaches to teaching students who are language disordered are ________ and ________.

7. Hypernasality, breathiness, and hoarseness are characteristics of ________ disorders.

8. The most common types of speech disorders are in the area of ________.

9. A cleft palate may not only result in problems with speech, but also in problems in ________.

10. LEP is an acronym for ________.

True–false questions

1. Competence with language in the toddler and preschool years has a direct influence on a child's ability to later read and write. T F

2. In teaching and promoting communication skills in children, the research has not yet indicated which approach is most effective. T F

3. Language must always be transmitted through oral modes; that is, speech. T F

4. In identification, assessment, and remediation, language problems are more complex than are speech disorders. T F

5. Language can exist without speech but speech cannot exist without language. T F

6. Itard believed that Victor was an idiot because he had been left in the wilds; he therefore thought that appropriate environmental conditions would humanize the boy. T F

7. When small children are acquiring language, they learn all aspect of language simultaneously. T F

8. Aphasia is a language problem that arises from structural or orofacial problems. T F

9. By the time a child is six years old, all the semantic components of language are developed. T F

10. Speech and language emerge at different times, with language preceding speech. T F

Short-answer questions

1. Briefly define the terms *syntax, semantics,* and *pragmatics.*

2. Between birth and eighteen months, children progress through various stages of language and speech development. Outline the major stages.

3. Speech disorders are classified into a number of major categories. List and briefly describe three categories.

4. Identify the major tasks of a speech/language clinician.

5. List and explain three major types of educational interventions provided for children with delayed or disordered language.

Applications

1. In the educational journals, find three articles relating to
   - language disorders in children who are autistic; or
   - using peer-mediated strategies with preschool children with language delays and disorders.

   Present a report consisting of a description, comparison, and evaluation of the three articles. (See Application Question 1 in Chapter 1 of this study guide for report format.)

2. Secure a copy of the test manuals, materials, and record forms for a language test. Read and study these materials thoroughly. Before using the test with a child, you should first observe a competent examiner administering, scoring, and interpreting the test. As well, practise administering, scoring, and interpreting the test on one of your peers. Any work with children should initially be under the supervision of a competent examiner, if possible. When you feel ready, administer the test to a child. Follow all test directions, score carefully, then interpret very cautiously.

3. Reread the three sections of the case study about Ashley in Chapter 4 of the text. Using only the information presented, outline an IEP for Ashley. Fill in the IEP sections on
   - child data
   - IEP data
   - assessment results
   - present levels of functioning
   - long-range goals (provide goals for oral language and reading)
   - short-term objectives (three objectives for each of the above goals)

Activities

1. In 1800, Jean Marc Itard undertook the training of Victor, a boy of about fourteen years of age who had been found running wild in the forest near Aveyron. Itard, who believed that Victor was idiotic because of lack of environmental stimulation, developed structured and systematic sense training methods to improve Victor's visual, auditory, and motor skills. Itard's memoirs and reports to the French Ministry are contained in *The Wild Boy of Aveyron* (1932, New York: Century). Obtain a copy of this book and from it write a paper on Itard's work with Victor.

2. Find a child between eighteen and twenty months of age. Spend at least an hour with the child and note all utterances. Revisit the child in about three months and again note all utterances. Compare your two assessments in terms of advances in vocabulary and syntax usage.

3. Record three people reading a passage of about one hundred words. Describe each voice in terms of loudness, pitch, nasality, breathiness, hoarseness, and other identifying characteristics.

4. Visit a nursery school that includes children with disabilities. Observe one child for at least a full morning or afternoon session. Note the child's language, and then compare it to the language levels that are appropriate for that age. Note the child's major strengths and deficits.

Portfolio item

One way to examine disabilities and societal perceptions is through the media. Find a movie that relates to disability. Some examples are *The Miracle Worker, Rain Man,* and *Children of a Lesser God.*

Present a report. First, provide a brief overview of the theme and the story in the movie. The major portion of the report should then be on the issues that the portrayal raises for you personally and new ways that you perceive disability and societal reactions.

Chapter 5

Children with Learning Disabilities

Learning outcomes

After reading this chapter, you should be able to:

- Understand the common elements found in most definitions of learning disabilities;
- Understand the developmental consequences of learning disabilities;
- Understand the diversity of causes and symptoms of learning disabilities;
- Recognize the relationship between learning disabilities and other mild forms of disability;
- Understand the many forms of intervention used with students with learning disabilities.

Introduction

Perhaps more than any other field of exceptionality, learning disabilities have generated controversy, confusion, misconceptions, and polarization among concerned professionals. This happens in part because learning disabilities does not concern a single, easily identifiable disability and children with learning disabilities do not form a unified, homogenous group. Rather, learning disabilities is a syndrome, a group of related and overlapping conditions that includes vastly different populations who reveal a wide variety of behavioural, learning, social, and interpersonal problems.

Definitions of learning disabilities

The category of learning disabilities is still not well understood by many educators, psychologists, and parents. Because of the heterogeneous nature of the learning-disabled population and the many characteristics displayed, it is extremely difficult to arrive at an accurate and universal definition of learning disabilities. The fact that no universally accepted definition exists leads to problems with prevalence, etiology, and assessment.

While there are many definitions of learning disabilities, most share some common elements.

Neurological dysfunction

This is a medically oriented criterion that views most learning disabilities as resulting from minimal brain dysfunction.

Uneven growth pattern

Children with learning disabilities display a wide range of abilities and disabilities, manifested as peaks and valleys in performance.

Difficulty in academic tasks

The most noticeable manifestations of learning disabilities are learning deficits; children with learning deficits fail to learn by traditional methods in traditional classrooms. Specific problems may occur in the acquisition of speech and oral language, in reading, in written language, in handwriting, in spelling, or in arithmetic. Depending on the definition, thinking, motor skills, perceptual skills, and psychosocial skills could be added.

Discrepancy between potential and performance

A discrepancy between potential (as measured on tests of mental ability) and performance (demonstrated on achievement tests and academic tasks) is the most important characteristic differentiating students with learning disabilities from those with other exceptionalities.

Exclusion of other causes

Children whose exceptionalities are primarily the result of other causes are excluded in most definitions of learning disabilities. This is an administrative arrangement and does not imply that otherwise-disabled students may not have learning disabilities.

Average or above-average intelligence

Generally, youngsters with learning disabilities are considered to be of average or above-average intelligence.

Social deficits

Some definitions define learning disabilities strictly in terms of intellect and achievement; others include emotional and social complications that may adversely affect school learning and achievement.

Prevalence of learning disabilities

Given the definitional difficulties, it is very hard to estimate the true prevalence of learning disabilities. Most Canadian studies place the number of seriously learning-disabled students at from 2 to 4 percent of the school-aged population. Among this population, boys outnumber girls by about four to one. The reasons for the sex-ratio differences are unclear.

Classification of learning disabilities

Across the country, different classification schemes for learning disabilities are used. Students may be classified as having mild, moderate, or severe learning disabilities, or general or specific learning disabilities.

As in other fields of exceptionality, classification systems and terminology in the field of learning disabilities have evolved and changed. Much of the early terminology was drawn from neurology. The most pervasive term is *dyslexia,* which refers to difficulties with reading. The terms *dyslexia* and *learning disabilities* are not synonymous.

Etiology of learning disabilities

Experts do not agree on the causes of learning disabilities any more than they agree on definitions. Numerous etiological factors have been proposed.

Minimal brain dysfunction

Traditionally, *minimal brain dysfunction*, which refers to some damage or insult to the brain, has been viewed as the root of most learning disabilities.

Biochemical disturbances

Some researchers view learning disabilities as the result of physiological problems or biochemical disturbances. Benjamin Feingold popularized the notion of relating allergies to hyperactivity after he studied the effects of food dyes, flavours, and artificial preservatives on children.

Genetic factors

Especially in the area of reading difficulties, there is a tendency for learning disabilities to run in families. Reading retardation may be an inherited form of difficulty in some cases, but it is not possible to pinpoint the particular aspects that are genetically determined.

Maturational lags

Other researchers have focused on the slower development of children who are learning disabled in some areas. They see a **maturational lag** as contributing to the problem. A maturational lag means that a child is slow to reach some developmental milestones.

Environmental factors

Poor teaching, described as *dyspedagogia* or maleducation, is a type of poor environment that may underlie the problems exhibited by some students. As well as teaching failure, dyspedagogia includes a child's poor physical condition, poor school attendance, and lowered motivation.

Developmental consequences of learning disabilities

So many characteristics have been attributed to the learning-disabled population that a review of the symptoms would seem to indicate that nearly everyone suffers a learning disability. However, for the child who is learning disabled, the difficulties are chronic, academically debilitating, and lie outside the normal range.

Cognitive development

By definition, students with learning disabilities possess average or above-average intelligence. In most cases, students with learning disabilities do not have deficits in the actual ability to learn. They seem to have performance deficits rather than ability deficits; that is, they are weak in the development of learning and problem solving strategies and have deficiencies in metacognitive skills. Their learning strategies—or lack of them—prevent them from using their basic abilities to the best advantage.

Communication

A significant relationship exists between learning problems and language deficits. Many children with learning disabilities have speech and language problems; deficits may occur in expressive or receptive language or in speech. Youngsters who are learning disabled may manifest problems in articulation, syntax, grammar, or pragmatics. These children may be very literal in their responses, indicating that they miss the subtleties and nuances of the language.

Academic achievement

Academic underachievement is the major characteristic of students with learning disabilities. Reading, written expression, and mathematics are the chief areas of difficulty.

Reading

A large percentage of students with learning disabilities have reading difficulties. The reading problems vary in nature; students may have early difficulties with phonological awareness, be unable to deal with symbols, synthesize parts of a word into a whole, or organize words into meaningful clusters; they may miss or confuse important details. Poor reading leads to poor spelling, and spelling impairments are endemic among the learning disabled population. **Phonological awareness** is the ability to blend, segment, rhyme, or in other ways manipulate the sounds of spoken words.

Written expression

These students have great difficulties with written expression, showing poor spelling, gross disorganization, disconnected thoughts, incorrect syntax, and poor grammar. For some students, handwriting is clearly deviant. Writing may show incorrect letter formation, reversals, transformations, uneven slant, and no relationship of the graphics to the paper lines. **Story grammar** describes the typical elements found in stories, such as theme, characters, and setting.

Mathematics

A substantial number of students with learning disabilities meet problems with mathematics. Difficulties may be related to perception, directionality, abstract thinking, memory, or reading.

Perceptual development

Perception involves the use of the senses to recognize, discriminate, and interpret stimuli. Students unable to process perceptions accurately are said to have perceptual disorders, sometimes referred to as psychological processing deficits.

Children with learning disabilities may have problems with perception and with recognizing, discriminating, and interpreting incoming stimulus data. Difficulties may be in visual processing, auditory processing, or haptic perception.

Motor development and coordination

Haptic problems, those that include touch, body movement, and position in space, are thought to be uncommon. Some children may have difficulties with **body image**—the knowledge of their own bodies and their relationship to the environment. Others have problems with **laterality** and **directionality**. Children who have not developed hand dominance by age five or six may have laterality problems that lead to confusion in directionality and left–right discrimination.

Youngsters with perceptual-motor impairments have difficulty in identifying or reproducing information received through the senses. General uncoordination refers to a lack of muscular control. Such children may be clumsy, have an awkward gait, or show other fine and gross motor deviations.

Social and emotional development

Significant numbers of children with learning disabilities suffer social and emotional complications, which may exist alone or may contribute to learning deficits. Problems occur in social adjustment, social perception, self-concept, and motivation.

Many students with learning disabilities lack systematic and organized judgment. They have difficulty in perceiving the affective status of others, have problems in socializing, in making friends, and in establishing positive family relationships. Pupils who are learning disabled tend to be rejected by their peers; they receive less-favourable responses from both peers and teachers.

Poor academic behaviours, the inability to achieve, the lack of success, and the non-reinforcing experiences that are the lot of many youngsters who are learning disabled bring about other reactions. Children with learning disabilities often have poor **self-concept** and poor self-esteem. They may also show an external locus of control, learned helplessness, and poor motivation.

An external locus of control develops when students believe themselves to be controlled by outer, rather than inner, forces. This accompanies learned helplessness, the belief that any efforts will not result in desired outcomes. Individuals expect to fail and consequently lose motivation.

Social and emotional problems can lead students with learning disabilities to develop an **emotional overlay**—adverse emotional or behavioural problems that develop as a function of a learning disorder.

Co-occurring disabilities

Children who are caught in a cycle of frustration and failure may react with poor behaviour. Children with learning disabilities show many externalizing behavioural disorders such as aggression, antisocial behaviour, and conduct problems. Teenage students may display impulsiveness, low frustration thresholds, irritability, low self-esteem, and suggestibility. Under some conditions, these behaviours result in antisocial acts.

Attention deficits compound the problems of students with learning disabilities. These children tend to be less attentive in school and demonstrate less task-oriented behaviour and more non-constructive off-task behaviour.

Cultural and linguistic differences

In the field of learning disabilities, the number of linguistic-minority students placed in learning disabilities programs is growing disproportionately. Limited English proficiency (LEP) is often identified as a learning disability because the characteristics of second-language learners, especially in the early stages of second-language acquisition, are similar to behaviours associated with certain categories of exceptionality, specifically learning disabilities and communication disorders.

Assessment of learning disabilities

Identification and measurement of learning disabilities serves to pinpoint atypical behaviour, explain it, differentiate it from other exceptionalities, and use results to plan efficient program implementation. Currently, no single identification procedure exists; varied identification and diagnostic measures are employed.

Identification of students who are learning disabled involves screening and diagnosis. Screening examines large groups of children to find those performing above or below the norm. Diagnosis investigates selected children to determine the precise nature of their difficulties. Diagnostic data are obtained through informal testing and formal standardized testing.

Psychological processing

Psychological processing (more often called *learning styles* today) refers to how an individual processes sensory information and puts it to meaningful intellectual use. Hence, tests of psychological processing are often used.

Intervention with children who have learning disabilities

Because of the heterogeneous nature of the learning-disabled population, a wide variety of intervention approaches and techniques have been employed. Research does not support any single approach or method.

Medical intervention

The medical community maintains an active interest in children with learning disabilities, and extensive medical research is reported each year. The current focus of medical interest includes drug therapy and diet management.

Psychopharmacological management

Drug therapy with children who are learning disabled has increased in recent years. A variety of drugs are prescribed to control hyperactive and inattentive behaviour. (See Chapter 7.)

Diets

Dr. Benjamin Feingold popularized the notion that food dyes and colourings are linked to hyperactivity. Feingold's K.P. Diet restricts or eliminates the intake of suspected foods that may adversely affect the child.

Technical aids

Computer technology holds promise for students with learning disabilities. Programs include learning packages, voice printers, programs to teach logic and develop learning strategies, and programs to develop and enhance self-concept.

Educational intervention

Almost all students with learning disabilities are adequately served in general classrooms with some curriculum adaptations and support. Some students receive resource-room assistance.

Service delivery models

While almost all students with learning disabilities are educated in general classrooms, research supports a continuum of services. Without a continuum of services, some students who are learning disabled flounder in traditional classrooms.

In question are the competencies of general classroom teachers, few of whom possess the breadth of knowledge or the competencies to meet the individual needs of students with learning disabilities. Too, students themselves are ambivalent about in-class or pull-out programs.

There is no research evidence that any one service delivery model meets the needs of all students; indeed, empirical research in the field so far fails to support the efficacy of inclusion for students with learning disabilities.

Educational approaches

A diverse range of approaches has developed in the field of learning disabilities. These can be grouped into three general categories: traditional approaches, behavioural approaches, and cognitive approaches. Traditional approaches that sought to remediate processing deficits are rare today and the focus is now on behavioural (skills) or cognitive (strategy training) approaches.

Behavioural (skills) approaches

In the behavioural or skills approach to the remediation of learning disabilities the focus is on a student's ability to perform specific academic tasks through the provision of direct instruction in areas of deficit. Instruction begins at the child's level of skill acquisition.

Task analysis is an important aspect of the skills approach. Using task analysis, the teacher breaks a skill down into its components and teaches in small building steps.

Cognitive approaches

Good students plan how to learn and understand the strategies that help them learn efficiently. Students with learning disabilities often lack awareness of the metacognitive strategies that help them learn.

The major approaches today are cognitive approaches that stress teaching students to develop metacognitive skills and to use **learning strategies** effectively. Once they are trained in these areas, students with learning disabilities show considerable improvement in academic functioning.

What are metacognitive processes?

Within the general concept of **metacognition**, there are two types of behaviour. The two behaviours comprising meta-cognition are knowledge and skill, alternatively referred to as *cognitive strategies* (control executive strategies) and *learning strategies.*

Strategy training

Research findings indicate that children with learning disabilities in general lack comprehension monitoring skills and efficient task strategies. They show significant improvement following strategy training (also known as learning–thinking instructional programs, cognitive training, and cognitive behaviour modification), which typically provides the learner with a set of self-instructional steps to increase effectiveness in the acquisition, organization, and expression of information. **Attributions** are the reasons that people give for what happens to them.

Curriculum

Students with learning disabilities require a variety of curricular adaptations directed to their unique and individual needs. For example, the teacher may need to adjust language programming and explore different approaches and techniques in teaching reading. Remediation in mathematics may require carefully structured and sequenced instruction, along with the use of much concrete material.

Key Terms

attributions
body image
directionality
emotional overlay
laterality
learning strategies
maturational lag
metacognition
perception
phonological awareness
psychological processing
self-concept
story grammar
task analysis

Practice Questions

Multiple-choice questions

1. The largest single focus of programming for children who are exceptional in many school districts is
   a. mental retardation.
   b. behavioural disorders.
   c. learning disabilities.
   d. physical disabilities.
   e. sensory deficits.

2. The classification of learning disabilities is hampered because
   a. learning disabilities do not fit into any of the traditional categories of disabling conditions.
   b. learning disabilities constitutes a syndrome, not a unitary concept.
   c. the category of learning disabilities encompasses a complex group of behaviours and conditions.
   d. students with learning disabilities display varied characteristics.
   e. all of the above

3. Within the learning disabled population, prevalence estimates indicate that
   a. boys outnumber girls.
   b. girls outnumber boys.
   c. most learning disabilities can be overcome, so elementary-aged pupils outnumber secondary students.
   d. no adults are considered to be learning disabled.
   e. the highest prevalence is found among preschool children.

4. According to the text, the major issue in the field of learning disabilities today is
   a. the formulation of a universally accepted definition.
   b. clear determinations of prevalence.
   c. finding effective assessment measures.
   d. determining the combination of traits that call for special placement.
   e. deciding on appropriate instructional strategies.

5. The field of learning disabilities has shown unparalleled growth in the past three decades because
   a. increasing numbers of children previously categorized as mentally retarded are now termed learning disabled.
   b. the strength of the ACLD (CLDA) combined with massive research has propelled learning disabilities to prominence.
   c. learning disabilities have become easier to identify and diagnose.
   d. parents and teachers prefer the label of learning disabilities.
   e. all of the above

6. In the area of learning disabilities, the *discrepancy criterion* refers to
   a. uneven growth pattern.

b. a gap between potential and performance.
c. difficulties in processing information.
d. problems in social functioning.
e. problems in the language arts.

7. In the classroom, children who are learning disabled generally
   a. perform as well as their non-disabled peers.
   b. do well in all subject areas except reading.
   c. are less attentive and demonstrate less task-oriented behaviour.
   d. demonstrate few learning problems in content areas such as science and social studies.
   e. are generally well accepted by peers and teachers.

8. Various factors seem to account for the higher prevalence of males among the learning-disabled population. According to explanations put forward,
   a. boys show more overt and acting-out behaviour than do girls and are therefore more likely to be identified as learning disabled.
   b. family and twin studies show that dyslexia in families is more common in males than females.
   c. genes thought to influence reading disability are found in the area also thought to influence certain aspects of male development.
   d. males have more problems overall with reading than do females.
   e. all of the above

9. Many approaches have been attempted in the field of learning disabilities. Today, we totally discount
   a. psychological processing approaches.
   b. processing tests and measures.
   c. special diets.
   d. psychopharmacological management.
   e. None of the above are totally discounted.

10. Mrs. Jones is positive that her three-and-a-half-year-old son, Jimmy, has a learning disability. She tells the pediatrician that Jimmy never sits still, forgets what she tells him, and does not have the language skills that his sister had at the same age. The pediatrician explains that he cannot determine if Jimmy is really learning disabled because
    a. hyperactive behaviour is not a part of the learning disabilities syndrome.
    b. language problems are not generally characteristic of young learning disabled children.
    c. Jimmy is very well coordinated, and clumsiness is characteristic of children with learning disabilities.
    d. the category of learning disabilities is intimately tied to academic performance and Jimmy has not yet demonstrated academic performance.
    e. Jimmy is too young to assess for any type of learning or behaviour problem.

11. A conclusion that may be drawn about dietary treatment for children with learning disabilities is that
    a. the approaches are never effective in the alleviation of learning disabilities.
    b. the techniques have heightened the problems in many children.

c. the approaches are fads and should never be considered in the treatment of learning disabilities.
d. research is ongoing and results so far are equivocal.
e. diet modification is considered the most efficient approach to alleviate learning disabilities in young children.

12. Carl is meeting increasing problems with his peers and his teachers. The research on the social interactions of students with learning disabilities shows that
    a. Carl is unusual; most children with learning disabilities are well accepted by their peers.
    b. Carl fits the pattern: children with learning disabilities are poorly accepted by peers although well accepted by teachers and other adults.
    c. students with learning disabilities meet social difficulties with both teachers and peers.
    d. there is no difference in peer interaction between students with learning disabilities and their normally developing peers.
    e. none of the above

13. When identifying learning disabilities, the most common discrepancy measure is between
    a. age and grade placement.
    b. grade-level expectations and grade placement.
    c. achievement areas such as reading and math.
    d. tested potential for academic tasks and actual academic performance.
    e. academic and social domains.

14. A maturational lag refers to
    a. slowness to reach developmental milestones.
    b. peaks and valleys in performance.
    c. general incapacity across all academic areas.
    d. a developmental delay.
    e. innate differences in attention, behaviour, and perception.

15. Rosebriar Elementary School initiates a program to prevent learning disabilities. To do this, school personnel concentrate on
    a. prevention of neurological damage.
    b. identification of learning disabilities in the preschool years.
    c. curriculum designed to meet the unique needs of individual students.
    d. identification of high-risk students for kindergarten placement in resource rooms.
    e. all of the above

16. Match the individual to the statement.
    a. A. Strauss
    b. N. Rockefeller
    c. J. Hinshelwood
    d. B. Feingold
    e. S. Kirk
    ___ named the field of learning disabilities
    ___ wrote *Congenital Word Blindness*
    ___ wrote about his own dyslexia
    ___ devised the K.P. Diet
    ___ studied children with brain damage

Recall questions

1. Strauss contributed to the development of the field of learning disabilities. The five behaviours known as the Strauss syndrome are hyperactivity, ________, ________, ________, and ________.

2. An internal knowledge of the differences between left and right is ________; an awareness of left and right outside the body is ________.

3. An individual's belief that any efforts will fail to result in desired outcomes is referred to as ________.

4. An analysis of the behavioural components and prerequisite skills of a task is known as ________.

5. Mary consistently mixes up /b/ and /d/ in her reading and writing. Mary may have difficulties in visual and/or auditory ________.

6. Samuel Orton coined the term *strephosymbolia,* which means ________.

7. The notion that food substances and hyperactivity are linked was popularized by ________.

8. A disturbance in the ability to express thoughts in writing is ________.

9. The term *dyspedagogia* refers to ________.

10. The blanket term used to refer to the strategies that control learning is ________.

True–false questions

1. In the field of learning disabilities, many definitions have emerged but no consensus yet exists. T F

2. Children with learning disabilities can be viewed as a homogeneous group of students with similar learning deficits. T F

3. It is relatively easy to distinguish children who are learning disabled from those who are behaviourally disordered. T F

4. Visual closure means the ability to sight an object with only one eye. T F

5. Reading difficulties represent the most common specific academic disability seen in students with learning disabilities. T F

6. Students with learning disabilities lag in academic achievement. To bridge the gap, they should be given more homework than their non-disabled peers. T F

7. Dietary control has been conclusively shown to help in alleviating learning disabilities in large numbers of children. T F

8. Research has shown the traditional ability or process-training approaches for the remediation of learning disabilities to be successful with nearly all students. T F

9. Concrete objects should not be used to teach math to children who are learning disabled as they only add to incoming stimuli. T F

10. The great majority of students with learning disabilities also have Attention Deficit Disorder. T F

Short-answer questions

1. There are more boys than girls among the learning disabled population. List five factors that have been put forward to account for this.

2. Many of the widely used definitions of learning disabilities share some common elements. List five criteria for learning disabilities that commonly appear.

3. *Dyspedagogia* is a coined term that has been used to describe factors that may contribute to mild learning disabilities. List five elements that may be involved in dyspedagogia.

4. List and explain the subskills that make up visual processing.

5. Written language presents great difficulty to many students with learning disabilities. List the areas in which problems may be manifested. Include spelling and handwriting difficulties.

Applications

1. In the educational journals, find three articles relating to one of the following topics:
   - early identification of learning disabilities; or
   - metacognitive strategy training with students with learning disabilities.

   Present a report consisting of a description, comparison, and evaluation of the three articles. (See Application Question 1 in Chapter 1 of this study guide for report format.)

2. From the relevant chapters, list ten characteristics of children categorized as learning disabled, mildly intellectually disabled, and behaviourally disordered. Chart these. Compare the characteristics for similarities and differences.

3. Danny, the child in the case study in Chapter 5, is described as "fairly typical of children with learning disabilities." Given the developmental consequences of learning disabilities as detailed in the text, explain why Danny would be considered a fairly typical child.

4. The IEP for Danny in the text stresses reading, creative writing, and mathematics. Add to the IEP by writing two long-range goals for handwriting. Add three short-term objectives for each handwriting goal.

Activities

1. Try these measures to judge handedness. Note whether your left or right hand is dominant.

- Clasp your hands. The dominant thumb tends to be on top.
- Stand opposite a partner. Close your eyes and raise your hands slowly to shoulder height. The dominant hand tends to be a little higher.
- Comb your hair. In which hand did you hold the comb?
- Take a piece of notepaper and punch a small hole in it. Through the hole sight an object on the wall. Now bring the paper in toward your nose. Your dominant eye will tend to continue to sight the object.
- Take two pieces of paper and a pencil. Use each foot to sign your name. You will tend to get a better signature with the dominant foot.

Portfolio item

Although there are many persons with disabilities in North American society, their representation may not be reflected in the popular media. To find out whether this is true or not, watch television for at least three hours. As you do so, keep a log in which you note each program and each advertisement. How many people with disabilities of any type were shown? Then note what were they doing. Were they shown in a positive or a negative manner? Try to explain the reasons for any under-representation that you found.

Chapter 6

Children with Intellectual Disabilities

Learning outcomes

After reading this chapter, you should be able to:

- Understand the definitions of mental retardation and adaptive behaviour;
- Recognize the risk factors that can result in mental retardation;
- Relate the category of mental retardation to other forms of mild or significant disability;
- Recognize the developmental consequences of the different levels of intellectual disability;
- Understand accommodations, adaptations, and modifications that teachers can make to assist learners with special needs.

Introduction

Essentially, the term *intellectual disability* refers to delayed intellectual growth that is manifested in immature reactions to environmental stimuli and below-average social and academic performance.

Definitions of intellectual disabilities

No universally accepted definition of mental retardation exists. Over the years, definitions have undergone change and modification as more has been learned about people with intellectual disabilities, their potential, and the developmental consequences of the condition. Today's definitions are flexible. They focus on the interplay between the individual and the environment rather than viewing mental retardation as a condition existing solely within the individual.

The most commonly used definition is that first proposed by the American Association on Mental Deficiency (AAMD) in 1959 and revised by the American Association on Mental Retardation (AAMR) in 1993. Under this definition, *mental retardation* refers to significantly subaverage general intellectual functioning resulting in or associated with impairments in adaptive behaviour that are manifested during the developmental period.

Subaverage general intellectual functioning

Individuals are not considered intellectually disabled unless they score below 70 IQ on a standardized test of mental ability; that is, two or more standard deviations below the mean.

Adaptive behaviour

Adaptive behaviour is an increasingly important element in definitions of intellectual disability. In general, **adaptive behaviour** refers to how well an individual adapts to the environment; that is, the degree and efficiency with which an individual meets the standards of personal independence and social responsibility expected of a particular age or cultural group. The level of skill development and the relationship of skill development to developmental trends are the two major elements of adaptive behaviour.

Developmental period

Under the AAMR definition, the developmental period refers to the time between the child's conception and the eighteenth birthday.

Classification of intellectual disabilities

Most professionals classify mental retardation on a range of severity as proposed by the AAMR. Levels are mild, moderate, severe, and profound. Some educators continue to use the terms *educable mentally retarded* (mild), and *trainable mentally retarded* (moderate).

Divisions based on severity or any other classification schedule are arbitrary. There is much overlap and blurring among categories. As well, as in all areas of special education, new trends are apparent in terminology in the field of intellectual disabilities. Terms such as *mentally retarded, intellectually challenged*, and *developmentally disabled* are all used.

Classification by needs

Rather than severity, a new system changes dependency to support needs, keys terms to the level of services required, and describes them in ways that are prescriptive for programming needs. Specifically, it replaces the levels of mild to profound with *intermittent, limited, extensive,* and *pervasive*, which refer to the supports needed.

Prevalence of intellectual disabilities

It is extremely difficult to accurately estimate the prevalence of mental retardation. This is because different IQ cut-off points are used; data gathering differs; there are various ways of defining adaptive behaviour; there tend to be differences in prevalence in relation to different geographic areas and different socio-economic groups; and different age groups demonstrate different prevalence rates. There are also gender differences that confound estimates. There are more boys than girls in the identified population of children with intellectual disabilities. Finally, the movement among categories, specifically for students with mild disabilities, tends to muddy figures.

Today, there is much blurring among the traditional categories of children who are exceptional. This is particularly true among groups termed *mildly disabled*: those identified as mildly mentally retarded, learning disabled, and mildly behaviourally disordered. Among other things, this movement among categories means that mental retardation is a shrinking category and that children referred to as mildly mentally retarded display more serious learning problems than in the past.

Current estimates place the number of persons with intellectual disabilities at about 1.5 percent of the population. Of these, the great majority fall into the category of mildly intellectually disabled.

Etiology of intellectual disabilities

Because of the medical orientation in which the roots of mental retardation are deeply embedded, etiological considerations remain important in this field. A wide range of agents can lead to intellectual disabilities. But while there are more than 200 known causes, only in about 6 to 15 percent of cases can the etiology be accurately pinpointed.

Genetic defects

PKU and galactosemia are two genetic disorders that have the potential to cause intellectual problems.

Chromosomal problems

Down syndrome is the most common form of chromosomal disorder. The recent discovery of fragile X syndrome has attracted interest because of its unique inheritance pattern, the wide variability in accompanying disabilities, and the gender differences among persons affected.

Infections and intoxications

Among infections, rubella, syphilis, pediatric AIDS, meningitis, and encephalitis can all lead to intellectual disability. Intoxicants and drugs can damage the cognitive functioning of a child.

Environmental influences

Often, genetic factors interweave with environmental conditions to further affect a child's development.

Developmental consequences of intellectual disabilities

Intellectual disability does not characterize a homogeneous group of children, nor can it be considered a specific disorder or disease. Individuals who are intellectually disabled demonstrate diverse characteristics and are an extremely heterogeneous population. When IQ can be changed, it is called **trait plasticity**.

Physical development

Children with mild intellectual disabilities usually show no pathological signs of disease or injury. But as the severity of disability increases, so does the prevalence of physical problems. Persons with moderate, severe, and profound disabilities are likely to have additional disabling conditions such as poor speech, inadequate social skills, poor motor development, incontinence, behavioural and psychiatric disorders, sensory impairments, seizures, and cerebral palsy. Survival rates are lower among those who are mildly disabled than the general population.

Cognitive development

Cognition is the process of recognizing, identifying, associating, and inferring meaning beyond the figural information provided by the environment. By definition, intellectual disability means deficits in **cognitive development**; that is, the way individuals understand and cope with their world. Therefore, the most noticeable effect of intellectual disabilities is on a child's ability to learn. However, the differences in learning are quantitative rather than qualitative. Children learn in the same way as their normally developing peers but more slowly and with more restricted ceilings.

Children with mild intellectual disabilities are the largest group of learners in this population. These children demonstrate wide diversity in academic and behavioural performance; they learn at a rate of half to three-quarters that of non-disabled children and can usually reach the academic standards of the later elementary-school grades. They develop adequate social, personal, and communication skills. As adults, they function in a variety of contexts.

Persons with moderate intellectual disabilities have limited intellectual abilities. They have problems in abstracting and generalizing and are not ready for much academic work until their early teens. They show rather clear-cut deficits in adaptive behaviour. Individuals who are severely retarded have many learning difficulties. People who are profoundly retarded are some of the most seriously impaired of all people who are disabled.

Learning and memory

Memory is often explained through an information processing model that includes a sensory register, short-term memory, and long-term memory. Students who are intellectually disabled have memory problems, especially in regard to short-term memory.

Communication development

Language and speech problems are typical of children with intellectual disabilities; their language levels are often below their general mental age levels. Language problems are related to the severity of disability but not to the etiology of the condition.

Academic achievement

In general, pupils categorized as mildly intellectually disabled tend to underachieve in all academic areas. Individuals who are moderately retarded have limited intellectual ability, difficulties in working with abstract ideas, and problems in generalizing learning to new situations. Children and young adults who are severely or profoundly retarded experience major challenges to successful adaptation.

Social and emotional development

In general, students with intellectual disabilities are not well accepted by their peers. These children often show special personal and social problems and develop poor self-concept.

Learning problems lead to lowered motivation. Children soon come to expect failure, which then results in poor motivation and the development of an outward locus of control.

Behaviour

Children with mental retardation have a higher rate of behavioural disorders than do other children. As well as behavioural disorders, there exists a significant correlation between the level of retardation and psychiatric processes.

Maladaptive behaviour, which includes both inappropriate behaviours and **self-injurious behaviours**, is found across the spectrum of the population of intellectual disabilities but is more common in persons who are severely and profoundly retarded.

Co-occurring disabilities

Across the spectrum, persons with intellectual disabilities show more co-occurring conditions than do the rest of the population. Epilepsy is the most frequent additional disability in children with mental retardation.

Down syndrome

Apart from their physical stigmata, children with Down syndrome are prone to a range of sensory impairments and very serious health problems. Only within recent years has the lifespan of children with Down syndrome begun to approach that of the general population.

Cultural and linguistic differences

Although there is an over-representation of students from culturally and linguistically diverse groups in programs for intellectual disabilities, there is far greater reluctance today than in the past to refer students to this category. Caution results from the growth of the field of learning disabilities, the inclusive movement, the overlap among categories, and a number of court cases in the United States.

Assessment of intellectual disabilities

Procedures may include direct testing, ecological or functional assessment, or some other assessment procedure. The tools administered depend on the strengths and needs of the child. A test that suits a child who is mildly disabled, for example, will likely be inappropriate for one with severe retardation.

Screening

For children with moderate to profound intellectual disabilities, screening may not take place simply because the clear-cut organic or psychological signs that accompany severe disabilities make it possible to identify them in infancy. On the other hand, teachers are often the first to recognize mild disabilities.

Assessment of intelligence

To fulfill the criteria for intellectual disabilities, identification first stresses IQ levels and adaptive behaviour. When assessing children, the reliance is not solely on IQ instruments. Tests of mental ability are seen as only one measure in the total assessment of a child.

Assessment of adaptive behaviour

There exists no simple, quantifiable, and reliable method for assessing individuals for levels of adaptive behaviour. Adaptive behaviour is usually judged by scales or inventories that are completed by someone close to the individual being assessed.

Intervention with children who have intellectual disabilities

Many forms of intervention are available to assist individuals who are intellectually disabled and their families.

Medical intervention

Medical intervention is directed primarily toward the prevention or correction of organic conditions that may lead to retardation.

Technical aids

Many adaptive devices are used with people with intellectual disabilities. Computers are used in the classroom.

Educational intervention

Intellectual disabilities are related to delayed intellectual development in areas considered important for school success. Achievement is related to the degree of disorder, and various settings and strategies are directed toward this population.

Service delivery models

The trend today is to include students with intellectual disabilities in general classrooms. Placements for students with more significant intellectual disabilities may be in a range of settings: the general classroom, self-contained classrooms with academic or nonacademic integration, special classes, or group homes.

Educational approaches

There are three major goals in the education of students with intellectual disabilities: productivity, independence, and participation. To accomplish these goals, students are presented instruction in the areas of academic, social, self-help, community living, and vocational skills.

Students who have mild intellectual disabilities

The actual curriculum objectives are the same for students with mild intellectual disabilities as for their peers. Students require instruction in basic academic skills, particularly basic literacy and numeracy.

Students who have moderate intellectual disabilities

For children with moderate disabilities, the curriculum is structured around basic academics and functional skills, which include self-help and daily living skills, vocational skills, and communication training. When functionality is the core of the curriculum, it is referred to as a functional approach or life-skills instruction.

Functionality, which includes self-help skills, life skills, and social skills, is an important element of adaptive behaviour. Functional skills are those that help children to get along in their current and future environments. Functional skills include dressing, eating, and toileting, as well as the skills needed for participation in routine home and community activities such as playing with siblings, helping with simple chores, and eating at a fast-food restaurant.

Students who are severely and profoundly disabled

For children who are severely and profoundly disabled we must redefine the term *education* beyond its traditional academic limits. The major educational goals are to decrease dependence on others, increase awareness of environmental stimulation, teach basic communication and self-help skills, and push achievement levels higher.

Social intervention

Many advocacy groups of parents and professionals exist to serve individuals with intellectual disabilities. The Canadian Association for Community Living, for example, promotes the welfare and rights of persons with intellectual disabilities.

Key Terms

adaptive behaviour
cognition
cognitive development
self-injurious behaviours
trait plasticity

Practice Questions

Multiple-choice questions

1. The most noticeable consequences of intellectual disabilities involve
   a. the effects on the individual's ability to learn.
   b. parent–child relationships.
   c. peer interactions.
   d. sibling relationships.
   e. physical and motor functioning.

2. The idea that persons with intellectual disabilities formed one homogeneous population was first discredited by
   a. Stanley Bijou.
   b. John L. Down.
   c. Howard Grossman.
   d. Edgar Doll.
   e. Alfred Binet.

3. The AAMR has presented a new classification of mental retardation that classifies by needs. The needs classification does all of the following, except
   a. joins needs and severity classifications.
   b. changes dependency to support needs.
   c. keys terms to the level of services required.
   d. describes needs in ways that are prescriptive for programming needs.
   e. replaces severity levels with the supports needed.

4. Lance is a child with a severe intellectual disability. He needs pervasive supports. Such supports are characterized by
   a. constancy.
   b. high intensity.
   c. provision across environments.
   d. potentially life-sustaining components.
   e. all of the above

5. A psychologist would administer an IQ measure to a child suspected of being mildly intellectually disabled in order to
   a. determine if the child meets the criteria for mental retardation of two standard deviations below the norm.
   b. decide on an appropriate placement for the child.
   c. begin the process of writing an IEP.
   d. provide the classroom teacher with ideas for instruction.
   e. determine an educational program for the child.

6. Under the AAMR definition of mental retardation, the developmental period refers to the time between
   a. conception and birth.
   b. conception and the eighteenth birthday.
   c. birth and eighteen years.
   d. birth and twelve years.
   e. conception and death.

7. Organic causes of mental retardation are divided into the categories of
   a. genetic factors and brain damage.
   b. chromosomal and genetic factors.
   c. infections and intoxications.
   d. environmental and genetic influences.
   e. prenatal and postnatal difficulties.

8. In the etiology of intellectual disability, *tuberous sclerosis* is classified as a(n)
   a. chromosomal abnormality.
   b. gestational disorder.
   c. infection.
   d. intoxication.
   e. gross brain disease.

9. Reduction in the rate of intellectual disabilities has resulted from
   a. significant changes in the rates for severe and profound retardation.
   b. equally significant changes in the rates for moderate retardation.
   c. changes in the way we now define and label the condition, particularly mild retardation.
   d. more flexible criteria for diagnosis and labelling.
   e. a preference for very specific labels.

10. One of the major rationales for the inclusion of students with exceptionalities into general classrooms is social interaction. The research on students with intellectual disabilities indicates that these students
   a. are generally popular and well liked.
   b. get along the same as everyone else.
   c. are well accepted by their peers but not by teachers.
   d. are not well accepted by peers generally.
   e. are accepted by same-sex peers but not by the opposite sex.

11. In the past two decades, the category of learning disabilities has been the subject of intense research and that of mental retardation has been shrinking. This happened as
   a. parents and educators tended to prefer the term *learning disabilities* to *mental retardation.*
   b. huge amounts of research and funding have been directed toward learning disabilities.
   c. children previously referred to as mentally retarded are being labelled as learning disabled.
   d. the category of learning disabilities has expanded dramatically to include more and more children.
   e. all of the above

12. Worldwide, the most common clinical cause of mental retardation is
   a. fragile X syndrome.
   b. Down syndrome.
   c. infantile autism.
   d. Heller's disease.
   e. Asperger's syndrome.

13. Both Down syndrome and fragile X syndrome are chromosomal aberrations. However, there are differences. Research shows that
   a. fragile X is a type of X-linked disorder; Down is not.
   b. Down syndrome means extra chromosomal material; fragile X does not.
   c. fragile X is passed through the generations; Down is not.
   d. to some extent, Down is related to the age of the mother; fragile X is not.
   e. all of the above

14. Language and speech problems in individuals who are intellectually disabled are related most specifically to
    a. the level of disability.
    b. the etiology of the retardation.
    c. time of onset of the condition.
    d. the actual speech-making mechanism.
    e. social interactions in early childhood.

15. Today, we would be most likely to find the child described as *mildly intellectually disabled* in a
    a. general classroom.
    b. self-contained classroom.
    c. special school.
    d. residential school.
    e. clinic.

16. Match the person to the idea or event.
    a John L. Down
    b. Henry Goddard
    c. Edgar Doll
    d. John F. Kennedy
    e. Benge Nirje
    ___ applied the principles of normalization
    ___ called together a panel on mental retardation in the early 1960s
    ___ in the 1800s, differentiated among types of mental retardation
    ___ introduced the concept of adaptive behaviour
    ___ defined sub-groups in mental retardation

Recall questions

1. The WISC-III is a widely used measure of mental ability. WISC-III is an acronym for ________.

2. In the formal assessment of intellectual disabilities, the two major initial areas of concern are ________ and ________.

3. The majority of children identified as intellectually disabled fall into the ________ level of severity.

4. Children who manifest deficits in adaptive behaviour but whose IQ scores fall within the normal range would be classified as ________ rather than mentally retarded.

5. When children lose their initiative and grow overly dependent on letting others tell them what to do, they have developed an outward ________.

6. The highest mortality rates are among persons in the ________ severity level of intellectual disability.

7. Three major goals in the education of students with severe and profound intellectual disabilities are to teach basic communications skills, to ________, and to ________.

8. Any self-inflicted, repetitive action that leads to laceration, bruising, or abrasions of the client's own body is referred to as _______.

9. When no clear-cut evidence of an organic cause for an intellectual disability can be found, the condition is referred to as ________ mental retardation.

10. Decreases in the prevalence rates of conditions such as Tay-Sachs disease and Down syndrome are attributed to ________.

True–false questions

1. Persons with profound intellectual disabilities are more likely to be medically fragile than are persons identified as mildly intellectually disabled. T F

2. Although scales of adaptive behaviour are widely used in the area of intellectual disabilities, there remain problems with the scales that relate specifically to whether or not professionals need to even assess adaptive behaviour. T F

3. The AAMR's most recent definition of mental retardation emphasizes the support needs of individuals. T F

4. Significantly subaverage general intellectual functioning adequately defines mental retardation. T F

5. Current prevalence estimates show that approximately 5 percent of the population is intellectually disabled. T F

6. Down syndrome is classified as a genetic problem; fragile X is an inborn error of metabolism. T F

7. Severe and profound mental retardation is closely tied to economic status. T F

8. Males affected by fragile X syndrome usually show distinct physical stigmata. T F

9. *Maturation* refers to the degree to which an individual meets the standards of personal independence and social responsibility expected of a particular age or cultural group. T F

10. In the population of children with intellectual disabilities, boys outnumber girls. T F

Short-answer questions

1. The AAMR definition of mental retardation includes three major elements. List and briefly explain each.

2. There are three major types of Down syndrome. Briefly explain each type in terms of time of occurrence, prevalence, and developmental consequences.

3. List four instruments that are used for the assessment of adaptive behaviour.

4. The developmental consequences of intellectual disability vary according to severity. List and compare the possible developmental consequences of mild and moderate intellectual disabilities.

5. Speech and language problems are common among individuals with intellectual disabilities. List the types of problems that may be apparent.

Applications

1. In the educational journals, find three articles relating to one of the following topics:
   - including children with severe and profound intellectual disabilities in the regular classroom; or
   - normalization and deinstitutionalization of persons who are severely and profoundly disabled.

   Present a report consisting of a description, comparison, and evaluation of the three articles. (See Application Question 1 in Chapter 1 of this study guide for report format.)

2. You are teaching a small group of grade-three students to multiply by two. Prepare a lesson plan using the specific steps of direct instruction as detailed on p. 207 of the text.

3. Reread the case study on Nicholas that begins on p. 175 of the text. In the psycho-educational assessment, the psychologist administered an IQ measure as well as tests of language and reading and math readiness. What classroom measures would be valuable to add to the psychologist's results? Also use the text's appendix on assessment tools to detail additional measures that could be used with Nicholas, specifically to further assess language and adaptive behaviour.

4. Reread the brief case study on Ben on p. 198 of the text. Another skill that Ben needs is using public transportation. List the areas and activities that could be included in teaching Ben to use the bus, subway, or streetcar.

Activities

1. Children can typically repeat sentences only at the level of their individual syntax development. Ask children of various ages (from two to eight) to repeat these sentences: "The little boy skated on the frozen pond with his friends. The little boy was hit by a snowball." Record the children's responses; evaluate in terms of age and norms for language development.

2. In the United States, a number of court cases have concerned misdiagnosis of students as mentally retarded on the basis of IQ test results. One of the most important cases was Larry P. vs Riles. Research this case, stressing the use (or misuse) of IQ tests.

3. Research one type of co-operative learning strategy. Explain how you would use it in a classroom, the most appropriate grade levels for implementation, and the subject area or areas. Stress how you would adapt the process to allow a student with an exceptionality to participate and contribute fully.

Portfolio item

A number of films have been produced that deal with mental retardation, such as *Forrest Gump* and *The Other Sister*. Other films deal with people whose intellectual disabilities were altered, such as *Molly* or *Charlie*. View a film that has a person with an intellectual disability as a central character. Write a brief overview of the plot and the theme of the film. Then discuss the perceptions and treatment of the individual as portrayed in the film. Write about your own perceptions and how the portrayal affected you.

End Test 2

1. The educational approach that is suitable for students with special needs is
   a. peer tutoring.
   b. co-operative learning.
   c. Computer Assisted Instruction.
   d. small-group work.
   e. all of the above

2. *Individualization* for a student with special needs is best described as
   a. a teaching approach that stresses peer tutoring and one-to-one instruction.
   b. a plan on how to organize instruction.
   c. direct instruction methods.
   d. time in the resource room with a specially trained teacher.
   e. all of the above

3. Given the discussion on prevalence, sex differences, and changing rates of diagnosis, the individual most likely to be classified as having mild intellectual disabilities is
   a. two-month-old Mary.
   b. ten-year-old Tom.
   c. forty-year-old Janet.
   d. three-year-old Jane.
   e. All are likely to be classified as mildly mentally retarded.

4. Mental retardation appears to be a shrinking category of exceptionality because
   a. substantially fewer children with mental retardation are being born.
   b. many more children are labelled as learning disabled than mentally retarded.
   c. mental retardation is particularly difficult to identify and diagnose.
   d. the parameters of the definition of mental retardation are too obscure.
   e. children today tend not to be labelled at all.

5. The correct sequence of normal language development is
   a. crying, babbling, cooing, telegraphic speech.
   b. crying, cooing, babbling, holophrasic speech.
   c. holophrasic speech, crying, cooing, babbling.
   d. babbling, lalling, cooing, holophrasic speech.
   e. Children pass through different sequences.

6. Although integration as practised in the 1960s, mainstreaming, and full inclusion are not the same, they share one common factor. This is
   a. the need for co-operation and collaboration between general teachers and special education personnel.
   b. the gradual elimination of special classes and special education.
   c. the teaching of all children in general classrooms.
   d. the elimination of the continuum of educational services.
   e. all of the above

7. Under the United States definition of severe handicaps, a child so classified would demonstrate which of the following behaviour(s)?
   a. severe language deficits or absence of forms of verbal contact
   b. self-mutilation and self-stimulation
   c. failure to respond to social stimuli
   d. temper tantrums
   e. all of the above

8. The school-based team is preparing IEPs for children identified with special needs. In general, the most complex and time-consuming IEP will be for a child with
   a. visual impairment.
   b. mild intellectual disabilities.
   c. moderate intellectual disabilities.
   d. multiple gifts and talents.
   e. severe language disabilities.

9. Speech disorders associated with cleft palate are due to
   a. neurological dysfunction.
   b. structural defects.
   c. intellectual disabilities.
   d. sensory deprivation.
   e. poor learning.

10. When viewing the broad field of learning disabilities, it is correct to state that
    a. learning disabilities can be easily identified by a common trait.
    b. learning disabilities concern a single, easily identifiable disability.
    c. children with learning disabilities form a unified homogeneous group.
    d. learning disabilities is a syndrome.
    e. there are more commonalities than differences among the population of students with learning disabilities.

11. The *prosody* of a language refers to the
    a. morphology.
    b. phonemes.
    c. stress, rhythm, and pitch.
    d. semantics and grammar.
    e. pragmatics and proxemics.

12. Of the following, the major characteristic of students who are learning disabled is
    a. hyperactivity and inattention.
    b. an inability to learn adequately through traditional teaching methods.
    c. laziness and lack of motivation.
    d. perceptual dysfunction.
    e. minimal brain dysfunction.

13. Efficient speech and language in a child underlie school success because
    a. early speech and language development impacts on later ability in reading and writing.
    b. communication skills predict social acceptance in middle childhood.
    c. children with speech and language difficulties have more social and emotional problems than do their normally developing peers.
    d. teaching and learning are essentially linguistic activities, and children with speech and language problems are at risk for educational failure.
    e. all of the above

14. Studies on early intervention with children with Down syndrome show that
    a. declines in development can be halted if intervention begins when the child is between two and three years of age.
    b. the rate of development of Down syndrome babies is normal at first but slows down at about two years of age.
    c. Down syndrome infants receive the same scores as normally developing children on tests of intellectual ability at ten months of age, but lower scores at two years of age.
    d. the rate of development of children with Down syndrome is slower than that of normally developing children from birth and the intellectual profiles of Down children are not malleable.
    e. none of the above

15. Three-year-old Tommy likes to push a large box around the room but he cannot yet tie his shoelaces or control a paintbrush. This happens chiefly because
    a. all the other children like to push boxes and Tommy imitates them.
    b. the parts of the brain that control the large motor functions for pushing are more developed than the parts needed for tying and painting.
    c. Tommy has been taught to push but not to tie.
    d. Tommy's leg muscles are growing faster than his hands and fingers.
    e. the teacher allows pushing but does not promote tying or painting.

16. When a child has difficulty in remembering words, the condition is referred to as
    a. dysnomia.
    b. dysarthria.
    c. dysnosia.
    d. dysgraphia.
    e. dyslexia.

17. Intellectual disability is best described as
    a. an illness.
    b. a disease.
    c. a hereditary condition.
    d. delayed intellectual growth.
    e. All of the above are descriptors.

18. Although Hesh is nearly eight years old, he still has problems dressing and undressing himself, especially with coats and sweaters. Hesh may be having problems in the development of
    a. directionality.
    b. metacognition.
    c. visual discrimination.
    d. body image.
    e. locus of control.

19. Adverse emotional or behavioural problems that develop as a function of a learning disorder are referred to as a(n)
    a. internal locus of control.
    b. external locus of control.
    c. framework for social non-acceptance.
    d. emotional overlay.
    e. all of the above

20. Achievement tests are part of the battery used in the identification of students with possible learning disabilities because
    a. achievement test results correlate highly with WISC-III scores.
    b. the definitional discrepancy clause requires assessment of school achievement.
    c. achievement tests compare a child to his or her peers.
    d. most teachers can administer achievement tests.
    e. all of the above

21. With fragile X syndrome, it is true to say that
    a. physical anomalies are more closely related to retardation in females than in males.
    b. there is a strong relationship to childhood schizophrenia.
    c. the condition has been among the catalogue of causes of mental retardation since the 1920s.
    d. the number of physical anomalies correlates with the degree of retardation.
    e. All of the above are true.

22. An inability to read normally as a result of damage to the brain is referred to as
    a. dysgraphia.
    b. dyscalculia.
    c. dysnomia.
    d. dysphasia.
    e. dyslexia.

23. When compared to her peers, Alice seems to find it difficult to understand the teacher's directions and to express her needs verbally. Alice has a(n)
    a. articulation disorder.
    b. language disorder.
    c. fluency problem.
    d. voice disorder.
    e. speech dysfunction.

24. Phonological awareness is related to
   a. early literacy.
   b. the ease and the speed of the reading process.
   c. children's reading and spelling delays.
   d. problems in areas such as written expression.
   e. all of the above

25. The child who cannot cope with school but functions quite adequately in other environments is often referred to as a(n) ________ child.
   a. learning disabled
   b. behaviourally disordered
   c. six-hour retarded
   d. emotionally disturbed
   e. ADHD

26. Match the term to the definition.
   a. vocalization
   b. modulation
   c. respiration
   d. articulation
   e. phonation
   ___ the ability to produce sound
   ___ generation of speech sounds by modification of the vocal tract
   ___ the ability to control the loudness of the sounds produced
   ___ the air stream that produces speech
   ___ vocal tone production (5 x 1)

27. Throughout history, many famous people have overcome disabilities. Match the disability to the person.
   a. Helen Keller
   b. George VI
   c. Auguste Rodin
   d. Nelson Rockefeller
   ___ deaf-blindness
   ___ learning disabilities
   ___ stuttering
   ___ reading difficulties (4 x 1)

28. Match the term to the description.
   a. dyscalculia
   b. dysgraphia
   c. dysnomia
   d. dyslexia
   e. dysphasia
   ___ problems with the comprehension or use of language
   ___ difficulties with numbers
   ___ reading difficulties
   ___ forgetting words and their meanings
   ___ problems with writing (5 x 1)

29. Cluttered speech and stuttering are essentially the same condition. T F

30. There are close connections between speech and language problems and other disabilities. T F

31. In the correction of minor speech disorders, incidental teaching is preferable to direct instruction. T F

32. The ideal of full inclusion is not universally shared and it is not endorsed by all of those concerned with the education of children with learning disabilities. T F

33. Intelligence tests alone give sufficient information about the strengths and weaknesses of a child with intellectual disabilities for the purposes of educational programming. T F

34. It is now recognized that a child can score in the low range on an intelligence test but still be able to function adequately in society. T F

35. All students with exceptionalities require the same type and intensity of special education intervention. T F

36. The ACLD is the major parent body in the field of mental retardation. T F

37. Almost all speech and language delays and disorders can be corrected by the classroom teacher. T F

38. Classification by needs rather than classification by severity has been universally accepted in the field of mental retardation. T F

39. An instructional program for students with moderate levels of intellectual disabilities should focus on the development of functional and daily living skills. T F

Total /50

Section 3

Children and Youth with Behavioural Disorders

Children with behavioural disorders are not rare and almost everyone has come into contact with one of these children at some time. These are youngsters who are in conflict with themselves and those around them. They fail to establish close and satisfying ties with other people. Some youngsters are withdrawn; the great majority strike out with hostility and aggression.

Many and varied approaches have been used with students with behavioural disorders, but no single approach works effectively in every child. Of the many factors involved, one of the most important is the diversity of the population. The category of behavioural disorders includes conduct disorders, delinquency, anxiety and withdrawal, and attention deficit hyperactivity disorders. Of the extremely serious disorders, childhood schizophrenia is one of the most important (see Chapter 13).

Chapter 7

Children and Youth with Behavioural Disorders

Learning outcomes

After reading this chapter, you should be able to:

- Recognize that the category of *behavioural disorders* is fluid, increasing, and encompasses many groups;
- Understand the various classifications and sub-groups within the area of behavioural disorders;
- Understand the different conceptual models and how they underlie etiological consideration and direct treatment;
- Understand the developmental consequences of the different categories of behavioural disorders;
- Recognize the varied assessment procedures in the field of behavioural disorders, with particular reference to functional assessment;
- Detail methods of medical, therapeutic, and educational intervention for students with behavioural disorders;
- Discuss the validity of inclusive schooling for all students with behavioural disorders.

Introduction

Children and adolescents with behavioural disorders are not rare, and most of us have come into contact with or observed such young people. Special education for students with behavioural disorders is a fairly modern development. It was not until the 1950s that it really emerged.

No single approach suits each child with a behavioural disorder, and the approach that works today may not work tomorrow. Teachers employ various methods of discipline and management.

Definitions of behavioural disorders

Deviant behaviour has been defined and conceptualized in many ways. Many disciplines have contributed and definitions have been proposed from a variety of perspectives and disciplines. Even so, there is not a universally accepted definition of behavioural disorders. Of the many reasons for this, some of the most important are:

- there is no such thing as a typical student who is behaviourally disordered;
- there exists no adequate definition of mental health;
- if we cannot define normalcy, then it is difficult to define behavioural disorders;
- normal children demonstrate varied behaviour;
- disturbed children exhibit varied behaviours;
- the behavioural problems change as children grow older;
- behavioural disorders cannot be measured quantitatively;
- many disciplines have contributed to the field of behavioural disorders and each views the problems from a slightly different perspective;
- legal and educational terms differ;
- social and cultural expectations vary;

- behavioural disorders correlate with teacher tolerance levels and disruptive behaviour is often in the eye of the beholder;
- behavioural disorders are often associated with other disabilities.

Although there is not a universally accepted definition of behavioural disorders, most definitions share some common elements. Children with behavioural disorders exhibit behaviour that is chronic; violates cultural and social norms; and affects the child's self-esteem, interpersonal relationships, and probably school achievement.

Prevalence of behavioural disorders

Estimates of the prevalence of behavioural disorders vary tremendously, chiefly because of the lack of a clear and precise definitional construct. The best available research data indicate that 6 to 10 percent of school-age children exhibit serious and persistent behavioural problems.

The greatest proportion of the behaviourally disordered population falls in the mild and moderate ranges. Boys outnumber girls in every classification, with first-born males more prone to disturbed behaviour. In school, the prevalence is low in the early years but reaches a peak in the middle grades. Prevalence then drops off during the secondary years (except for delinquency).

Classification of behavioural disorders

The words used to describe students with inappropriate behaviours have evolved over the years. Today, *behavioural disorders* is an encompassing term although some researchers prefer to use *children in conflict.*

Although a number of systems have developed, very few professionals working with children who are behaviourally disordered are satisfied with the current classifications available.

Clinical classification

The American Psychiatric Association provides a classification system for a variety of behavioural disorders.

Classification by severity

The population of children and youth with behavioural disorders may be classified in terms of the severity of the disorder: mild, moderate, severe, and profound.

Dimensional classification

Quay and his colleagues outline a classification system for behavioural disorders that groups behaviours into six clusters or dimensions: conduct disorders, anxiety and withdrawal, socialized aggression, immaturity and attention problems, motor excess, and childhood psychoses. Dimensions similar to these have been found with remarkable consistency in many samples of children.

Classification by behavioural type

Definitions of behavioural disorders are based on excesses of deficits of social behaviour. Following this, behaviours are often described as externalizing or internalizing.

Etiology of behavioural disorders

Many factors are proposed to account for behavioural disorders. However, the etiology is most unclear for mild problems.

In order to explain behavioural disorders, their etiology, and their treatment, a number of conceptual models have emerged. The models differ considerably in the importance they attach to the etiology of the problems and to the treatment approaches prescribed.

Biophysical model

The biophysical approach views the problems as related to biology. Disorders may be inherited or acquired pre-, peri-, or postnatally. They may also be due to accidents, disease, or malnutrition.

Although some evidence links risk from genetic and constitutional conditions and prenatal and birth factors to behavioural disorders, the findings are inconclusive. It is more likely that biological and environmental factors combine to trigger behavioural disorders.

Psychodynamic model

The psychodynamic model, which arose from the work of Sigmund Freud, was influential in establishing the terminology, definitions, and classification of emotional disturbance. Advocates believe that traditional psychoanalytic concepts can be employed to find and treat the causes of behavioural disorders in children.

Psycho-educational model

Approaches focus on the underlying problems of the child as well as school success. Teachers stress academics and affect.

Behavioural model

Behaviourists try to understand the causes of behavioural disorders by observing the relationships among the environmental factors that elicit and maintain deviant behaviour. They believe that all behaviour is learned; therefore, behavioural difficulties represent inappropriate learning.

Ecological model

The ecological approach emphasizes the need to look at the total interaction of children with their environments. The ecological model presumes that aberrant behaviour is the result of a variety of interactions and transactions between individuals and the environment.

Psychosocial model

This approach focuses on the family and extra-familial influences. Much research is directed toward family structures and functioning as possible causes of behavioural disorders. Factors include parental divorce, separation, absence, conflict, neglect, hostility or illness, and inconsistent or lax discipline in the home. The risk for behavioural disorders increases with the number of variables present.

Social agencies other than the family that influence a child's cognitive, social, and emotional development are known as extra-familial influences. Schools, peer groups, and television are included.

Holistic model

The most encompassing approach is the holistic model. Stress is placed upon employing many disciplines in the treatment of children who are behaviourally disordered.

Characteristics of children and youth with behavioural disorders

More than a hundred characteristics have been attributed to children with behavioural disorders. These children have been described as cantankerous, disruptive, lacking in social skills, disliked, rejected, generally difficult, and by many other unsavoury terms. Generally, such children demonstrate behaviours that do not compare favourably with those shown by normal children; behaviours that are generally unacceptable to the child and to those in the environment; behaviours that are comparatively high in number; and behaviours that interfere with the child's academic and social performance.

Conduct disorders

Hyperaggressive and highly disruptive children constitute the major portion of school-aged behaviourally disordered pupils. Conduct-disordered children display antisocial behaviour—behaviour that is disruptive, distressing, and not age-appropriate. They may be disobedient, destructive, defiant, assaultive, impertinent, and jealous. Their behaviour is resistant to change through the usual forms of disciplining.

Oppositional defiant disorders are conditions in which children argue repeatedly with authority figures, show resentment, and often throw temper tantrums, although physical aggression is limited.

Aggression is of more concern to teachers than any other behavioural disorder. Aggressive behaviour is learned in many ways: by observing parents, siblings, friends, and characters on television and in the movies. Children are more likely to be aggressive if they have opportunities to practise aggression and if no unpleasant consequences generally follow.

Socialized aggression

Children and youth in this category are hostile, disobedient, and destructive, and often display both physical and verbal aggression. While similar in many ways to students with conduct disorders, they are also active in delinquent gangs and loyal to delinquent friends.

Sometimes these students are categorized as behaviourally disordered and sometimes as socially maladjusted. The difference lies in the perception that behavioural problems are distressing to children, while social maladjustment does not necessarily result in persistent distress. Delinquency refers to antisocial behaviours; delinquent behaviour is an illegal act by a juvenile. Juvenile offences are increasing, with more offences by younger children and by females.

Delinquency continues to baffle sociologists, criminologists, and educators. Contributing factors may include unfortunate family relationships, low self-concept, and fear of failure. Delinquent youth may suffer social anomie; they do not internalize a coherent set of values and standards for the self-regulation of behaviour.

Anxiety and withdrawal

Anxiety is a fear with a future reference. Anxious and withdrawn children internalize their behaviour. They may display nausea, pains, headaches, fears, obsessions, shyness, nightmares, crying, depression, and self-consciousness. Some children suffer **phobias**—intense fears that have no rational basis. School phobia may be accompanied by physical illness associated with tension and extreme emotion.

Severe behavioural disorders are by far the most prevalent conditions associated with suicidal behaviour. Many studies have confirmed the link between suicidal behaviour and emotional instability.

Immaturity

Little is known about the special nature of immature children. They appear to be clumsy, socially inadequate, passive, easily frustrated, and messy. They lack initiative, have short attention spans, and prefer younger playmates.

Attention problems and motor excess

Attention Deficit Hyperactivity Disorder (ADHD) is an area of intense interest and research in contemporary special education. It is characterized by a cluster of behaviours, of which the most prominent are **impulsivity, attention disorders**, and **hyperactivity**.

Students with attention disorders have difficulty in focusing and maintaining attention and therefore have problems in appropriate school performance. Children are often impulsive; they do things without thinking and do not learn from experience. They also tend to **perseverate.** Hyperactivity is an excess of motor activity for a child's age and situation. Hyperactive children display rates of motor activity that are too high and too intense for their age group. The excessive, non-purposeful movement of the hyperactive child disturbs others and disrupts a classroom.

Developmental consequences of behavioural disorders

Because the behaviours and the population are so heterogeneous, a profile of a typical child with behavioural disorders cannot be drawn. Each child is unique.

Cognitive development

Many students with behavioural disorders may be slightly below the norm in cognitive development.

Academic performance

Children with behavioural disorders do not achieve well academically. They usually lag behind in reading, arithmetic, and spelling. The behaviour often hinders efficient learning in conduct-disordered children. Anxious children develop a defeatist attitude that hinders social development. The timid and passive behaviour of anxious and withdrawn children interferes with the adequate utilization of potential. The general characteristics of ADHD—inattention, distractibility, impulsivity, and hyperactivity—can cause or compound academic problems.

Communication

Communication problems, per se, are not characteristic of students with behavioural disorders. However, a number of students with speech/language problems do show behavioural disorders.

Social development

Socialization is the means by which individuals become acceptable members of their society. Many children with behavioural disorders do not have **social competence** and lack **social skills**.

Social cognition is the knowledge and cognitive activities used by people in dealing with the social world. **Prosocial behaviour** is voluntary behaviour intended to aid or benefit others.

Highly aggressive children have few friends and probably meet school failure. Children with personality disorders develop strategies to cope with anxiety. In doing so, they forego assertive, independent behaviour and instead exhibit low self-concept, poor self-esteem, and withdrawn behaviours.

Cultural and linguistic differences

Today, a high proportion of students served under the categories of behavioural disorders or serious emotional disturbance are from culturally and linguistically diverse groups. Misdiagnosis is often a culprit; equally important are the ideologies and expectations of school systems, which can have an immediate and profound effect on behaviour. Behaviour considered normal and adaptive in a subculture may be looked upon as deviant or inadequate by members of the dominant group.

Assessment of children and youth with behavioural disorders

Because the behaviours attract attention, it is easier to identify behavioural disorders than to define or classify them. However, a number of screening and diagnostic procedures have developed to identify youngsters who deviate significantly in behaviour.

Screening may begin with parents or teachers. Informal measures include teacher observations, teacher rating scales, children's ratings, and behavioural analysis techniques such as direct observation.

Functional assessment

Functional assessment relies on the systematic administration and interpretation of quite a range of indirect and direct measures of student behaviour; for example, parent and child interviews, observation, direct observation, plotting the identified behaviour, and experimental modification of a student's environment. The focus is on the function of a behaviour—what purpose does that behaviour serve for a student, how to reduce or eliminate the behaviour, and how to replace it with a more acceptable alternate behaviour.

Observation

One of the most potent processes, teacher observation, tries to answer the question When is a behavioural disorder a behavioural disorder? Teachers look for form- the form or shape of a behaviour that involves a description of the behaviour itself, such as a temper tantrum—as well as for chronicity and frequency.

Direct observation

Direct observation, a structured behavioural analysis technique, is the cornerstone of behavioural functional assessment. Observers record instances of specific behaviours to establish the frequency, durability, and age-appropriateness of a behaviour. Data recording may be as simple as a narrative system, or it may be more sophisticated with codes to score behavioural deviations, language skills, motor behaviour, and so on. **Event sampling** is used to determine the frequency or length of a specific behaviour.

Rating scales

Teacher judgment measures (teacher ratings of behaviour) are the most widely used tools for diagnosing conduct disorders in a classroom setting.

Formal assessment

In psycho-educational assessment, diagnosticians may use measures that assess mental ability and performance.

Ecological assessment

Ecological assessment includes an examination of the materials, methods, and curriculum, as well as teacher expectations, discipline, cultural and social factors, and so on.

Social skills assessment

The purpose of social skills assessment is to ascertain whether or not children possess social skills.

Assessing ADHD

To be diagnosed as ADHD, a child must exhibit eight of fourteen symptoms appearing in DSM-IV that reflect attention difficulties, impulsivity, or motor hyperactivity, with onset before the age of seven. Assessment requires parent and teacher interviews, parent and teacher rating scales, and direct observation.

Intervention with children and youth who have behavioural disorders

Childhood antisocial behaviour predicts problems in adjustment and health in later years, especially in boys. Children do not grow out of aggressive behaviour but continue to indulge in such activities as they mature. In attempts to overcome the problems, many methods and models are used with students with behavioural disorders.

Medical intervention

Drug therapy is commonly employed. The psycho-stimulants—methylphenidate (Ritalin) and dextroamphetamine (Dexedrine)—are the most commonly recommended. Positive effects of stimulant drug dosage include increased signs of happiness, friendliness, and co-operation. However, drug therapy with students with ADHD, other behavioural disorders, and learning disabilities remains a hotly debated issue.

Therapy and counselling

Therapy and counselling are widely used techniques. Therapies include individual and **group therapy**; music, art, pet, and play therapy; and **bibliotherapy**.

Educational intervention

Methods for intervention have generally been developed according to the various conceptual models.

Service delivery models

For many school-age children with mild behavioural disorders, the general classroom is the common placement. But what about students with serious and violent behaviour? Whether they belong in the regular classroom is an ongoing argument. Teachers must take into account the needs of other students and the discipline of the class.

Educational models

There are real differences between the conceptual models of behavioural disorders. Although current educational programs are generally based upon psycho-educational or behavioural approaches, no single model has proven adequate in the management of all children who are behaviourally disordered.

Psychotherapeutic intervention (psychodynamic approach)

Psychoanalytic approaches view disturbed behaviour as a pathological imbalance in the mind and therefore aim toward symptom removal. Psychodynamic approaches see little value in altering observable behaviour, but focus on the underlying pathology. These approaches concentrate on helping children to understand and alter the inner turmoil and conflict that are viewed as the primary causes of the deviant behaviour. Individual, group, and family therapy are important dimensions.

Psycho-educational approaches

Psycho-educational models combine aspects of psychodynamic theory with the acquisition of academic and daily living skills. Educational practices focus on uncovering the underlying pathology in order to improve psychological functioning. As teachers help children to understand the underlying causes of their behaviours, they also stress academic success in order to enhance self-concept.

Behavioural approaches

The behavioural approach is the preferred method of many educational practitioners. Behaviourists focus on observable behaviour and use structured methods in order to establish, improve, or eliminate certain behaviours. To accomplish this, they use reinforcers to increase desirable behaviours and aversive methods to decrease or extinguish undesirable behaviours.

Ecological approaches

The ecological approach sees behavioural disorders as a mismatch between children and their environments. In order to overcome behavioural problems, changes are made in both child and environment so that more constructive interactions can take place. In **role playing**, participants assume a specific role in a demonstration or simulation.

Promoting social skills

Training in **social skills** is a particularly important academic feature for children with behavioural disorders because instruction helps children to make and keep friends and get along with adults, and helps aggressive children to modify their behaviour.

Curriculum

In planning curriculum for pupils with behavioural disorders, teachers must blend academic and affective components. Instruction may include art, drama, music, dance, role-playing, and bibliotherapy. Teachers must be concerned with classroom management, behaviour management, discipline, and preventative discipline.

Programs addressing school violence

There are common features of school-wide behavioural management systems. These are a total staff commitment to managing behaviour, whatever approach is taken; clearly defined and communicated expectations and rules; consequences and clearly stated procedures for correcting rule-breaking behaviours; an instructional component for teaching students self-control and/or social skill strategies; and a support plan to address the needs of students with chronic, challenging behaviours.

Social intervention

This form of intervention encompasses a variety of services directed toward assisting behaviourally disordered children and their families. It includes outpatient, home care, day treatment, and residential treatment programs, as well as foster care.

Key Terms

anxiety
attention disorder
bibliotherapy
event sampling
group therapy
hyperactivity
impulsivity
oppositional defiant disorders
perseverate
phobias
prosocial behaviour
role playing
social cognition
social competence
social skills
socialization
therapy

Practice Questions

Multiple-choice questions

1. The greatest number of school-aged children with behavioural disorders are categorized as
   a. conduct disordered.
   b. anxious and withdrawn.
   c. phobic.
   d. socialized aggressive.
   e. immature.

2. Figures on the prevalence of behavioural disorders in the school-aged population show that
   a. girls outnumber boys in every category.
   b. lack of teacher tolerance may be inflating prevalence estimates.
   c. the great proportion of students fall into the severe category of behaviour disorders.
   d. prevalence is highest during the secondary-school years.
   e. numbers are actually on the decrease.

3. In children with behavioural disorders, the problems are chronic. Chronicity refers to behaviours that
   a. last six months or longer.
   b. violate social or cultural expectations.
   c. do not match teacher expectations.
   d. fluctuate and decline.
   e. are characterized by much overt aggression.

4. In the entire area of behavioural disorders, many conceptual and administrative difficulties continue to exist. All of the following statements are true about the field except
   a. even today, this field is in many ways both confused and confusing.
   b. terminology is inconsistent and much dissatisfaction exists with current definitions.
   c. treatment regimes and interventions vary.
   d. many provisions are now being made for students at secondary levels.
   e. there is considerable debate about how to subdivide the various disorders in a reliable and helpful way.

5. On the playground, seven-year-old Jimmy constantly fights with other children. In the classroom, he demonstrates both physically and verbally aggressive behaviour. Jimmy would be characterized as
   a. immature.
   b. anxious.
   c. withdrawn.
   d. conduct disordered.
   e. juvenile delinquent.

6. Andrew swears, screams, and has tantrums in the classroom. Although his teacher has many ideas about Andrew and his behaviour, she is most correct in saying that
   a. "He cannot help the poor behaviour and there is an underlying thread of depression."
   b. "He goes home every night and plans ways to bother me in the classroom."

c. "Andrew enjoys the behaviour and the attention it brings."
d. "Punishment is the only way to cure this behaviour."
e. "The behaviour is the fault of the home environment, and it is the parents who should cure the behaviour."

7. The three primary characteristics of Attention Deficit Hyperactivity Disorder are
   a. inattention, impulsivity, and hyperactivity.
   b. distractibility, poor metacognitive skills, academic deficits.
   c. outward locus of control, learned helplessness, emotional overlay.
   d. perseveration, haptic problems, poor body image.
   e. social skill deficits, neurological dysfunction, immaturity.

8. Educators use the term *antisocial behaviour* rather than *delinquency* because
   a. delinquency is a term with a legal connotation.
   b. antisocial behaviour is a more restrictive term.
   c. the educational and legal systems hold very different views about the problems.
   d. delinquency includes too broad a range of behaviours.
   e. none of the above

9. All the following are general characteristics of children with behavioural disorders, except that the
   a. manifested behaviours do not compare favourably with those displayed by other children.
   b. behaviours are generally acceptable to the child.
   c. number of behaviours is comparatively high.
   d. behaviours interfere with the child's performance in and out of school.
   e. behaviours usually result in social rejection.

10. The most frequent phobic reaction among school-aged children is ________ phobia.
    a. school
    b. spider
    c. stranger
    d. animal
    e. food

11. Research indicates that
    a. temper tantrums are common among four- and five-year-olds.
    b. unfocused temper tantrums increase during the preschool period.
    c. temper tantrums are more common after age six.
    d. in children with behaviour disorders, tantrums are more likely to persist than they are in other children.
    e. all of the above

12. Behavioural approaches to the treatment of behaviour disorders focus on
    a. reinforcers and rewards.
    b. punishments and detentions.
    c. class meetings and role playing.
    d. individual and group counselling.
    e. social skills instruction.

13. All of the following statements refer to individual psychotherapy, except
    a. there is a transaction between the child and the therapist.
    b. the approach is founded on the belief that all behaviour is learned.
    c. the approach relies on discussions of feelings and motivations.
    d. the inner conflicts of the child are viewed as essential starting points.
    e. it evolved from the work of Freud at the opening of the 20th century.

14. The biophysical model of behaviour disorders focuses on
    a. behaviours that are learned.
    b. helping children to overcome inner turmoil.
    c. behaviour modification.
    d. specific physical etiologies.
    e. various therapies, such as play therapy.

15. Bibliotherapy refers to
    a. behaviour modification techniques.
    b. reading stories with positive role models.
    c. writing lines.
    d. a form of contingency contracting.
    e. time out.

16. Match the conceptual model of behavioural disorders to the statement.
    a. biophysical
    b. holistic
    c. ecological
    d. psychodynamic
    e. behavioural
    f. psycho-educational

___ stresses underlying tensions as well as academic performance
___ looks at genetic and chemical causes
___ encompasses all models
___ focuses on underlying pathologies and tensions
___ stresses observable behaviour
___ examines the interaction of a child and the environment

Recall questions

1. Quay and his associates identified six clusters or dimensions of disturbed behaviour: conduct disorders, ________, ________, ________, ________, and ________.

2. The ________ approach is the most encompassing conceptual model in the field of behavioural disorders.

3. Those who believe that all behaviour is learned and can therefore be changed or "unlearned" belong to the ________ school of psychology.

4. Among the population of students with behavioural disorders, the greatest number of school-aged children with behavioural disorders are those classified as ________.

5. Any form of behaviour designed to harm or injure another living being who is motivated to avoid such treatment is referred to as _______.

6. DSM is the ________; it is published by the APA, the ________.

7. Individual, group, and family therapy are important dimensions of the ________ approach to the treatment of behavioural disorders.

8. The psychotherapeutic procedure where the therapist interprets the child's play as the basis for alleviating problems is known as ________.

9. In behaviour therapy, rewarding a behaviour in the belief that this will encourage its recurrence is known as ________.

10. *Enuresis* is a term that refers to __________.

True–false questions

1. When teachers select a model to intervene with students with behavioural disorders, the research literature suggests that they should select one model because studies show that programs with a solid philosophical base are the most successful. T F

2. In general, children simply grow out of behavioural disorders, especially conduct disorders. T F

3. Since 1845, when the condition was first identified, the terminology and diagnosis of hyperactivity in children has remained relatively stable. T F

4. Many more boys than girls at the elementary-school level suffer from school phobia. T F

5. Empirical evidence now links behavioural disorders to very specific genetic causes that can be identified and treated. T F

6. ADHD is characterized by clusters of behaviours—impulsivity, hyperactivity, juvenile delinquency, and social anomie. T F

7. Distinctions between normal and disturbed behaviour should be seen as differences in degree rather than in kind. T F

8. In the area of behavioural disorders, psychotherapeutic approaches try to help the child overcome distress by seeking the underlying causes of the problem. T F

9. Because of increased understanding of the condition, juvenile delinquency is on the decline. T F

10. According to the holistic model, behavioural disorders result solely from illness and childhood trauma. T F

Short-answer questions

1. Identify five factors that hinder a clear determination of the prevalence of behavioural disorders in school-aged children.

2. List the six dimensions of behaviour outlined by Quay and his colleagues.

3. Much research and theory has focused on family structures and functioning as possible causes of behaviour disorders. List five family variables that have been found to be related to behavioural disorders.

4. List and briefly describe four models or approaches used in the treatment of behaviour disorders.

5. List and briefly describe five proposed causes of juvenile delinquency.

Applications

1. In the educational journals, find three articles relating to one of the following topics:
   - the use of token economy systems with students who are behaviourally disordered; or
   - the increase in suicide rates among older adolescents.

   Present a report consisting of a description, comparison, and evaluation of the three articles. (See Application Question 1 in Chapter 1 of this study guide for report format.)

Activities

1. Drug therapy to control children's behaviour and learning is on the increase. Interview a pediatrician or a psychiatrist involved with the diagnosis of children with behavioural disorders and find out their views on drug therapy.

2. Observe in a classroom for a full morning or afternoon session. Use a time sampling technique to record the on-task, off-task behaviour of three children. Chart the baseline.

3. Visit a classroom that stresses behaviour modification as a means to achieving academic success. Record your observations and feelings.

Portfolio item

Television viewing is a common experience for most children. However, American television is often violent and observation of aggression on television is a likely cause of aggressive behaviour with both long-term and progressive effects.

Spend three hours watching television. Divide the time between a prime-time adult show, an evening show for children and adults, and children's cartoons. Chart the incidences of physical and verbal violence in each group. Discuss your findings in essay form.

Section 4

Children Who Are Gifted, Talented, and Creative

Individuals with outstanding skills and abilities are described as gifted, talented, and creative. In order to reach their full potential, gifted and talented children need suitable challenges and profitable educational experiences.

Many people believe that gifted youngsters are so smart they can make it on their own. Others support the idea that giftedness needs to be fostered and nurtured. Opponents of special education for gifted pupils fear that an elite may be created that will jeopardize the principle of democratic education. Advocates believe that special education is vital if children who are gifted are to realize their full human potential. Hence, while many issues circulate in the education of students with gifts, talents, and creativity, the major issue is whether a public education system that is philosophically and administratively egalitarian in nature should provide special services for children who are already well-endowed.

Chapter 8

Children Who Are Gifted, Talented, and Creative

Learning outcomes

After reading this chapter, you should be able to:

- Differentiate between giftedness, creativity, and talent;
- Appreciate why students who are gifted require special education;
- Understand the measures used to identify and assess students who are gifted;
- Explain the various approaches to accommodating giftedness employed in schools and the pros and cons of each approach.

Introduction

Giftedness is a somewhat abstract term applied to people who, by virtue of outstanding abilities, are capable of high performance. Several variables figure in the scenario of giftedness, including aptitude, creativity, personality, and motivation.

Gifted, creative, and talented students have special educational needs: they may learn in ways different from other students; they are more curious; and they think more abstractly. At the same time, students who are gifted are vulnerable to the same forces that affect other children and youth and can become frustrated and bored in unstimulating learning environments.

Definitions

There exists little consensus regarding definitions in the field of gifted and talented education. This is because of the diversity of the population, the difficulties in defining intelligence and giftedness, and a lack of knowledge of the relationships among various components.

Today's definitions are flexible and inclusive enough to encompass a range of gifts, talents, and creative aptitudes. Most stress the necessity of special educational intervention.

There are two major ways of viewing giftedness. Some researchers and practitioners look at giftedness as potential. Others see it as product; that is, the attributes of identified gifted individuals and their potential value to society.

Joseph Renzulli's definition leans toward giftedness as product. When Renzulli undertook research with adult gifted individuals, he discovered that gifted and talented persons possess high ability, high creativity, and high task commitment.

Prevalence of giftedness

With no universal definition of giftedness, it is difficult to accurately estimate the prevalence of children who are gifted and talented. In general, giftedness is said to occur in 2 to 5 percent of the school-aged population.

Classification of giftedness

It is difficult to arrange the gifted population into precise categories. Too, many terms are used to describe gifted individuals. *Genius* has traditionally been used to indicate a particular aptitude or capacity in any area. *Creativity* refers to the process of bringing new, different, and unexpected responses to a given situation. Remarkable early development is termed **precocity**. *Talent* refers to a specific dimension of skill in a certain area. *Atypical abilities* are exceptional strengths in a relatively narrow area.

Gifted children

Giftedness is the possession of special abilities. In the classroom, this is often seen as **academic ability**; that is, intellectual ability as measured by performance on IQ tests and standardized tests of academic achievement.

Academic ability refers to intellectual ability measured by performance on IQ and standardized tests of academic achievement. **Academically talented students** are generally considered to be those scoring at the 95th percentile or higher on these measures.

Creative children

Creativity is the process of bringing new ideas to different problems. Researchers have identified four components: fluency of ideas, or producing a number of responses to a given stimulus; flexibility, or shifts in thinking from one category to another; originality, or unusual and clever responses; and elaboration, or the addition of details to basic ideas or thoughts.

Talented children

Some children who are gifted may have special talents that they begin to nurture early. **Talent** is above-average performance. It refers to a specific dimension of a skill in areas such as music, visual arts, drama, athletics, and particular academic domains.

Leaders

Leadership is the ability to produce positive change that is self- or group-enhancing.

Factors contributing to giftedness

Individuals who are gifted and talented form a heterogeneous population. It is not exactly clear which particular factors contribute most to giftedness. However, the interplay of genetic and environmental variables is important.

Genetic factors

Most authorities now hold that genetics are at least as important as environmental factors in determining intelligence.

Environmental factors

A stimulating environment is vital to the nurturing of innate gifts and talents. Children who are gifted are more likely to come from families that provide the general advantages of higher socio-economic homes.

Developmental consequences

Individuals who are gifted tend to be superior in many ways. However, gifted individuals are a heterogeneous population, displaying disparate characteristics. Individual differences run the gamut of possibilities. The true extent of the variations is not known because of the difficulties in identifying all gifted youngsters.

Physical development

As a group, youngsters who are gifted tend to exceed the average in physical ability.

Academic development

Students who are gifted learn more quickly and more easily than do their non-gifted peers. They are ahead in academic achievement and tend to like school.

Social and emotional development

Generally, children who are gifted are emotionally stable, self-sufficient, and less prone to neurotic and psychotic disorders than others. They tend to have wide and varied interests. Although modestly gifted children are well liked by their peers, group pressures, especially during adolescence, may result in conflict between a highly developed personal ethical system and a desire for popularity. Modestly gifted students seem to have more favourable profiles in terms of personality and peer acceptance than do students who are highly gifted.

Behaviour

Just because they are gifted is no reason to always expect good behaviour from these children. Like other youngsters, behaviour falls across a range.

Ethical development

Children who are gifted appear to develop ethical concerns earlier than do their normally developing peers.

Cultural and linguistic differences

Many students who are non-white, non-middle-class, or from language minority groups are not identified and taught as gifted learners. A major reason accounting for under-representation is an implicit demand that children always manifest giftedness in the same way—the same equating with the majority culture's definitions of giftedness.

Assessment of giftedness

The issue of identification is highly problematic among the gifted and talented school-age population and contentious among their educators. There are so many areas of functioning to be assessed and at the moment there is no adequate single identification procedure, or combination of procedures, that will effectively identify all gifted and talented children.

The Terman studies

In 1922 Lewis Terman, an American educator and psychologist, undertook a longitudinal study of 1528 California school children. Terman's research had profound implications for the field of gifted education and remains the paramount work in the area. Terman's study dispelled some traditional myths about gifted individuals; established the IQ test as the sole criterion in the identification of giftedness; and lent credibility to the notion of special education for youngsters who are gifted.

Multiple intelligences

Emphasis on the IQ test as the sole criterion in the identification of giftedness remained predominant until the 1960s. A multidimensional theory of intelligence proposed by the psychologist J. P. Guilford, the Structure of Intellect, includes 120 different types of intelligence grouped into three dimensions: operations, contents, and products.

When Howard Gardner proposed an alternate theory of multiple intelligence, he departed from Guilford's more traditional psychometric approach. In essence, Gardner holds that many forms of thinking are prominent both inside and outside of school. The capabilities that people develop fall into seven areas: linguistic, logical-mathematical, spatial, bodily, kinesthetic, musical, interpersonal-intrapersonal, and naturalistic. Most people are not gifted or even highly competent in all seven areas. Gardner believes that development of high-level competence requires innate capacity, motivation, and opportunity.

Assessment measures

No single measure, or group of measures, has proven infallible in the identification of children who are gifted. A variety of measures are used. The most effective identification procedures include a combination of standardized tests of mental ability and achievement, assessments of performance, and rating scales. Other techniques are nominations by teachers, parents, and peers; previous school history; family history; interviews; case studies; and observations.

Tests of mental ability

Promising students are often administered individual intelligence tests. The Stanford-Binet Individual Intelligence Test and the Wechsler Intelligence Scale for Children (WISC-III) are the most commonly used measures.

Group tests

Some schools begin by screening students with standardized group intelligence tests. However, all currently available group intelligence tests have a high prevalence of under-identification and over-identification of exceptional children, particularly with reference to creative divergent thinkers and very young children.

Achievement tests

Achievement tests can be employed systematically to identify children with gifts and talents who are already achieving at a high level academically.

Portfolios

Portfolios are emerging as a promising tool for the ongoing assessment of students who are gifted.

Observation

Especially for young children, observation is one of the most potent ways to identify those who are potentially gifted.

Teacher nomination

Teacher nominations are founded on the premise that teachers know and can identify their gifted students. However, classroom teachers are relatively poor at this activity. Rating scales help to objectify and document teacher judgment.

Parent nomination

Parents are more accurate at identifying children who are gifted and talented than are classroom teachers. Different socio-economic groups tend to rate children differently, while some parents may be unaware of their child's outstanding accomplishments.

Peer nomination and self-nomination

Increasingly, peer nominations are providing positive results in identification procedures. Self-nominations are also used, especially at secondary levels.

Measuring creativity

The assessment of creativity presents a challenging paradox: how to devise a standardized means to capture non-standard behaviour. Popularly employed measures of creativity include the Torrance Tests of Creative Thinking, the Creativity Assessment Package, and parts of the SOI Learning Abilities Test.

Leadership

In order to assess leadership, observations of performance together with a rating checklist are most appropriate.

Visual and performing arts

Although talent in the visual and performing arts is still predominantly determined by expert judges in audition settings, a range of measures have been devised, especially in the areas of art and music.

Problems in identification

Whatever method of identification is used, some special populations of children who are gifted are often overlooked. This is most pronounced among gifted underachievers, gifted females, gifted children who are also disabled, and gifted children from different cultural backgrounds.

Gifted underachievers

Many children who are gifted and talented do not reach their full potential. **Underachievers** are those students about whom we can make a reasonable prediction of academic potential that is not fulfilled. Many factors contribute. These include an unfavourable self-concept, the necessary conformity of the traditional classroom, and the lack of effort necessary in the early grades, which eventually becomes a self-defeating cycle.

Females who are gifted

Of the gifted youngsters who become underachievers, many are female. In early adolescence, girls face conflicts between traditional sex roles and gifted behaviour. Females have fewer opportunities to explore their interests and more pressure to conform. Traditional roles are further reinforced by parents, teachers, and peers.

By an overwhelming margin, men achieve outstanding status and recognition more frequently than do women of the same age. Social and cultural expectations appear to underlie the discrepancy; although more women are entering non-traditional professions, the numbers remain small.

Gifted students who are disabled

Children who are gifted with disabilities form a minority within a minority. However, the proportion of gifted children among disabled groups is thought to parallel that of the non-disabled population.

When a child has a disability, many people focus on the handicap and cannot accept the child's unique pattern of strengths and weaknesses. They see the many contradictions in the performances of these children as part of the disability, not the giftedness.

Gifted students who have learning disabilities

When a student who is gifted also has a learning disability, the two conditions can mask each other. The giftedness helps the child get through school, but the learning disability overwhelms the giftedness.

Gifted children who are culturally different

In assessing giftedness in children from different cultural backgrounds, it is important to be aware of the cultural mores of the particular society. Certain traits that define giftedness in the dominant culture may be seen as inappropriate by other groups.

Intervention with students who are gifted, creative, and talented

Children who are gifted and talented require special provisions if they are to realize their full human potential. Without educational opportunity and challenge, children who are gifted may hide their abilities, bury them in underachievement, or become school dropouts.

Technical aids

The use of educational technology is important in the education of gifted and talented students. Computer technology allows such children access to advanced instruction and to phenomena otherwise beyond their reach.

Educational intervention

Nobody is sure of the best way to educate students with gifts, and it is true to say that there is a lack of systematically developed models and systematic experimental evaluation of programs and program models with explicit goals, objectives, and specified outcomes. Numerous models and programs have been attempted, all intended to come to grips with three major problems: the balance between the quest for excellence and a zeal for equality; the wide range of abilities among the gifted population; and teachers' lack of special instructional methods.

Service delivery models

Currently, the three most common types of educational provisions for students who are gifted are enrichment, ability grouping, mentoring, and acceleration. While the research sees acceleration as efficient for academic progress, it does not provide clear evidence for or against mentoring, ability groupings, or classroom enrichment.

Debate about the full inclusion of students who are gifted is ongoing. Advocates of special programming contend that gifted education and gifted students are in deep trouble without grouping practices. Opponents contend that special programs for the gifted run counter to the spirit of inclusive classrooms.

Educational approaches

The difference between the education of students who are gifted and other learners is a matter of degree. Students who are gifted need many opportunities for self-directed learning.

Acceleration

Acceleration allows students who are gifted to progress through the educational system at their own rates. Several variations are possible: early admission to kindergarten, grade skipping, and rapid progress through a non-graded school system.

Ability grouping

Ability grouping refers to removing children from heterogeneous settings and placing them in special groups according to their ability. This may be on a full or part-time basis and may mean travelling to a single school within a district.

Mentor programs

Mentor programs join the community to the school in providing an additional learning experience for gifted students.

Enrichment

Enrichment means providing special activities in an otherwise regular classroom. The activities are broader and deeper than the regular curriculum, designed to challenge and interest gifted children while focusing on each child's unique pattern of strengths and weaknesses.

Renzulli's Enrichment Triad Model, designed for implementation within the regular classroom, provides three types of enrichment activities on three increasingly complex levels: all children in a class can accomplish level-one activities; gifted children are challenged and rewarded by level-three activities.

The Revolving Door Identification Model was designed to overcome problems related to student selection, motivation, and interests. Students choose their own programs, earn the right of participation, and are never permanently in or out of the program. The Autonomous Learner Model for secondary levels is designed to meet the socio-emotional needs of gifted students.

Curriculum

The differences between the regular program and the program for students who are gifted is one of degree. Some classroom practices currently being studied include independent projects, creative writing on self-selected topics, teaching thinking skills, encouraging discovery, and using classroom questioning that encourages reasoning and logical thinking.

For individual students, teachers can use **independent studies**, individualized learning experiences that allow students to select a topic, define problems or questions, gather and analyze information, apply skills, and create a product to show what has been learned.

Key Terms

academic ability
academically talented students
enrichment
independent studies
precocity
talent
underachievers

Practice Questions

Multiple-choice questions

1. The best reason for considering children who are gifted as exceptional is that
   a. they require special education if they are to attain their full potential.
   b. they deviate significantly from the norm.
   c. they sometimes experience serious difficulties.
   d. their deviation is above the norm.
   e. they challenge and sometimes frustrate teachers.

2. The major argument against providing special programs for children who are gifted is that
   a. they are too expensive.
   b. they may create an elite.
   c. they may be too stressful for some children.
   d. gifted children will do well anyway.
   e. all of the above

3. Currently, no universally accepted definition of giftedness exists because
   a. special educators have not viewed definitions as being of primary importance.
   b. the heterogeneous nature of the population and the disparate characteristics displayed make definitions very difficult.
   c. children who are gifted have been almost completely ignored in the school system.
   d. special education for youngsters who are gifted is still a novel venture.
   e. little research has been undertaken in this area.

4. Theories of multiple intelligences are attributed to
   a. Jean Piaget and Jerome Bruner.
   b. Howard Grossman and Edgar Doll.
   c. Guy Henry and Lewis Terman.
   d. J.P. Guilford and Howard Gardner.
   e. Sigmund Freud and Leo Kanner.

5. For an underachieving student who is potentially gifted, the most appropriate identification measure among the following would be
   a. an individual IQ test.
   b. a group intelligence test.
   c. teacher nomination.
   d. achievement tests.
   e. measures of creativity.

6. Someone who defines giftedness in terms of product would look at
   a. IQ levels.
   b. task commitment.
   c. the potential value of a contribution to society.
   d. "school-house" giftedness.
   e. results of tests of creativity.

7. *Talent* refers to
   a. a specific dimension of skill in a particular area.
   b. the process of bringing new and unexpected responses to a situation.
   c. remarkable early development.
   d. flexibility and creativity.
   e. the ability to effect positive change that is self- or group-enhancing.

8. Two high-school students, A and B, agreed to have their IQs assessed. Both scored almost three standard deviations above the mean. Years later, A is working in the dress department of a large store. B has published a number of highly acclaimed books on child development that influence both parents and teachers. Under current definitions of giftedness
   a. B is gifted because she has made a significant contribution to society.
   b. both A and B are gifted because their tested IQs are in the top one percent of the population.
   c. A is gifted because she has gifted potential.
   d. although A is gifted, B is more so because she has made valuable contributions.
   e. the best answer here is to say that it depends on whether you, the reader, believe that giftedness is product or potential.

9. You are teaching a grade-four math class that has a child identified as gifted. According to the research, this child
   a. can cover two years of standard content in one year.
   b. will be at class level as math is a subject that is developmental in nature.
   c. may have difficulties with math because of its mechanical nature.
   d. will not willingly participate in the practice associated with math.
   e. all of the above

10. To determine his sample for his study of giftedness, Lewis Terman began with
   a. teacher, parent, peer, and self-nominations.
   b. teacher nominations and group intelligence tests.
   c. the Structure of Intellect test.
   d. the WISC-III and the Stanford-Binet Individual Intelligence Test.
   e. non-verbal measures of mental ability.

11. The major conclusion that can be drawn about programs for students who are gifted is that
   a. the best programs are those that are quite different from the general curriculum of the general classroom.
   b. differences between the general classroom curriculum and that for gifted students are a matter of degree.
   c. enrichment programs provide the most effective means to stimulate gifted learners.
   d. resource programs are extremely rare and don't work that well, anyway.
   e. all of the above

12. A psychologist suggests accelerating a student identified as gifted. The research indicates that the most likely comment of a classroom teacher would be
    a. "What a good idea!"
    b. "Yes, I think he needs the challenge."
    c. "Acceleration will harm the child socially."
    d. "Please move him; he's a nuisance in my class."
    e. "No, I believe I can help him with a special enrichment program."

13. The myth that "the cream will rise to the top" is attributed to
    a. Francis Galton.
    b. Lewis Terman.
    c. Cesare Lombroso.
    d. Guy Henry.
    e. J. P. Guilford.

14. In a grade-three classroom, a school psychologist wishes to discover those children who have gifted potential. To determine potential, the psychologist would
    a. examine students' performance in academic subjects.
    b. administer the WISC-III.
    c. use performance assessments.
    d. review students' portfolios.
    e. talk to the teacher.

15. In the whole area of the education of children who are gifted, talented, and creative, the most deeply investigated subgroup comprises those who
    a. show high levels of creativity.
    b. are talented in the arts.
    c. possess high IQs.
    d. show leadership ability.
    e. are precocious.

16. Match the procedure to the definition.
    a. curriculum telescoping
    b. horizontal enrichment
    c. vertical enrichment
    d. self-directed learning
    ___ moving through a curriculum more rapidly
    ___ examining a certain curriculum area in more depth
    ___ doing additional independent work based on interest
    ___ providing students autonomous control of their learning

Recall questions

1. The first full-scale longitudinal study of giftedness was undertaken by ________.

2. According to Guilford's Structure of Intellect, there are ________ types of intelligence, in the three major areas of ________, ________, and ________.

3. Under Renzulli's definition of giftedness, individuals must possess the three components of ________, ________, and ________ in order to make remarkable achievements.

4. Remarkable early development is referred to as ________.

5. Dyssynchrony in young children refers to ________.

6. Gifted and talented children are recognized as exceptional because ________.

7. Two major contributors to theories of multiple intelligences are ________ and ________.

8. Special abilities, aptitudes, or accomplishments in a narrow field are called ________.

9. Research on the subject areas that students who are gifted particularly enjoy indicates that in school they are more likely to excel in areas such as ________ and ________, and least likely to enjoy ________.

10. The most commonly used IQ test to determine high intellectual functioning is the ______.

True–false questions

1. To reach their full potential, gifted students must be provided with suitable challenges and profitable educational experiences. T F

2. When Lewis Terman undertook his study of giftedness, he contended that giftedness encompasses both talent and creativity. T F

3. Because a stimulating environment is so vital in the development of giftedness, genetics actually have little effect on an individual's giftedness. T F

4. Individuals who are gifted, especially those who excel in the arts, are more prone to mental disease. T F

5. Research evidence clearly supports in-classroom enrichment programs as the most appropriate model for the education of students who are gifted. T F

6. The major opposition to acceleration programs arises from the fear of the social and emotional consequences of placing children who are gifted away from their chronological peer groups. T F

7. The Autonomous Learner Model and the Enrichment Triad model are essentially the same in practice. T F

8. Joseph Renzulli's definition clearly points to the characteristics that contribute to giftedness and talent; however, it does not resolve the problem of identifying potential gifts and talents. T F

9. It is safe to assume that teachers will consistently identify the highly creative child. T F

10. Children from minority groups are less likely to be identified as gifted than children from majority groups. T F

Short-answer questions

1. Identify three ways in which the category of gifted and talented is different from all other areas of exceptionality.

2. Many techniques are employed in informal and formal identification of children who are gifted. Identify five commonly used techniques.

3. List five reasons why group intelligence tests are problematic in the identification of pupils who are gifted.

4. Many barriers are presented to the gifted female. Identify and list five of these barriers.

5. List five pros and five cons related to the acceleration of students who are gifted.

Applications

1. In the educational journals, find three articles relating to one of the following topics:
   - identification and/or programming for gifted students who are also disabled; or
   - providing enrichment for gifted students in the general classroom; or
   - issues and problems in the area of the education of gifted and talented students.

   Present a report consisting of a description, comparison, and evaluation of the three articles. (See Application Question 1 in Chapter 1 of this study guide for report format.)

2. There are many tests to assess creativity available. Secure a copy of one test. Read the manual carefully. Administer the test to other students in your class. If possible, also administer it to young children. Score the children's responses using the manual. Did you see major differences between the efforts of the adults and those of the children? Can you explain why?

Activities

1. On p. 536 of the text (Chapter 15) is a letter written by the parent of a particularly precocious gifted eight-year-old boy. Imagine that you are a teacher writing back to the father. What type of advice could you give him about handling the child in the home, about interaction with his sibling, and about school programming? Explain any other approaches the parent could take to ensure that the child reaches his full potential.

2. Briefly describe a unit of study in social studies or math that you teach to your regular class. Now describe how this unit can be individualized for two groups of special learners: those who are gifted and those who are intellectually disabled. Stress content and pace. Keep in mind that material needs to be more concrete for disabled learners and more abstract for those who are gifted. With pace, remember that gifted students may learn much faster than others; students with intellectual disabilities learn at about half the rate. Show the adaptations to your lessons that will allow gifted children the opportunity to extend and expand their abilities and children with intellectual disabilities to obtain more drill and practice.

3. In the text, re-read and analyze the components of the sample enrichment unit on p. 310. Choose any area from the science curriculum of your province and develop a similar unit, following the same progression.

4. Attend a meeting of a local parents' association for gifted and talented youngsters. You may be able to interview some of the parents about special education for students who are gifted and talented. Prepare a series of questions that you could use in the interviews.

Portfolio item

Research and write a biography of an individual with a disability who contributed to the arts in some way. For example, John Milton, Beethoven, or Stevie Wonder.

End Test 3

1. A qualitative conception of exceptionality holds that
   a. the differences are a matter of degree.
   b. environment is a major contributor to exceptionality.
   c. people who are disabled think and learn in ways that are different.
   d. all children with special needs must be educated in general classrooms.
   e. children with special needs should be provided with the same quality of life as everyone else.

2. Of the following teaching functions, which is unique to the special education teacher?
   a. assessment of student behaviour
   b. design of instructional programs
   c. management of the learning environment
   d. implementation of remedial programs
   e. none of the above

3. For the general classroom teacher, the most important components of an IEP are
   a. long-term goals and short-term objectives.
   b. assessment results.
   c. IEP data.
   d. duration of services.
   e. who will take responsibility.

4. The related terms are
   a. self-concept, locus of control, learned helplessness.
   b. self-concept, body image, directionality.
   c. locus of control, school achievement, laterality.
   d. learned helplessness, anxiety, directionality.
   e. processing difficulties, locus of control, haptic processes.

5. For a student with behavioural disorders, success in the general classroom depends on a number of additional factors. What must be present is (are)
   a. support services.
   b. curriculum adaptations and modifications.
   c. acceptance by the other students.
   d. classroom teacher's experience with and exposure to children who are exceptional.
   e. all of the above

6. All of the following statements refer to behaviour therapy except
   a. it is concerned with producing behaviour.
   b. it is concerned with finding and explaining the inner conflicts of the child.
   c. it views all behaviour as learned.
   d. it sees behaviour as open to modification through new learning.
   e. it arose from the work of psychologists such as B. F. Skinner.

7. In the field of intellectual disability, definitions remain a problem. It is true that
   a. no universally accepted definition exists.
   b. definitional attempts have involved many disciplines.
   c. definitions have changed as more is learned about intellectual disabilities.
   d. today's definitions are more flexible than in the past.
   e. all of the above are true

8. Children with Down syndrome often have problems in acquiring and using language. Studies of language acquisition and development in these children indicate that
   a. the problems begin in infancy, when Down babies vocalize less frequently than other infants.
   b. the sentence acquisition in toddlers is delayed.
   c. articulation problems often result from the facial anomalies that accompany Down syndrome.
   d. the use of functional speech is often delayed.
   e. all of the above

9. Classroom enrichment means
   a. a child spending time in a special class.
   b. providing special activities in an otherwise regular class.
   c. allowing the child more drill and practice in certain skill areas.
   d. a full-time special class.
   e. none of the above

10. Although youngsters who are gifted tend to be well liked by their peers, the most popular seem to be those who
   a. challenge teachers.
   b. are intelligent but athletic and non-studious.
   c. are intelligent, studious, and non-athletic.
   d. help others to complete assignments.
   e. are exceptionally gifted.

11. Cleo has problems with the /th/ sound but can produce it correctly when prompted by her teacher. Cleo has a(n) ________ problem.
   a. articulation
   b. phonological
   c. receptive language
   d. voice
   e. dysfluency

12. A 17-month-old child looks at her mother and says, "Mommy milk." This is an example of
   a. a presentence.
   b. babbling.
   c. telegraphic speech.
   d. echolalia.
   e. motherese.

13. In the formation of aggressive behaviour, the most important influence comes from
   a. temperament and temperamental traits.
   b. parents' attitudes and child-rearing strategies.
   c. peers and gangs.
   d. television and other media.
   e. academic ability and school difficulties.

14. Bullying is today considered a major problem in our schools. Bullying is characterized by all of the following statements except
   a. bullying is a repeated action that occurs over a prolonged period of time.
   b. in bullying, there is an imbalance of power.
   c. the verbal, psychological, and/or physical negative actions of bullying are unprovoked.
   d. bullying is a form of aggression.
   e. more girls than boys bully.

15. Lewis Terman's study of giftedness may be described by all of the following statements except
   a. it represented the first full-scale longitudinal study of giftedness.
   b. it dispelled some traditional myths about gifted children.
   c. it established the IQ test as the sole criterion for the identification of giftedness.
   d. it lent credibility to the process of special education for gifted children.
   e. it had little impact on the field of gifted education.

16. According to Walberg, the approach with the best outcomes for learners with special needs is
   a. direct instruction.
   b. peer tutoring.
   c. whole-class instruction.
   d. resource room instruction.
   e. independent studies.

17. Conceptual models in the field of behavioural disorders differ considerably in how they view the causes of the problems. The model that sees behavioural disorders as almost exclusively the result of inner forces is
   a. biophysical.
   b. ecological.
   c. psychosocial.
   d. behavioural.
   e. psychodynamic.

18. Mr. L., an elementary teacher, is attending a professional meeting to learn more about psychotherapeutic intervention techniques. Of the following, Mr. L. would be likely to choose the workshop on
    a. new genetic findings.
    b. drug therapy.
    c. ecological assessment.
    d. token economies.
    e. play therapy.

19. Social-skill deficits are common among children and youth with
    a. behavioural disorders.
    b. learning disabilities.
    c. mental retardation.
    d. ADHD.
    e. all of the above

20. Given a normal curve, a theoretical 2.27 percent of the population might be expected to fall two or more standard deviations below the mean. In reality, about ____ percent of the population meets the AAMR definition of retarded.
    a. 1 to 1.5
    b. 3 to 5
    c. 6 to 8
    d. 10 to 12
    e. 0.1 to 1

21. In school, fourteen-year-old Jim shouts, swears, and is physically violent. Although he often loses control, Jim is deeply concerned about this behaviour and is working to overcome it. In educational terms, Jim would best be described as
    a. a juvenile delinquent.
    b. socially maladjusted.
    c. immature and hyperactive.
    d. incorrigible.
    e. anxious and withdrawn.

22. Mrs. J. teaches kindergarten and Mrs. L. teaches grade six. While Mrs. L. often has lessons that last thirty or forty minutes, Mrs. J changes activities often. The difference between the kindergarten and the grade-six class is that
    a. kindergarten children are likely to become bored and disruptive more quickly than are older students.
    b. young children have shorter attention spans than older students.
    c. in the kindergarten class, the curriculum is so heavy that the teacher must instruct as much as possible.
    d. older children need much drill and practice but younger children need much instruction and little practice.
    e. all of the above

23. In children, creativity is most apparent
    a. in the preschool years.
    b. during the first three years of school.
    c. in grades three to six.
    d. in junior-high-school students.
    e. at secondary levels.

24. Children who are gifted and talented are recognized as exceptional because
    a. giftedness is closely correlated with behavioural problems.
    b. they require special help to reach their full potential.
    c. such a designation builds awareness in teachers.
    d. these children will never achieve without special help.
    e. all of the above

25. In his 19th-century study of gifted individuals, Francis Galton took as his subjects
    a. eminent British women.
    b. men and women of the British working class.
    c. a group of British parliamentarians.
    d. his own family.
    e. eminent British men.

26. The clinical classification of behavioural disorders comes from
    a. factor analysis.
    b. the AAMR.
    c. DSM-IV.
    d. observations of children.
    e. behavioural type.

27. Social autopsies form part of a ____ strategy.
    a. co-operative learning
    b. bibliotherapy
    c. role playing
    d. social-skills training
    e. peer tutoring

28. All of the following statements about childhood aggression are true, except
    a. normally developing children rarely use aggressive behaviour.
    b. aggression is more prominent in males.
    c. aggression is more tolerated in boys.
    d. aggressive behaviour becomes more acceptable to children as they grow older.
    e. aggression is characteristic of many students with behavioural disorders.

29. All of the following are known as pioneers in the education of gifted children, except
    a. Louis Terman.
    b. Francis Galton.
    c. Henry Goddard.
    d. Joseph Renzulli.
    e. Guy Henry.

30. Follow-up studies of Terman's gifted subjects showed them to be superior in
    a. educational achievement.
    b. emotional stability.
    c. occupational achievement.
    d. production, such as writing and patents.
    e. all of the above

31. Match the person to the event or finding.
    a. Charles Bradley
    b. Jacob Periere
    c. Lewis Terman
    d. John Down
    e. Jean Marc Itard
    ___ first to use drug therapy with children
    ___ pioneer French special educator
    ___ worked with Victor, the so-called wild boy
    ___ differentiated among forms of mental retardation
    ___ pioneer in the education of students with gifts (5 x 1)

32. Match the researcher to the field of expertise.
    a. Herbert Grossman
    b. Alfred Strauss
    c. Joseph Renzulli
    d. Samuel Kirk
    e. Lewis Terman
    ___ adaptive behaviour
    ___ early research on giftedness
    ___ brain-damaged children
    ___ enrichment models
    ___ first definition of learning disabilities (5x 1)

33. Match the individual to the statement.
   a. Lewis Terman
   b. Joseph Renzulli
   c. Catherine Cox
   d. J. P. Guilford
   e. Guy Henry
   ___ longitudinal study of giftedness begun in 1922
   ___ multidimensional concept of intelligence
   ___ models for enrichment such as the Enrichment Triad
   ___ first to use the term *gifted*
   ___ early classes for gifted students (5 x 1)

34. Some researchers dispute the category of ADHD because such children are already served under the category of learning disabilities. T F

35. A self-contained classroom for students with behavioural disorders should be isolated from the rest of the school to ensure quiet and privacy. T F

36. Peter is an academically talented student. The research literature indicates that he would find an independent study preferable to co-operative learning. T F

37. Joseph Renzulli's definition of giftedness is universally accepted by today's educators. T F

38. If we were to examine preventative measures for behavioural disorders, we would focus upon aspects of nutrition, neglect, abuse, and pathological family climates. T F

Total /50

Section 5

Children with Sensory Impairments

In normally developing children, speech and language acquisition occurs spontaneously and effortlessly. Hearing infants take in, process, and organize the language they hear and eventually recreate for themselves the language of their culture. For children who are hearing impaired, the acquisition of speech and language is inevitably hindered or halted. In fact, the loss of easy acquisition of speech and language is the major result of hearing impairment.

The education of students who are visually impaired has undergone a dramatic restructuring in recent years. Most children with visual impairments, no matter how severe, are now in public school classes. In addition, a new emphasis is placed on the development of residual vision, which has led to a reassessment of traditional definitions and classification systems. There is a new stress on braille literacy and the continuing development of sophisticated optical and travel aids.

Chapter 9

Children with Hearing Impairments

Learning outcomes

After reading this chapter, you should be able to:

- Differentiate between the categories of deaf and hard of hearing;
- Understand the developmental consequences of hearing loss, especially in relation to language and speech acquisition;
- Recognize some of the technical aids that assist persons who are deaf;
- Identify the variety of communication modes used in the education of students with hearing impairments;
- Understand the nature of deaf culture and the deaf community and how it impacts on contemporary education for students who are deaf.

Introduction

Hearing loss is one of the least recognized and most misunderstood disabilities. Severe and profound hearing loss (deafness) is a low-incidence condition; however, milder forms of hearing impairment (hard of hearing) are widely prevalent.

The greatest single result of serious hearing impairment is the concomitant impairment in communication skills. For children, hearing impairment poses a serious threat because hearing is so critical for learning.

The human ear

The ear is one of the most complex organs in the human body. It is the mechanism that collects sound, processes it, and transmits it to the brain where it is decoded into meaningful stimuli. The anatomy and physiology of the human hearing mechanism is usually discussed in terms of the external, middle, and inner ear.

The external ear

In the external ear is the auricle, or pinna, which collects and funnels sound. There is also an external canal, or meatus, which is a wax and hair-lined canal that funnels sound and also protects the hearing mechanism. The tympanic membrane, or **ear drum,** is a concave mechanism that vibrates when struck by sound waves.

The middle ear

In the middle ear are the malleus, incus, and stapes, (hammer, anvil, and stirrup), the three tiny bones that span the middle ear cavity and transmit sound from the ear drum to the oval window at the entrance to the inner ear. The Eustachian tube connects the middle ear to the nasopharynx. It serves to equalize air pressure.

The inner ear

The inner ear is called the **labyrinth**. It contains the **cochlea**, a tiny, fluid-filled, snail-shaped structure of specialized cells that translates the mechanical sound impulses into neural impulses of electricity ready to be sent to the brain. The auditory nerve relays messages to the brain where they are decoded into meaningful input. The **vestibular mechanism** or semicircular canals are an organ of balance.

Sequence of hearing

- Sound waves enter the ear, travel through the external canal, and vibrate the ear drum.
- The vibrations of the ear drum move the bones of the middle ear.
- The footplate of the stapes moves the oval window and sets the cochlear fluid in motion.
- The movement causes the hairs immersed in the cochlear fluid to move. This stimulates the attached cells to send a tiny electrical impulse along the fibres of the auditory nerve to the brain.
- In the brain, impulses are translated into meaningful sound.

Definitions of hearing impairment

A number of definitions and classification systems exist to describe those with hearing impairments.

Hearing impairment is a generic term indicating a hearing disability that may range in severity from mild to profound. A **hard-of-hearing person** is one who, generally with the use of a hearing aid, has residual hearing sufficient to enable successful processing of linguistic information through audition. A **deaf person** is one whose hearing disability precludes successful processing of linguistic information through audition, with or without a hearing aid.

Prevalence of hearing impairments

It is very difficult to arrive at a true determination of the prevalence of hearing impairments. This is the result of inconsistent definitional data; confusion in identification and reporting; survey problems; problems in early identification; the problems of increasing prevalence with age; and the difficulties in identifying and reporting individuals with multiple disabilities.

As well, much of the research related to hearing impairment has been directed toward deafness rather than mild hearing loss. However, even mild hearing losses can result in educational difficulties.

Classification of hearing impairments

A number of classification systems exist in the field of hearing impairment. The orientation of the classifier determines the classification system used.

Classification by severity level

Severity classifications are based on hearing acuity and frequency response, which are measured in terms of decibels (dB) and hertz (Hz). A **decibel** is a unit of intensity or loudness. The number of decibels indicates the degree of loudness. The cycles per second or frequency of sounds, **hertz** (Hz), indicates the pitch of sound. Most English sounds fall in the range of 500 to 2000 Hz, the **speech range**.

A common way to classify individuals who are hearing impaired is by the degree of hearing impairment, whether mild, moderate, severe, or profound. Measures of loss of sound intensity (dB) and sound frequency (Hz) determine the extent of the hearing impairment.

Classification by site of loss

As well as a severity-of-loss classification, hearing impairment is defined in relation to the site of the loss. Problems of the middle and outer ear are referred to as **conductive hearing losses**. Inner ear losses, which mean permanent damage to the cochlea or auditory nerve, are known as **sensorineural impairments**.

Classification by etiology

A **congenital hearing impairment** is present at birth; losses acquired through accident or disease after birth are known as **adventitious hearing impairments**.

Classification by age of onset

Hearing impairments and delays in speech and language are intimately related. Therefore, educators are most concerned with the time of onset of a hearing loss. If a child has developed adequate speech and language prior to the onset of the problem, the results may not be as educationally devastating. The later in life the hearing impairment occurs, the more linguistic capabilities a child is likely to have.

Children with **prelingual deafness** are those in whom deafness was present early in life, or before the development of speech and language. Children with **post-lingual deafness** are those in whom hearing impairment occurred after the development of speech and language. The cutoff point is generally set at two years of age.

Etiology of hearing impairments

The causes and treatment of the physical manifestations of hearing impairment are the venue of medical personnel and audiologists.

Impairments of the outer ear

Outer ear impairments may be due to external otitis, wax build-up, or to a perforated ear drum. **Auditory atresia**, a condition in which the pinnae or the external canals are unformed or undeveloped, also leads to mild or moderate conductive hearing loss.

Impairments of the middle ear

Middle ear hearing impairments are generally more serious than those of the outer ear although most are medically correctable. The most common form of medically correctable middle ear hearing impairment is caused by **otitis media**, a condition in which the middle ear lining becomes inflamed and the cavity fluid-filled.

Otosclerosis, a hereditary problem, causes hearing loss in the middle ear when the functioning of the three small bones of the ossicular chain is hampered by a knob-like growth. Other middle ear problems result from blows to the head, falls, and congenital defects.

Impairments of the inner ear

The most severe hearing impairments occur in the inner ear. Five major causes account for childhood deafness: heredity, maternal rubella, meningitis, Rh factor, and prematurity.

Apnea—failure to breathe immediately after birth—is another commonly reported cause of hearing problems.

There are about sixty types of hereditary deafness, which can occur alone or with other disabilities as part of a syndrome. Maternal rubella is the most common cause of deafness from external sources. Meningitis is a potential cause of hearing handicaps and other conditions. Premature and low-birth-weight infants are at higher risk for hearing impairment.

In adults, **presbycusis** is the most common cause of auditory defect. Another condition, **Ménière's disease,** is characterized by nausea, vertigo, and tinnitus (throbbing or ringing in the ears).

Syndromes

Hearing loss can occur alone or in a syndrome. The most common is Usher's syndrome.

Developmental consequences of hearing impairments

Although the major consequences of hearing impairment are speech and language problems, other domains may be affected.

Cognitive development

Over the years, ideas about intelligence and cognitive development of individuals who are hearing impaired have altered. In the early part of this century, researchers saw deaf individuals as functioning intellectually slightly below the norm. By mid-century, deaf people were seen to have normal intellectual capacity but were also seen to be qualitatively different in some ways. Today it is acknowledged that the mental ability of individuals who are deaf falls along the normal curve.

Communication

Speech and language are the areas most affected in individuals who are hearing impaired. The degree of loss, age of onset, use of amplification, and many other variables affect speech and language acquisition.

Mild and moderate hearing losses allow individuals to communicate orally because the voice sounds of conversational speech remain audible. However, the language abilities of children suffering from recurrent or untreated otitis media may be delayed or disordered.

For children who are deaf, speech is inaudible, which inevitably leads to significant problems in language learning and speech acquisition. Even under optimal conditions, the language and speech levels of most deaf children lag in comparison to those of their hearing peers.

Academic achievement

The academic achievement of children who are deaf closely correlates with their language acquisition. Students who are deaf appear to be uniformly educationally lagging by three to five years. The lag is less in mechanical skills, such as arithmetic computation and spelling, and greatest in areas that are language dependent. Reading is particularly retarded; the typical student who is deaf graduates from school reading at about a grade-three level.

Social and emotional development

The deaf population demonstrates higher rates of emotional instability, neuroticism, and social maladjustment than do non-impaired persons. The severity and type of hearing impairment correlates with social maladjustment patterns.

Co-occurring disabilities

It is estimated that 33 percent of persons with hearing impairments have additional disabilities. Emotional disorders, intellectual disabilities, and learning disabilities are the most common additional conditions.

Family variables

Deaf children who have deaf parents have different experiences and tend to perform better on all measures than do deaf children who have hearing parents.

Hearing children of deaf parents

Hearing children of deaf parents often show deviations and delays in language development.

Assessment of children who have hearing impairments

Measuring a hearing impairment is quite complicated because measurement must incorporate the physical, psychological, and educational aspects as well as the impact on speech and language acquisition and development.

Measurement of hearing loss

Audiology is the science of hearing impairments, their detection, and their correction. Audiologists use three major types of hearing assessments: pure-tone audiometry, speech audiometry, and specialized tests for very young or difficult to assess children.

Pure-tone audiometry

The degree of hearing loss can be ascertained through pure-tone audiometry, which establishes an individual's **threshold of hearing**—the level at which a person can first detect sound. The audiometric data from pure-tone tests are plotted on an audiogram, a chart of hearing.

A hearing problem may be first identified through screening procedures. The most common screening instrument is the sweep test, which uses a portable audiometer to present tones at 20 to 25 dB across a range of frequencies.

Speech audiometry

Speech audiometry tests the level at which speech is detected. The level at which a person detects and understands speech is known as the **speech reception threshold** (SRT).

Tests for young children

Because very young children cannot undertake formal procedures, other methods are used, including electrophysiological assessment, behavioural assessment, and psycho-educational assessment.

Electrophysiological assessment

In electrophysical assessment, brain activity in response to sound is shown on charts. Acoustic impedance audiometry allows the audiologist to assess the movement of the tympanic membrane and middle ear bones to accurately detect conductive hearing loss.

Behavioural assessment

Behavioural testing includes observation of behaviour and reflexes, and play audiometry. Reflex audiometry, used with infants, assesses normal reflex reactions to sound. Play audiometry uses pure tones, but the child responds as part of a game.

Psycho-educational assessment

Non-verbal scales are most appropriate in the intellectual assessment of children who are hearing impaired. Popular measures include the Performance Scale of the WISC-III, the Goodenough-Harris Drawing Test, Raven's Progressive Matrices, and the Leiter International Performance Scale.

Intervention with children who have hearing impairments

Individuals with hearing impairments require different types of intervention in health care, rehabilitation, therapy, and education. Generally, intervention includes two major components: medical or corrective procedures and special education and related services.

Medical intervention

Many conductive hearing losses can be corrected. Antibiotics and surgical myringotomy are used to alleviate otitis media. Microsurgery helps otosclerosis, while otological surgeons can reconstruct the middle ear or its components.

Cochlear implants

Cochlear implants are a relatively new development to aid those with sensorineural hearing impairments. Electronic implants are used to stimulate the auditory nerve.

Technical aids

Many technical devices aid individuals who are hearing impaired. Personal hearing aids are now tiny and unobtrusive.

Amplification

Hearing aids can be worn by infants as well as by children and adults. In the classroom, children may use FM systems, some with direct audio input systems. Classroom FM systems have a teacher microphone and student receiver that allows the child to receive the teacher's message from any classroom location with good sound and clarity.

Most children who are hearing impaired benefit from amplification; even those who are profoundly deaf may hear distorted fragments of sound that aid in speech and language acquisition. But even though hearing aids help children to develop the use of residual hearing, improve audition and speech, and enlarge vocabulary and language ability, amplification cannot correct hearing or completely eliminate the problems of deafness.

Vibrotactile devices

Vibrotactile devices were developed to provide additional sensory input during speech training. The child can feel speech differences with the device attached to the hand or arm.

Telephone devices

The telecommunication device (TDD), sometimes called the TTY (teletypewriter), offers persons who are deaf direct telephone access to each other and to community services.

Household devices

A number of tools are available for adults who are hearing impaired. As well as the teletyper and printer for telephoning, there is a range of household signalling devices.

Captioned films

Captioned television and captioned films are a boon to the hearing impaired population.

Educational intervention

Programming for children who are hearing impaired ranges along a continuum of educational placements and services. In Canada, the most popular delivery models are itinerant programs, resource rooms, part-time integration, self-contained classes, day schools, and residential schools.

Service delivery models

Although contemporary views of special education favour inclusion, the issue is not simple in the education of students with severe hearing impairments. Many educators argue for placement in the regular classroom; others stress that the needs of students who are deaf are better met in settings where students find easier communication and social interactions.

Educational interpreters

When a child with a hearing impairment is placed in a regular classroom, an oral or manual interpreter aids in communication.

Educational approaches

Since the very beginning, the question of the most appropriate communication mode has been the most contentious issue in the education of deaf students. Educators divided themselves into two opposing camps. Those termed *oralists* viewed deafness as a human handicap to be overcome and invoked the primacy of speech and speech reading. On the other side, *manualists* saw deafness as a human difference and held that the deaf population needed their own unique sign language.

Under the two major philosophies of manual and oral, a number of methods and approaches developed. These include:

- **Acoupedic** methods, oral approaches that eliminate visual cues. They stress the development of residual hearing through amplification and auditory training.
- Oral/aural methods, which evolved through a number of stages. A pure oral method stressed speech, speech reading, and writing, while forbidding all natural gestures. Later, the oral method stressed speech, speech reading, and amplification but allowed natural gestures. Today's oral/aural methods focus on speech, speech reading, amplification, and auditory training.
- **Speech reading,** the ability to understand speech through observing lip movements and facial expressions. It is a difficult skill to acquire. Articulatory movements are very rapid and only about a third of English sounds are visible on the lips. Moreover, speech reading depends on the observer possessing a strong language base.
- Cued speech, an oral method in which eight hand configurations are used to aid discrimination in speech reading.
- The Rochester method, an oral approach that uses finger spelling in conjunction with speech, speech reading, and amplification.
- Total communication, which attempts to combine the best elements of the manual and oral methods. Speech, speech reading, and amplification are used simultaneously with a school-based manual system.
- American Sign Language (ASL), a true manual, ideographic sign language with its own vocabulary, grammar, and word order. It is the preferred communication method of the majority of North American deaf adults.

Bilingual-bicultural programs

Many people who are deaf see ASL as the natural language of deaf individuals. They want deaf children taught ASL first and then later taught English in the school system.

Curriculum

The primary objective of education for students who are hearing impaired is language development. Language teaching centres on two major approaches: the formal or grammatical approach and the natural approach. In the grammatical approach, the student is taught the structural elements of language and uses this information to generate sentences. In the natural approach, language teaching parallels the progression in which hearing children acquire language.

Key Terms

acoupedic
adventitious hearing impairments
apnea
audiology
auditory atresia
cochlea
conductive hearing losses
congenital hearing impairment
deaf person
decibel (dB)
ear drum
hard-of-hearing person
hearing impairment
hertz (Hz)
labyrinth
Ménière's disease
otitis media
otosclerosis
post-lingual deafness
prelingual deafness
presbycusis
sensorineural hearing impairment
speech range
speech reading
speech reception threshold
threshold of hearing
vestibular mechanism

Practice Questions

Multiple-choice questions

1. Swimmer's ear is an infection of the
   a. inner ear.
   b. Eustachian tube.
   c. external auditory canal.
   d. middle ear.
   e. pinna.

2. Conductive hearing losses
   a. usually respond well to medical or surgical intervention.
   b. affect mainly the inner ear.
   c. are usually permanent.
   d. result from damage to the cochlea or the auditory nerve.
   e. are most often congenital.

3. Mother is worried about 20-month-old Peter, who does not seem to respond to voices or loud environmental sounds. When she takes Peter to an audiologist, the audiologist is most likely to use
   a. a sweep test.
   b. play audiometry.
   c. pure-tone audiometry.
   d. an articulation test.
   e. reflex audiometry.

4. Peter's audiogram shows a flat loss in both ears. Across the speech range, the loss is 110 dB bilaterally. This means that Peter
   a. can hear only very loud voices.
   b. cannot understand voices but can respond to many environmental sounds.
   c. can understand voice only if using a hearing aid.
   d. cannot hear and understand voices even with a hearing aid.
   e. can learn to respond to the voices of family members.

5. In educational terms, Peter would be classified as
   a. adventitiously deaf.
   b. prelingually deaf.
   c. post-lingually deaf.
   d. hard of hearing.
   e. conductively hearing impaired.

6. Interference with the transmission of sound through the outer and middle ear causes a ________ hearing loss.
   a. severe.
   b. profound.
   c. conductive.
   d. sensorineural.
   e. mixed.

7. The critical range of frequencies into which most human speech falls is
   a. 500–5000 Hz.
   b. 500–2000 Hz.
   c. 125–2000 Hz.
   d. 4000–8000 Hz.
   e. 500–8000 Hz.

8. When surgeons implant a device that delivers electrical stimuli to remaining auditory nerves, the procedure is known as a(n)
   a. vestibular reversal.
   b. cochlear implant.
   c. myringotomy.
   d. tympanic reconstruction.
   e. amplification.

9. The condition characterized by tinnitus, vertigo, and nausea is
   a. congenital hearing loss.
   b. Ménière's disease.
   c. Down syndrome.
   d. Usher's syndrome.
   e. PKU.

10. Deaf children of deaf parents form a distinct subgroup within the deaf population because
    a. they tend to do better in many areas of functioning than do deaf children of hearing parents.
    b. they suffer fewer additional disabling conditions than do other children who are deaf.
    c. they are introduced to an understandable system of communication early in life.
    d. deaf parents accept the condition more readily than do hearing parents.
    e. all of the above

11. When bicultural-bilingual education for students who are deaf is discussed, it is true that
    a. it is an educational procedure that is well-accepted by all those involved in the education of deaf students.
    b. it is promoted by the deaf community.
    c. it combines a school-based manual system with deaf culture.
    d. it is an old method of instruction, simply resurrected.
    e. it is used universally in schools for the deaf throughout North America.

12. Today, persons in the deaf community would consider themselves all of the following except
    a. a minority group.
    b. an ethnic group.
    c. a group to be considered within a multicultural society.
    d. a disabled group.
    e. a cultural group.

13. Balance, motion, and gravity are maintained by the
    a. vestibular mechanism.
    b. Eustachian tube.
    c. incus.
    d. cochlea.
    e. stapes.

14. When people refer to *the deaf*, they are referring to
    a. deaf students in residential schools.
    b. members of the deaf cultural group, or deaf community.
    c. all persons with hearing impairments.
    d. students who are hearing impaired in regular schools.
    e. persons with serious and profound hearing impairments.

15. In bilingual-bicultural education, students who are deaf are taught about deaf culture and the many people who contributed. The one person students would be unlikely to study in this context is
    a. Abbé de l'Épée.
    b. Thomas Hopkins Gallaudet.
    c. Edward Miner Gallaudet.
    d. John McGann.
    e. Henry Goddard.

16. Match the term to the description.
    a. decibel
    b. hertz

c. speech reception threshold
d. threshold of hearing
e. gain

___ amount of amplification
___ the smallest difference in loudness intensity that can be perceived
___ the level at which a person first detects a sound
___ the level at which an individual actually understands speech
___ the cycles of sound per second

Recall questions

1. Bilingual education for deaf students sees children instructed in two communication or language modes: ________ and ________.

2. Loudness of sound is expressed in ________; frequency is measured in ________.

3. The form in which the content of a message is expressed is referred to as the ________.

4. When a child is born with missing or underdeveloped pinnae or auditory canals, the condition is known as ________.

5. The ________ ear contains the malleus, incus, stapes, and the Eustachian tube.

6. The audiological procedure that checks middle ear function is ________ audiometry.

7. The classroom amplification system that works much like a radio is a(n) ________ system.

8. A child with a sensorineural hearing loss in both ears of 105 dB is in the ________ level of hearing impairment.

9. The communication method for deaf students that uses a school-based manual system combined with speech, speech reading, and amplification is ________.

10. The snail-like structure in the inner ear is the ______.

True–false questions

1. The IQs of deaf persons as a group are substantially lower than those of the rest of the population. T F

2. Speech reading is an easy skill to acquire because nearly all English sounds are visible on the lips. T F

3. Children who are deaf pass completely through the babbling stage of speech development. T F

4. People who are hearing impaired have a natural ability to speech read. T F

5. Cochlear implants restore normal hearing to a person with a sensorineural hearing impairment. T F

6. The first North American institution for the education of students with deafness was established by Edward Miner Gallaudet in 1819. T F

7. Play audiometry is an important part of electrophysiological audiological assessment. T F

8. All adult deaf persons in North America use ASL as their primary mode of communication. T F

9. As a communication mode and a method of instruction, cued speech is still widely used. T F

10. Richard has his hearing checked by an audiologist and is found to have a loss of 15 dB in both ears. Richard would be classified as hard of hearing. T F

Applications

1. In the educational journals, find three articles relating to one of the following topics:
   - the child who is hearing impaired in the family climate;
   - bilingual education and the education of children who are hearing impaired;
   - reading levels, reading remediation, or reading approaches for children who are hearing impaired.

   Present a report consisting of a description, comparison, and evaluation of the three articles. (See Application Question 1 in Chapter 1 of this study guide for report format.)

Activities

1. Organize a formal debate to discuss the following topic: Children who are deaf should be educated through bilingual methods; that is, English and ASL.

2. In your local area, find out what types of educational facilities are available for hearing-impaired preschool and school-age children. What communication systems are in use?

3. Research a pioneer in the history of the education of the deaf.

4. Imagine you are designing and planning a new house for a deaf couple. List all of the household devices and modifications needed.

Portfolio item

Invite a deaf person or someone knowledgeable in sign language to the class. Discuss sign language in terms of its history, structure, development, and value to deaf persons.

Chapter 10

Children with Visual Impairments

Learning outcomes

After reading this chapter, you should be able to:

- Understand the various types of visual impairments, with their causes and developmental consequences;
- Differentiate between legal and educational blindness;
- Identify the various devices used for reading and mobility;
- Understand the types of adaptations, modifications, and support necessary to successfully include a child with a severe visual impairment in the regular classroom.

Introduction

Most of us have a special fear of blindness; to many people, a world without images would seem bleak, frightening, and virtually impossible to navigate.

Visual impairments can be among the most severe of all physical disabilities. In children, visual impairments cause complex developmental problems that make special education a necessity. Unique education needs include, but are not restricted to, early intervention; concept development; listening, study, and research skills; alternative methods for reading, writing, and mathematical computation; sensory training; daily living, socialization, and recreational skills; sexuality, career, and vocational training; utilization of low vision; accessibility to technology; orientation and mobility training; and meaningful transition programs.

The visual system

The entire visual system consists of the eye, nerve pathways, and the brain. Visual impairments result when there is interference with the passage of light as it travels to the brain.

The eye

The human eye is wrapped in three layers of tissue. The outer layer consists of the sclera and cornea. The middle layer contains the iris and lens, along with muscles and fluids. The retina, the actual seeing part of the eye, forms the inner layer. The most sensitive spot on the retina is the fovea, which possesses a rich supply of light-sensitive nerve cells, the rods and cones.

Sequence of vision

- When light reflected from an object hits our eye, the light rays pass through the cornea, where they are refracted.
- From the cornea, the light rays pass through the aqueous humour and proceed on their journey to the lens and the vitreous humour.

- The rays are then directed to the central part of the retina. This area contains rods and cones, which are light receptor cells. These are then stimulated by the light rays and consequently converted to electro-chemical energy.
- The energy is further transmitted through the optic nerve to the visual centre of the brain, where the visual information is interpreted.

Definitions of visual impairment

The category of visual impairment includes both blind persons and those with low vision. Two major types of definition exist—legal and educational.

Legal definitions

Legal blindness is defined as an acuity measure of 20/200 or less in the better eye with correction, or visual acuity of more than 20/200 if the widest diameter of the field of vision subtends an angle no greater than 20 degrees.

Low vision (partially sighted) individuals are those with a visual acuity greater than 20/200 but not greater than 20/70 in the better eye, after correction.

Educational definitions

Educational definitions focus on **visual functioning** or visual efficiency. In this case, a child who is visually impaired is one whose visual abilities interfere with learning. A **child with a visual impairment** is one whose visual impairment interferes with his or her learning and achievement, and requires adaptations in the presentation of learning experiences, the nature of the materials used, and/or in the learning environment.

Prevalence of visual impairments

Severe visual impairment is a low-incidence disability. The number of school-age children with visual impairments severe enough to require special education services is estimated to be about one in 1000.

Classification of visual impairments

Visual impairments include a range of degrees and types. At one end of the spectrum are blind persons; at the other are individuals with minor problems. Most visually disabled people have low vision. Even with correction, their vision is lower than normal.

Classification by degree

Individuals with visual impairments may be classified in terms of the type and degree of disability as follows:

- Near normal vision.
- Moderate visual disability.
- Low vision (partially sighted or severe visual disability).
- Blindness (profound visual disability).

Classification by age of onset

Congenital low vision refers to conditions that are diagnosable at birth or shortly thereafter. **Adventitious low vision** refers to conditions caused by accident or disease some time after birth.

Etiology of visual impairments

Hereditary factors are a leading cause of blindness in children under one year of age. Infectious diseases, including rubella, meningitis, encephalitis, and taxoplasmosis, also cause severe visual impairments. Other etiological factors include metabolic and vascular diseases, prematurity, birth trauma, hydrocephalus, nervous system infections, anoxia, and brain hemorrhages.

Visual problems arise from any interference with the passage of light from its entry to the eye through to its meaningful interpretation by the brain. Visual impairments are classified as refractive disorders, eye pathologies, and oculomotor disturbances.

Refractive errors

Refractive disorders are caused by irregularities in the shape or size of the eyeball, the cornea, or the lens. **Myopia, hyperopia, astigmatism**, and **presbyopia** are the major types of refractive disorders.

Disturbances of oculor motility

These are disturbances of eye movements. One such problem is **strabismus,** which is uncoordinated eye movement caused by improper muscle functioning. Amblyopia results from uncorrected strabismus. Diplopia is double vision. **Nystagmus**, a continual and involuntary movement of the eyeballs, is another oculomotor disturbance.

Eye pathologies

Eye pathologies are the result of damage to one or more structures of the eye. They include **glaucoma, cataracts**, **retinopathy of prematurity, retinitis pigmentosa**, macular retinal degeneration, **retinoblastoma, diabetic retinopathy,** retinal detachment, and optic nerve atrophy.

Other defects

Other eye defects include **colour blindness**, which stems from absent or malfunctioning retinal cone cells. **Albinism** is a condition in which pigment is lacking from all parts of the body, including the retina. Affected people often have **photophobia**. Cortical blindness occurs when there is some type of damage to the brain.

Syndromes

A number of syndromes are accompanied by visual defects. One of the most common causes of deaf-blindness is **Usher's syndrome.**

Developmental consequences of visual impairments

Individuals who are visually impaired do not form a homogeneous group. Even children with similar visual acuity may vary greatly in the utilization of their residual vision as well as the types of lighting and aids they require. The developmental consequences of total blindness differ in many respects from those related to low vision.

Motor development

Blindness imposes restrictions on a child's range and variety of experiences and ability to move freely within the environment. Children who are congenitally blind have little motivation to reach out into space and may be delayed in the area of motor development.

Cognitive development

The intelligence levels of persons who are visually impaired parallel those of the general population.

Perceptual development

Children who are blind build their knowledge on experiences with things that have smell, sound, and touch properties. They use synthetic touch: the tactual exploration of objects small enough to be enclosed by one or both hands. For larger objects, the person employs analytic touch, exploring the various parts of an object and then mentally reconstructing the parts.

Communication

Children who are blind acquire speech and language in the same manner as their sighted counterparts. They learn a great deal from voices and become adept at interpreting meaning from nuances and tone variations.

Academic achievement

Academic success for students with visual impairments is related to social, cultural, and familial factors rather than to the degree of visual impairment. Arithmetic, reading, and spelling may be problem areas.

Social and emotional development

Severe visual impairments impact negatively on spontaneous social interaction. Students with visual impairments may meet difficulties with their peers.

Co-occurring disabilities

About one-third of students with visual impairments have additional conditions. The most prevalent are emotional disorders, intellectual disabilities, and learning disabilities.

Assessment of children who have visual impairments

A comprehensive assessment of a child with a visual impairment takes into account two areas—medical diagnosis and treatment of the problem, and psycho-educational assessment that leads to efficient educational planning.

Screening

The most common screening procedure for visual acuity is the Snellen chart. Other screening measures include tests for visual field and muscle balance.
Children with serious visual impairments are likely to be identified during the preschool years, often at birth. More easily overlooked are children with mild visual problems. Teachers and parents should be aware of the signs of possible visual impairment.

Diagnosis

Diagnosis of visual impairment includes eye examinations and medical diagnosis. Diagnosis begins with an examination of visual acuity and visual fields, light sensitivity, and colour vision. Professionals trained to assess vision and diagnose problems include ophthalmologists and optometrists.

Psycho-educational assessment

It is not possible to use the same tests with blind as with sighted children because of the visual nature of many assessment measures. To assess the mental ability of blind students, psychologists use a battery of tests and rely on non-visual measures. Instruments include verbal versions of the Binet test and the verbal scale of the Wechsler scale.

Assessment is not restricted to IQ measures. It includes medical information, case histories, and data from developmental scales or checklists.

Intervention with students who have visual impairments

Intervention varies in type, intensity, and purpose, depending on the nature and degree of the visual loss as well as the unique goals of different professional disciplines. Generally, the major areas of intervention are habilitation (therapy) and education, which includes reading and optical enhancement, learning to use alternate modalities, and orientation and mobility training.

Medical intervention

Sophisticated medical technology for individuals with visual impairments takes many forms that include laser beam and surgical techniques, drug therapy, and artificial lens implants. Surgical intervention is required for retinal detachments, cataracts, and other medically treatable eye diseases.

Therapy

Occupational therapists may work with a child on the development of gross and fine motor skills.

Technical aids

More than 2000 technical aids, accessories, and devices exist for reading, mobility and orientation, and magnification.

Educational intervention

In recent years, there has been a movement from segregated residential school education for students who are severely visually impaired to placement in local schools. The needs of an individual student at a particular point in his or her educational career has been, and is, the deciding factor.

Service delivery models

Many boards retain a continuum of placement options that may include resource room programs, itinerant teachers, and special self-contained classes.

Successful inclusion of students with visual impairments depends upon the availability of specialist teachers, access to special equipment and optical aids, braille transcription services, and access to alternate programs. Special instruction for students who are blind includes braille reading and writing, orientation and mobility, the use of maps and technical and learning aids, and social and living skills. Pupils with low vision may require extra instruction in visual perceptual training, orientation and mobility, use of optical aids, and reading and writing.

Educational approaches

Education for students who are visually impaired can be clustered into seven major areas: regular curriculum; personal competence, such as self-help skills and daily living skills; orientation and mobility; communications skills; vocational guidance and career education; use of special aids and equipment; and visual stimulation.

Curriculum

In academic areas, students who are visually impaired follow the regular curriculum while being provided with special help in any areas of deficit and those in which specialized instruction is required.

Special aids and equipment

Reading aids include large-print materials, braille, and reading machines such as the Optacon and the Kurzweil reading machine.

Reading efficiency takes longer to develop using braille. Attention must be directed toward tactile tracking skills, reading posture, and hand coordination.

In the classroom, computers equipped with regular or braille keyboards and speech or braille output devices allow students to prepare assignments, keep files, and write programs. Paperless braillers are microcomputers with braille read-outs.

The Optacon, which converts print into a tactile array, is the most widely used reading device for individuals who are blind. The Kurzweil reading machine is designed for speech output. Variable-speed tape recorders are the most commonly used speech compressors. Closed-circuit television reading aids enlarge print to the size required by the visually impaired reader.

For writing, the slate and stylus are the braille version of pen and paper. The brailler allows the person to type braille.

Visual stimulation

Great strides have been made in the development of optical aids. **Low-vision aids** include handheld magnifiers and telescopes and stand magnifiers. Headborne aids include spectacles, clip-on aids, telescopes, and headband-style aids.

Orientation and mobility

Orientation and mobility are a daily issue in the lives of people who are visually impaired. **Mobility** refers to the knowledge of how to get from one place to another; **orientation** is the knowledge of location in space.

Orientation and mobility training teach individuals who are visually impaired to coordinate sensory impressions and engage all the remaining senses. The goal is to allow individuals who are blind to move in the environment with independence and confidence.

Mobility aids include the long or Hoover cane, dog guides, the Sonicguide, the laser cane, and the Mowat Sensor. Travel aids work on a radar principle, sending out beams of ultrasound that are reflected back to the device and converted into audible tones. The white, prescription, or Hoover cane is the mobility device most often recommended for people who are visually impaired.

Dog guides are used by only about one percent of the blind population. Owners must be older than sixteen years, emotionally mature, and responsible.

Personal competence

Young children may be instructed in self-help skills. Older students often require help in balancing interests, tackling new areas of learning, taking risks, and overcoming fear of failure.

Social intervention

The Canadian National Institute for the Blind is a national voluntary service for visually impaired Canadians.

Key Terms

adventitious low vision
albinism
astigmatism
cataract
child with a visual impairment
colour blindness
congenital low vision
diabetic retinopathy
glaucoma
hyperopia
low vision
low-vision aids
mobility
myopia
nystagmus
orientation
photophobia
presbyopia
retinitis pigmentosa
retinoblastoma
retinopathy of prematurity
strabismus
Usher's syndrome
visual functioning

Practice Questions

Multiple-choice questions

1. Blindness is defined as "central visual acuity of 20/200 or less." The numerals 20/200 refer to
   a. size of the chart letters.
   b. shape of the chart letters.
   c. width of the chart letters.
   d. distance from the chart.
   e. a fraction.

2. Three kinds of refractive errors that occur when light rays are not properly focused are
   a. myopia, hyperopia, amblyopia.
   b. myopia, astigmatism, hyperopia.
   c. hyperopia, myopia, nystagmus.
   d. astigmatism, nystagmus, hyperopia.
   e. amblyopia, hyperopia, astigmatism.

3. The legal definition of blindness includes visual acuity and
   a. the dependency of vision.
   b. retinal deterioration.
   c. macular area.
   d. the visual field.
   e. the convexity of the lens.

4. Sixty-year-old Bob Jones is suffering from a condition in which the increased intra-ocular pressure of the eye fluid is causing slow visual loss. Mr. Jones has
   a. congenital low vision.
   b. cataracts.
   c. glaucoma.
   d. strabismus.
   e. amblyopia.

5. In visual impairment, refractive errors are the result of
   a. problems with the image reflecting on the retina.
   b. cataracts.
   c. problems with the optic nerve.
   d. dysfunction of the cornea and lens.
   e. optic nerve atrophy.

6. Abu squints at the chalkboard and has great difficulty in identifying people and objects at a distance. Abu has a visual problem known as
   a. myopia.
   b. strabismus.
   c. hyperopia.
   d. nystagmus.
   e. presbyopia.

7. For children who can use their residual vision, the preferred term is
   a. visually impaired.
   b. blind.
   c. partially blind.
   d. physically handicapped.
   e. mobility restricted.

8. How children use their remaining sight is the major consideration of
   a. the educational definition of visual impairment.
   b. measures of visual acuity.
   c. the legal definition of blindness.
   d. the definition of low vision.
   e. none of the above

9. Children who have severe visual impairments or severe hearing impairments rely on other senses. Research shows that
   a. children who are blind have innate compensatory listening skills.
   b. children who are deaf have innate compensatory hearing skills.
   c. children with deafness or blindness only need practice to improve innate skills.
   d. listening and visual skills are not innate and are learned only after much practice.
   e. with some practice, all students learn appropriate listening or visual skills.

10. The braille system is used for reading by persons who are blind. Braille was
   a. universally accepted by all educators of blind students as soon as it was invented.
   b. generally accepted for English speakers but was found to be unsuitable for use in other languages.
   c. widely accepted by the beginning of the 20th century.
   d. only accepted once educators and scientists developed a scientific and mathematical code.
   e. accepted in North America, but not in Europe.

11. Of the following types of visual impairments, which would be most commonly seen in children?
   a. strasbismus and myopia.
   b. cataracts and glaucoma.
   c. diabetic retinopathy and glaucoma.
   d. retinalblastoma and albinism-related problems.
   e. astigmatism and nystagmus.

12. A visually impaired individual's knowledge of his or her position in space is referred to as
   a. mobility.
   b. directionality.
   c. laterality.
   d. orientation.
   e. body image.

13. The chief reason that special education exists for students who are visually impaired is
   a. to allow students who are visually impaired to avoid competition with their peers.
   b. to enable students who are visually impaired to reach their full capacity.
   c. to remediate emotional problems.
   d. to provide services not available in the regular classroom.
   e. all of the above

14. The cornea, lens, and aqueous humour function for
    a. protection.
    b. rotation.
    c. reflection.
    d. reception.
    e. refraction.

15. According to recent research on reading and braille, children who are blind
    a. should not be taught braille at all.
    b. should learn to use other reading aids.
    c. should have greater stress placed on braille reading.
    d. find braille so difficult that other modes are preferable.
    e. do not need braille today.

16. Match the term to the definition.
    a. fovea
    b. sclera
    c. retina
    d. cones
    e. rods

    ___ sensitive layer that lines the back of the eye
    ___ most sensitive spot on the retina
    ___ photoreceptors that collect light
    ___ tough covering of the outer portion of the eye
    ___ photoreceptors that collect light

Recall questions

1. Disturbances of eye movement are referred to generically as ________ problems.

2. Four types of refractive errors are ________, ________, ________, and ________.

3. Myopia is to nearsightedness as ________ is to farsightedness.

4. The tear film that is essential to the health of the cornea is provided by the glands of the ________ apparatus.

5. The portion of space as seen by the fixated eye is referred to as the ________.

6. The most common screening procedure used for the measurement of central visual acuity is the ________ chart.

7. Lack of skin pigmentation is referred to as ________.

8. ________ is a progressive hereditary disease that causes the retina to degenerate, resulting in night blindness and loss of peripheral vision.

9. The ________ is the mobility device most often recommended for blind persons.

10. It was the French priest ________ who gave deaf persons their own language of signs and the French teacher ________ who developed a six-dot cell system to help blind individuals to read more efficiently.

True–false questions

1. The majority of Canadian students who are visually impaired are educated in residential settings. T F

2. Presbyopia refers to visual problems resulting from disease. T F

3. A good braille reader can read as fast as a sighted reader. T F

4. Persons who are blind possess superior musical ability. T F

5. The extent to which a child can rely upon vision varies according to the degree of useful sight remaining. T F

6. Most adaptations for students who are visually impaired in a classroom are to assist with mobility. T F

7. Most children who are visually impaired can improve their visual functioning. The more children use their vision, the more they stimulate the pathways to the brain. T F

8. At the moment, the number of persons using braille is showing significant decreases. T F

9. You have a child with albinism in the classroom. For this child, especially strong light is needed. T F

10. A blind community exists, very similar to the deaf community. T F

Short-answer questions

1. Sketch and label a diagram of the human eye.

2. Individuals who are visually impaired may be classified into five major groupings. Briefly describe the visual characteristics of each group.

3. Identify and briefly explain three major causes of severe visual impairments in children.

4. Identify and describe four signs that might alert a teacher to a student's visual problems.

5. Identify and write one descriptive sentence about four types of mobility and travel aids that are useful to a blind person.

Applications

1. In the educational journals, find three articles relating to one of the following topics:
   - early intervention with infants who are severely visually impaired;
   - language development in children who are blind.

   Present a report consisting of a description, comparison, and evaluation of the three articles. (See Application Question 1 in Chapter 1 of this study guide for report format.)

Activities

1. Undertake a survey of your class. What percentage of people have myopia, hyperopia, or astigmatism?

2. Do a second survey on your class in health care. Check who has seen the following professionals in the last two years: general practitioner for a checkup; dentist for a checkup; ophthalmologist for eye checkup; audiologist or other personnel for screening of hearing. Tally the responses. Does any area seem underrepresented? Try to explain why.

3. Invite an adult who is blind who has a guide dog to the class. Discuss the pros and cons of various mobility guides.

4. In your local district, find out what types of educational programs are available for children who are visually impaired.

Portfolio item

A huge range of both low-tech and high-tech appliances and devices are available for persons with visual impairments. Visit your local branch of the Canadian National Institute for the Blind (CNIB). Make an inventory with descriptive notes of all the devices you see.

End Test 4

1. In today's special education, the dominant ideology is
   a. equal access to educational services.
   b. educational integration.
   c. the least restrictive environment.
   d. inclusion.
   e. All of these are part of the dominant ideology.

2. Within the categories used in the text, blindness and hearing impairments are classified as
   a. physical disabilities.
   b. health disorders.
   c. language disorders.
   d. sensory disabilities.
   e. technology-dependent conditions.

3. There are more boys than girls in the identified population of students with
   a. intellectual disabilities.
   b. learning disabilities.
   c. hearing impairments.
   d. visual impairments.
   e. all of the above

4. Which of these professionals are concerned with communication disorders?
   a. otolaryngologists
   b. speech pathologists
   c. neurologists
   d. audiologists
   e. all of the above

5. Neil meets problems in the comprehension of spoken language. He may have
   a. aphasia.
   b. a hearing impairment.
   c. a receptive language disorder.
   d. learning disabilities.
   e. any of the above

6. A child's acquisition and use of language is closely tied to
   a. cognitive development.
   b. self-concept.
   c. social interactions.
   d. a stimulating environment.
   e. all of the above

7. The pioneer educator of persons with visual impairment was
   a. Henry Goddard.
   b. Leo Kanner.
   c. Samuel Gridley Howe.
   d. Thomas Hopkins Gallaudet.
   e. Edward Miner Gallaudet.

8. Jane has problems perceiving the difference between words such as *bell, ball,* and *bill* when they are presented auditorily. Jane may have difficulties in the area of
   a. auditory closure.
   b. visual discrimination.
   c. auditory discrimination.
   d. visual figure-ground.
   e. visual closure.

9. A child said to be suffering from *dysgraphia* will show disturbances in
   a. the ability to express thoughts in writing.
   b. learning to read.
   c. handling numbers and arithmetic.
   d. attention and concentration.
   e. laterality and directionality.

10. Of the following techniques, which would be valuable for both visually impaired and hearing disabled children?
   a. reading material in braille
   b. raised maps
   c. classroom FM systems
   d. captioned films
   e. note-takers

11. The failure of the muscles to coordinate the two eyes is called
   a. albinism.
   b. nystagmus.
   c. presbyopia.
   d. strabismus.
   e. retinopathy.

12. Defects of colour vision arise from an absence or malfunction of
   a. cone cells.
   b. sclera.
   c. pupil.
   d. lens.
   e. iris.

13. The light receptor cells of the eye are embedded in the
    a. sclera.
    b. cornea.
    c. lens.
    d. iris.
    e. retina.

14. *Visual efficiency* refers to
    a. the degree of stress encountered when using vision.
    b. the amount of pressure placed on the eye muscles.
    c. the amount of information gathered in a short glance.
    d. how a person uses residual vision.
    e. how much a person can see without turning the head.

15. Which of the following would cause an adventitious hearing loss?
    a. auditory atresia
    b. genetics
    c. Rh factor
    d. childhood accidents
    e. rubella

16. For students classified as severely visually impaired, the major reading medium is
    a. large-print materials.
    b. Optacon.
    c. Perkins brailler.
    d. braille.
    e. Kurzweil reading machine.

17. Many approaches and communication modes have been used in the education of students with hearing impairments. Today, the dominant mode in North America is (are)
    a. school-based manual systems.
    b. American Sign Language.
    c. Rochester method.
    d. oral/aural methods.
    e. acoupedic methods.

18. You have a child in your class who has a visual impairment due to albinism. You would ensure that
    a. there is plenty of strong, natural light in the classroom.
    b. strong natural lighting is supplemented with good fluorescent lighting.
    c. all surfaces and the floor are kept brightly polished.
    d. the light is kept low.
    e. the light is muted most of the time, although strong light is provided when the student is reading.

19. In the oral/aural method of teaching deaf children, the stress is placed on
  a. speech, speech reading, and amplification.
  b. sign language and speech reading.
  c. cued speech.
  d. total communication.
  e. ASL and writing.

20. If a teacher wanted to implement a program for training social skills, the best way to determine the skills that should be taught is through
  a. informal natural observations.
  b. direct observation.
  c. standardized testing.
  d. peer- and self-nominations.
  e. dynamic assessment.

21. Mrs. Teacher is working with her class of children who are hearing impaired. She is teaching them how to write past-tense verbs. Her approach to language teaching is referred to as a ______ approach.
  a. natural
  b. grammatical
  c. language experience
  d. whole language
  e. dialect-based

22. To help a child who is hearing impaired in the regular classroom, the teacher should
  a. speak slowly and overenunciate to aid speech reading.
  b. keep light on the child's face for efficient speech reading.
  c. allow the child to make full use of visual and auditory clues.
  d. seat the child at the back of the room.
  e. all of the above

23. Which of the following statements does *not* refer to the braille system?
  a. The idea first came from Charles Barbier.
  b. The braille cell consists of six dots.
  c. All people who are visually impaired use braille.
  d. The braille system is used for reading.
  e. All of the above refer to braille.

24. When children who are blind learn to gauge distance and direction, they do so through
  a. sound localization and variations in sound.
  b. visual angle of perspective.
  c. an inborn obstacle sense.
  d. subtle changes in the slope and feel of the ground.
  e. Blind children use all of the above.

25. For persons who are blind, the most widely used reading device is (the)
   a. paperless brailler.
   b. Kurzweil reading machine.
   c. closed-circuit-television reading aid.
   d. Optacon.
   e. braille books.

26. Match the condition to the description.
   a. auditory atresia
   b. otosclerosis
   c. otitis media
   d. Ménière's disease
   e. presbycusis
   ___ hearing loss due to aging
   ___ lack of an outer ear opening
   ___ fusion of the three small middle ear bones
   ___ fluid in the middle ear
   ___ characterized by vertigo, nausea, and tinnitus

(5 x 1)

27. Match the terms to the description
   a. socialization
   b. sociability
   c. social skills
   d. social competence
   e. social cognition
   ___ responses in a given situation that prove effective or maximize the probability of producing, maintaining, or enhancing the positive effects for the interactor
   ___ knowledge and cognitive activities employed by people in dealing with the social world
   ___ the ability of children to successfully and appropriately select and carry out their interpersonal goals
   ___ willingness to engage others in social interaction and to seek their attention or approval
   ___ means by which individuals become reasonably acceptable and competent members of their society

(5 x 1)

28. Match the term to the definition.
   a. nystagmus
   b. diplopia
   c. presbyopia
   d. strabismus
   e. myopia
   ___ double vision
   ___ inefficient ocular motility
   ___ rhythmic involuntary eye movements
   ___ nearsightedness
   ___ visual loss due to aging

(5 x 1)

29. Match the pioneer to the area of special education.
 a. Samuel Kirk
 b. Valentin Haüy
 c. Michel Charles de l'Épée
 d. Lewis Terman
 e. Edgar Doll
 ___ learning disabilities
 ___ mental retardation
 ___ giftedness
 ___ blindness
 ___ deafness (5 x 1)

30. Match the person to the event or invention.
 a. Charles Barbier
 b. Frank Hall
 c. Samuel Gridley Howe
 d. Louis Braille
 e. John Barret McGann
 ___ opened a school in Toronto in the 1850s
 ___ invented a tactile communication system
 ___ revamped the Barbier system
 ___ invented the Perkins brailler
 ___ opened the first school for blind students in North America (5 x 1)

Total /50

Section 6

Children with Low-Incidence Disabilities

The extremely broad classification of children with special health care needs includes a huge number of conditions. About half of all childhood chronic health disorders are related to allergic and respiratory problems.

Normal development of the nervous system is necessary for efficient functioning. Damage or deterioration of the central nervous system is one of the most common causes of physical and neurological disabilities in children.

Pervasive developmental disorder is a general term used to describe individuals suffering from chronic and severe conditions that affect every aspect of their development. Childhood psychoses and infantile autism, two pervasive developmental disorders, represent the deepest forms of behavioural and emotional disorders both in terms of the impact upon the children and in terms of the effect on those involved in their lives. No other human behaviour is so removed from the range of normal experience and so difficult to understand.

Children with multiple disabilities show deficits in two or more areas of functioning. Because so many combinations of impairments are possible, these children form an extremely heterogeneous population.

Chapter 11

Children with Special Health Care Needs

Learning outcomes

After reading this chapter, you should be able to:

- Identify some of the more common health disabilities and their developmental consequences;
- Understand the special needs of children with health problems in educational settings;
- Prepare an emergency protocol.

Introduction

Special health care needs relate to diseases and conditions that affect the lives and functioning of children and adults. They include a huge range including cancer, diabetes, asthma and allergies, and genetic problems such as cystic fibrosis and muscular dystrophy. While special health care needs are medical problems that are handled within medical parameters, children with health care needs also present many educational challenges. All educational personnel must be familiar with the appropriate medical procedures and interventions that are part of the regular care of those students as well as those required in emergency situations. Educators must also be aware of the factors that put students at risk for difficulties. These include fatigue, limited vitality, short attention span, and limited mobility.

Definitions of special health care needs

One of the major difficulties in discussing health care needs (and neurological disorders) is the diversity of conditions and their sequelae. This leads to a range of overlapping descriptors that include:

- health impairments, which occur when the presence of a disease or medical condition interferes with school attendance and learning and hinders the ability to lead a normal life;
- physical disabilities, those that affect body systems; they include health disorders and problems related to mobility and motor skills;
- orthopedic conditions, those that arise from any cause and affect mobility;
- musculoskeletal impairments, specific disorders involving bones or muscles;
- neuromuscular diseases, which occur before, during, or after birth;
- technology dependent, which refers to conditions that require technological intervention;
- medically fragile children, who require specialized technological health care procedures for life support during the school day.

Prevalence of special health care needs

It is very difficult to accurately determine the incidence and prevalence of chronic health problems because of the variety of conditions; inconsistencies in defining various disorders; different data-gathering methods; limited nationwide health statistics; and multiple conditions that may be counted twice or may focus on only the primary disability.

Classification of special health care needs

Children with health care needs are primarily the concern of medical personnel. Education is concerned when the conditions impact negatively on learning and progress.

Cystic fibrosis

Cystic fibrosis is a genetically determined inborn error of metabolism involving the exocrine glands. It is the most lethal hereditary disorder affecting the Caucasian population.

Cystic fibrosis primarily affects the respiratory and digestive systems. Symptoms include the production of thick, sticky mucus, which clogs breathing and digestion and creates pockets of infection and dysfunction in the lungs. Intensive medical management is necessary: therapy, antibiotics, and diet.

Developmental consequences of cystic fibrosis

For children with cystic fibrosis, intellectual function is not impaired. The general classroom is the most appropriate option. However, accommodation must be made for frequent absences resulting from respiratory or digestive disorders.

It is on the family that a child with cystic fibrosis seems to have the greatest impact. For many families, everyday activities are dependent on the current health status of the ill child. Regimens of treatment, medication, feeding, positioning, and medical care can take up most of the day.

Diabetes mellitus

Diabetes mellitus is a disorder of sugar metabolism resulting from the failure of the pancreas to manufacture sufficient insulin. There are two major types of diabetes: insulin dependent and non-insulin-dependent. Insulin-dependent diabetes is usually of early onset while non-insulin-dependent diabetes ordinarily occurs after forty years of age.

Medical management revolves around diet, insulin injections, and exercise. Food intake, insulin, and exercise must be carefully balanced and monitored throughout the diabetic's life in order to prevent immediate and long-term complications associated with **hyperglycemia** (high blood sugar) or **hypoglycemia** (low blood sugar).

Developmental consequences of diabetes mellitus

No impediment of intellect is found in diabetic children. Children can participate in all school activities unless otherwise advised by a physician. In addition to regular education, children must be taught to manage their condition.

Cancer

About one hundred diseases characterized by the abnormal and uncontrolled growth of cells are subsumed under the general term *cancer*. Cancer is the second highest cause of childhood deaths in Canada; about two-thirds of these deaths result from leukemia.

Medical management of cancer includes surgery, chemotherapy, and/or radiation. The developmental consequences of cancer are associated with the type, extent, and location of the growth. In hospital, school progress is maintained by hospital teachers.

Developmental consequences of cancer

Apart from the condition itself, one of the major outcomes of cancer is the physical and emotional problems arising from treatment. Each child will have a unique experience at the hospital and in the diagnosis and treatment of a particular kind of childhood cancer.

Sickle cell anemia

Sickle cell anemia is an inherited condition in which, under certain conditions, there are changes in the red blood cells.

Allergies

An **allergy** is a hypersensitive reaction to something in the environment. There are two major categories of allergies. **Atopic allergies** are associated with hereditary and/or familial factors. **Non-atopic allergies** do not have a hereditary component but result from antibodies produced in response to allergens in the environment.

A huge range of substances cause allergic reactions. These are grouped into the categories of inhalants, contactants, ingestants, and injectants.

Asthma

Asthma, a high-incidence condition, causes narrowing and obstruction of the bronchial tubes. Attacks are characterized by coughing, wheezing, and shortness of breath.

Developmental consequences of asthma

School absenteeism is a major problem among children with asthma, especially in the first three years of school.

Children who are abused and neglected

Child abuse and neglect are the physical or mental injury, sexual abuse, negligent treatment, or maltreatment of a child.

Definitions of abuse and neglect

In a general sense, child abuse is defined as any interaction or lack of interaction that results in non-accidental harm to the individual's physical and/or emotional state. More specifically, physical abuse is non-accidental physical injury to a child; physical neglect is the failure of caretakers to meet a child's basic physical needs. Sexual abuse is the sexual exploitation of a child.

The family and child abuse

Child abuse and neglect cannot be attributed to any single cause, nor are they restricted to any socio-economic group. However, characteristics of child abusers have emerged. Abusive caretakers have little knowledge of good parenting and unrealistic expectations of children, and were often abused themselves.

In a family, some or all children may be abused. Particularly vulnerable to abuse are children with mental, physical, or behavioural anomalies.

Abuse is indicated by both physical and behavioural manifestations. Signs of sexual abuse are generally more subtle and difficult to see. The consequences of child abuse and neglect are varied. They may be manifested in failure to thrive, mental illness, personality disorders, school problems, lack of empathy, intense anger, and strong feelings of worthlessness.

Musculoskeletal impairments

These are impairments that affect body movement and functioning but are not the result of neurological damage. They affect physical development as well as **motor development.**

Limb deficiencies

Limb deficiencies include conditions in which there is a loss or absence of all, or parts, of a limb. **Congenital amputations** occur when infants are born missing all or part of a limb, a specific condition called *phocomelia.*

Acquired amputations, which may be the result of accident or disease, are more common than congenital amputations. Many children use a prosthesis, a device that serves as a substitute for a missing body part.

Spinal problems

There are three types of curvature of the spine: scoliosis, lordosis, and kyphosis. All can affect posture and mobility.

Muscular dystrophy

Atrophy occurs when there is muscle degeneration caused by neurological damage. **Muscular dystrophy** refers to a group of inherited conditions characterized by a degeneration of muscle fibres without neurological deficit.

There are a number of forms of muscular dystrophy; there is progressive muscle weakness in all. Duchenne's is the most common type of muscular dystrophy. It is sometimes referred to as *pseudo-hypertrophic muscular dystrophy* because it is characterized by an enlargement of the calves and sometimes the other muscles as a result of fatty deposits.

Duchenne's muscular dystrophy is transmitted from mother to son through a sex-linked recessive gene. Onset is early. By ten years of age the child is likely to be in a wheelchair.

Landouzy-Dejerine, or facioscapulohumeral, muscular dystrophy involves the face and muscles of the shoulder girdle. Inheritance is dominant and non-autosomal; the condition affects both sexes. The life expectancy of those with Landouzy-Dejerine muscular dystrophy is normal.

Arthritis

Arthritis is a common term for a variety of conditions involving inflammation of the joints. The cause is unknown and no cure exists.

Juvenile arthritis, or Still's disease, has a more favourable prognosis than does adult arthritis. However, children may suffer joint pains, eye and respiratory infections, enlarged spleen, and inflammation of the tissue covering the heart.

Assessment of children who have special health care needs

With the huge range of varied disorders that make up the category of health disorders, a single type of assessment procedure is not reasonable.

Intervention with children who have special health care needs

Health disorders require considerable intervention in the forms of education, therapy, and medical assistance. Social service agencies frequently become involved with them and their families. As they grow older, students may require counselling and other support for independent living.

Medical intervention

Medical interventions include diets, surgical procedures, drug therapies, and adaptive devices.

Therapy

Various types of therapy are necessary, including speech and language, occupational, and physical.

Technical aids

Many adaptive devices are used. These are explained in Chapter 13.

Educational intervention

Educationally, children with health problems are almost always placed in general classrooms. Curriculum changes are not necessary.

Service delivery models

In almost all cases today, children attend the general public school. The needs of children who are technology-dependent and/or medically fragile present greater challenges to the school system. They may be placed in a variety of educational settings depending upon the type and severity of the condition, the related services available, and the prognosis of the disability.

Curriculum

No special curricula exist or are really necessary for students with health problems.

Key Terms

allergy
asthma
atopic allergies
congenital amputation
hyperglycemia
hypoglycemia
motor development
muscular dystrophy
non-atopic allergies

Practice Questions

Multiple-choice questions

1. Of all children who have chronic health disabilities, the majority are affected by
   a. multiple sclerosis.
   b. allergies.
   c. cystic fibrosis.
   d. diabetes.
   e. cerebral palsy.

2. Conditions that impede bodily movements but are not the result of central nervous system damage are referred to as
   a. neurological disorders.
   b. sensory handicaps.
   c. congenital malformations.
   d. musculoskeletal impairments.
   e. pervasive developmental disorders.

3. Definitions in the area of physical and health disabilities are very untidy. This means that
   a. there is much overlap among categories.
   b. professionals prefer to dispense with definitions altogether.
   c. educators' classifications tend to be clearer than medical classifications.
   d. definitions and classification systems are of little value and rarely used today.
   e. new definitions are continually emerging.

4. Chronic health problems are best characterized as
   a. essentially medical conditions.
   b. specific conditions that retard academic performance.
   c. conditions requiring a range of technical equipment and aids.
   d. conditions that make special education a necessity.
   e. conditions that equate with cognitive dysfunction.

5. In the past, many children with physical disabilities were placed in special schools because
   a. general schools and classrooms were not equipped to physically accommodate them.
   b. general classroom teachers refused to accept them.
   c. they would have been neglected by other children.
   d. there were not enough trained aides available.
   e. it was thought that peers would not accept them.

6. The cyclic theory of child abuse holds that
   a. children learn parenting techniques from their own experiences in the family and abused children are likely to continue the cycle.
   b. men are more likely to break out of the cycle than are women.
   c. the majority of abused parents do not abuse their own children.
   d. whether parents continue the cycle of abuse is influenced by many aspects of their developmental history, not just the abuse.
   e. all of the above

7. Abnormally low levels of glucose in the blood are referred to as
   a. hypothermia.
   b. hypoglycemia.
   c. hyperglycemia.
   d. hyperthermia.
   e. hypermetabolism.

8. The most lethal hereditary disorder in the Caucasian population is
   a. cystic fibrosis.
   b. muscular dystrophy.
   c. Tay-Sachs disease.
   d. sickle cell anemia.
   e. hemophilia.

9. Diabetes mellitus may be described as
   a. a disorder of sugar metabolism.
   b. a disorder related to insufficient insulin manufacture.
   c. a disorder affecting both children and adults.
   d. a chronic disorder.
   e. all of the above

10. Educational personnel dealing with children with special health care needs are most involved with
   a. the medical prognosis of the disabilities.
   b. the etiology of the conditions.
   c. the factors that put children at risk for learning difficulties.
   d. physiotherapy.
   e. the risk factors that caused the condition.

11. All forms of muscular dystrophy are characterized by
   a. early onset.
   b. progressive muscle weakness.
   c. sex-linked inheritance.
   d. abbreviated lifespan.
   e. lowered intellectual performance.

12. A forward curvature of the spine is
   a. lordosis.
   b. kyphosis.
   c. amniosis.
   d. scoliosis.
   e. none of the above

13. Rheumatoid arthritis affects more
   a. boys.
   b. adult women.
   c. adult men.
   d. girls.
   e. numbers are consistent within these groups.

14. Children unable to attend school for extended periods of time will be educated by
    a. itinerant teachers.
    b. educational consultants.
    c. homebound teachers.
    d. therapists.
    e. parents.

15. A physician tells Colleen that she has atopic allergies. These allergies are related most specifically to
    a. hereditary factors.
    b. foods and food dyes.
    c. general poor health.
    d. climatic changes.
    e. could be any of the above

16. Match the condition to the description.
    a. cystic fibrosis
    b. Type I diabetes
    c. Type II diabetes
    d. sickle cell anemia
    e. asthma

    ___ a high-incidence and an increasing condition in most developed nations
    ___ a genetically determined inborn error of metabolism characterized by pervasive dysfunction of the exocrine glands
    ___ results from a defective recessive gene that causes the production of defective hemoglobin
    ___ an autoimmune illness caused by a pancreatic disorder that involves sugar metabolism and is usually associated with early onset
    ___ an autoimmune illness caused by a pancreatic disorder that involves sugar metabolism and ordinarily occurs after age forty

Recall questions

1. The causes of allergies in humans can be divided into four categories: inhalants, ________, ________, and ________.

2. When muscles are weakened as a result of nerve degeneration, the condition is referred to as ________; however, when muscle weakness is present but not due to nerve degeneration, the condition is known as ________.

3. ________ are conditions that impede bodily movements in the absence of damage to the central nervous system.

4. Most researchers look at child abuse within the broad categories of sexual abuse, ________, ________, and ________.

5. In terms of educational placement and setting, most children with special health care needs are educated in ________.

6. ________ is the most common lethal genetic disease found among Caucasians.

7. In sickle cell anemia, the _________ sickle and change shape.

8. Of muscles or nerves, in muscular dystrophy there are changes in the _______.

9. The type of diabetes that typically affects adults is ______.

10. The most common health disability seen among school-aged children is ______.

True–false questions

1. There are a number of forms of muscular dystrophy, all of which share the common characteristic of progressive muscle weakness. T F

2. Almost all children with chronic health care needs will require special education at some point in their school careers. T F

3. Asthma and allergies are high-incidence conditions. T F

4. Because the public is so aware of the problem, prevalence figures on child abuse are very accurate. T F

5. Screening for sickle cell anemia is carried out with amniocentesis. T F

6. Muscular dystrophy is a condition that involves hardening and scarring of the myelin sheaths. T F

7. A correlation has been found between child abuse and excessive crying. T F

8. Type II diabetes is found only in children. T F

9. Children with behavioural disorders seem to be particularly prone to child abuse. T F

10. Child abuse is a problem that has emerged only in our fast-paced, technological society. T F

Short-answer questions

1. Both behavioural and physical indicators of child abuse may be detected. List ten such indicators.

2. List the reasons why it is difficult to establish the prevalence of chronic health problems.

3. List the major groupings of agents that cause allergies.

4. List ten health difficulties of children with cystic fibrosis.

5. Describe the three major stages of the progression of muscular dystrophy.

Applications

1. In the educational journals find three articles relating to one of the following topics:
   - developmental consequences of child abuse;
   - new research findings on the etiology of muscular dystrophy.

   Present a report consisting of a description, comparison, and evaluation of the three articles. (See Application Question 1 in Chapter 1 of this study guide for report format.)

2. Reread the case studies in Chapter 11 about Czeslov, who has cystic fibrosis, and Bob, who is diabetic. For each of these students, plan an emergency protocol. Begin with an outline of the condition and problems that could emerge.

3. Research and prepare an essay on the prevalence, etiology, and developmental consequences of asthma in children. Stress prevalence rates in your own province or area.

Activities

1. In your province, what responsibilities do teachers have regarding cases of child abuse? Discuss these.

2. Do a survey of your class. Find out who suffers from allergies. Tally the results to find the most common allergies.

Portfolio item

Visit a shopping mall for an hour or so. Keep a brief diary of everything you do there. Now retrace your route to examine accommodations for persons with disabilities. Note, for example, accessibility such as ramps, widened doorways, special washrooms, and braille directions. Alternatively, check your own university or institution for means of access (ramps, doors, elevators, and so on) for persons in wheelchairs.

Chapter 12

Children with Neurological Disabilities

Learning outcomes

After reading this chapter, you should be able to:

- Demonstrate a working knowledge of the human brain and its function;
- Identify the major types of neurological disabilities, their etiology, and their developmental consequences;
- Understand the special classroom needs of children with neurological disabilities;
- Understand that different types of disabilities in this area mean different types of classroom environments and interventions;
- Identify a range of devices used for mobility by children with neurological and other motor disorders.

Introduction

A huge range of neurological disorders are found. Some are associated with impairments of the nervous system; others result from diseases and accidents. For many children, the decreased range of motion, the reduced strength of movement, or the addition of unwanted or uncontrolled movement can dramatically affect the way they perform.

The central nervous system

The human nervous system has two major components, the brain and the spinal cord. Neurons and glial cells are important to the central nervous system. Neurons (nerve cells), of which there are approximately twelve billion in the human nervous system, are the basic units of neurological function. The brain is a densely packed, complex organ that contains millions of nerve cells. As children grow and develop, there is a gradual coating of the neurons with myelin, a process that gives the brain weight, density, and increasing complexity. The myelin sheaths around individual nerves insulate them from one another and make it easier for messages to pass along the nerve pathways; they help speed up neural transmission and make the brain more efficient.

The brain

The cerebrum of the human brain—the gray matter that controls higher-level intellectual functioning—is subdivided into two hemispheres. Joining the two cerebral hemispheres is the corpus callosum, a thick, boomerang-shaped band of fibres. Each hemisphere is divided into four lobes: frontal, parietal, occipital, and temporal. The brain also contains four ventricles.

While the two halves of the human brain look like mirror images of each other, there are both structural and functional differences. A hemisphere is said to be dominant if one process is primarily housed there. In humans, the right hemisphere is specialized for holistic processing through the simultaneous integration of information. The left hemisphere controls verbal function and the linear, logical thinking associated with verbalizations. *Hemisphericity* is a person's tendency to rely more on one cerebral hemisphere than the other in processing certain types of information.

The spinal cord

The spinal cord is a pencil-thin, segmented collection of neurons that are related to specific parts of the body. Damage to the motor cells of the spinal cords results in **flaccid paralysis**, an inability to move muscles.

Definitions of neurological disabilities

Pupils who are physically disabled are those in whom a physical impairment, other than visual or hearing loss, interferes with the development of learning and requires special services.

Neurological impairments are a subcategory of physical disabilities. Neurological impairments result from damage to, or dysfunction of, the brain and/or the spinal cord that may occur pre-, peri-, or postnatally. The consequences of injury vary greatly. Damage to the motor cells of the spinal cord causes flaccid paralysis. Brain injuries may result in limited specific disorders or generalized problems.

Prevalence of neurological disabilities

Neurological disorders include a wide range of conditions. However, they are low-incidence conditions.

Cerebral palsy

Cerebral palsy (CP), caused by damage to the brain, is characterized by motor disorder and is often accompanied by other disabilities. Cerebral palsy is not contagious, progressive, or curable.

Classification of cerebral palsy

The topographical classification of cerebral palsy refers to the limb involved. The suffix *plegia* means paralysis. An individual with monoplegia would have one limb involved.

Cerebral palsy is also divided into five types according to specific motor patterns. Spastic (pyramidal) cerebral palsy is characterized by slow, laborious, poorly coordinated movement. It affects about 50 percent of the population affected with cerebral palsy.

The term *extrapyramidal cerebral palsy* includes the other four types. Athetosis is characterized by constant, involuntary, writhing movements. It affects about 25 percent of the population of individuals with cerebral palsy. Rigidity occurs when there is continuous diffuse muscle tension resulting in stiffness. The condition is rare. Tremors are involuntary, rhythmic movements of certain muscles. Ataxia is characterized by poor coordination of the movements associated with the maintenance of balance, posture, and spatial orientation. Ataxia affects about 15 percent of the population with cerebral palsy.

Developmental consequences of cerebral palsy

The consequences of cerebral palsy vary in relation to many factors: severity, additional disabilities, time of diagnosis and intervention, availability of services, and family attitudes and child-rearing practices. However, motor system damage will almost invariably result in some developmental lags.

Cerebral palsy is best viewed as a multi-disabling condition. Many children with cerebral palsy exhibit one or more additional impairments such as intellectual disability, learning disabilities, sensory loss, epilepsy, speech difficulties, and emotional disorders.

While people with cerebral palsy are represented across the full range of intellectual function, research indicates that intellectual disabilities are common. There is little evidence to link the severity of the intellectual impairment with a specific type of cerebral palsy, although the best mental development appears to be associated with hemiplegia.

Because cerebral palsy is essentially a motor disorder, speech difficulties are common in affected children. Children may have dysarthria, an articulation disorder associated with poor control of the speech muscles as a result of brain damage. Language disorders are less common than speech problems.

Many youngsters have visual defects and auditory problems. Other sensory problems and perceptual disorders are also prevalent. In addition, many children suffer some form of convulsive disorder.

Spina bifida

Midline defects result from a failure of the halves of the embryo to completely fuse. These defects, or *clefts*, may occur as cleft lip, cleft lip and palate, and in other parts of the body.

Spina bifida is a congenital midline defect of the spinal column in which one or more vertebrae fail to close during embryological development. The cause of spina bifida is unknown. Prevalence varies from country to country and even from region to region within a country. The condition is more likely to occur in lower socio-economic groups, in females, and may run in families.

Classification of spina bifida

Spina bifida is classified into three main forms. Spina bifida occulta is the mildest form, with limited or no consequences. In spina bifida with meningecele a sac of cerebrospinal fluid protrudes from the spine. Once the sac is replaced within the bony column, few problems ensue. Spina bifida with myelomeningocele, the most severe type, results in a protruding sac that contains parts of the spinal cord as well as cerebrospinal fluid.

Developmental consequences of spina bifida

Children with spina bifida occulta or with meningecele are likely to develop normally. In spina bifida with myelomeningocele the protruding sac contains not only cerebrospinal fluid but also parts of the spinal cord. Neurological damage is irreversible. The effects vary with the location of the sac on the spinal column. Lower-area defects cause fewer problems but may result in incontinence without paralysis. Many more difficulties result from higher sacs, including paralysis, loss of lower limb sensation, incontinence, kidney problems, and associated musculoskeletal deviations. Spina bifida is not associated with lowered learning ability. There may be ambulation difficulties and frequent absences from school.

Hydrocephalus

While hydrocephalus and spina bifida occur as solitary events, they are often found together. **Hydrocephalus** is a condition that is characterized by an excessive accumulation of cerebrospinal fluid in the brain, due to obstruction of the flow.

Developmental consequences of hydrocephalus

Without treatment, the child who is hydrocephalic develops an excessively large head. The accumulated fluid presses on the skull and on the brain tissue. This can result in mental retardation, motor disorders, and seizures, and may sometimes be fatal. A shunt that drains the fluid relieves the pressure and ameliorates or eliminates consequent difficulties.

Epilepsy

Epilepsy is defined as a condition produced by a sudden, violent, disorderly electrical discharge of brain cells. It is a chronic condition of various origins characterized by recurrent seizures.

Epilepsy is not a disease but a symptom of a disorder of the brain. However, not all brain-injured individuals will be epileptic and not all epileptics will be brain damaged. When evidence of brain damage is apparent the condition is known as symptomatic epilepsy. Idiopathic epilepsy refers to a condition of unknown origin.

Classification of epilepsy

Epilepsy includes many types of seizures. Generalized seizures are bilateral and symmetrical without local onset and are often accompanied by loss of consciousness.

Grand mal and petit mal are the most common types of generalized seizures. The grand mal seizure proceeds through relatively distinct stages that may include an aura, a cry, loss of consciousness, generalized body stiffness (the tonic phase), a clonic phase, regaining of consciousness, and deep sleep.

Petit mal is often referred to as an absence seizure. With petit mal, the child simply ceases activity and appears to stare vacantly. Although most petit mal seizures are very brief, some may be longer lasting.

Partial seizures begin locally and may or may not be accompanied by unconsciousness. The common feature of partial seizures is their local origin in the brain.

Jacksonian seizures are characterized by motor symptoms without impairment of consciousness. Psychomotor seizures include relatively complex, well-organized movements and sometimes clouding of consciousness and amnesia.

Developmental consequences of epilepsy

Children with idiopathic epilepsy are more likely to develop normally than are children with symptomatic epilepsy. The latter show a greater prevalence of mental retardation, sensory loss, and/or motor disabilities.

Many negative aspects are attached to epilepsy; the stigma may be worse than the condition itself. As well, epilepsy is a chronic condition; individuals cannot look forward to a cure nor can they predict when a seizure will occur.

Tourette syndrome

Tourette syndrome is a condition characterized by multiple, involuntary muscular and cerebral tics that wax and wane, remit, and change.

Head trauma

Traumatic Brain Injury is an increasing cause of disabilities in children, of whom many will require special education for short or long periods.

Developmental consequences of head trauma

Teachers familiar with students with TBI often report classroom difficulties. It is estimated that among children with mild head injuries, about 25 percent will require special classes; of children with serious injuries, about 50 percent will need special education.

Drug-exposed children

Some children who were exposed to drugs prenatally suffer adverse effects that include learning disorders and problems dealing with incoming stimuli.

Fetal Alcohol Syndrome (FAS)

Students with FAS may experience multiple behavioural difficulties. They have problems communicating their needs, are easily frustrated, have little control over their impulses, find it difficult to stay on task, are in constant motion, are nondisruptive, and cannot work independently for long periods.

Acquired Immunodeficiency Syndrome (AIDS)

AIDS is a condition caused by a virus, HIV, which seriously disrupts the body's immune system. In children, the prevalence of AIDS is on the increase, transmitted from an affected mother, through blood transfusion or, rarely, through the mother's milk.

Developmental consequences of AIDS

Pediatric AIDS is a severe medical condition as well as a potential neurological disability. The condition brings many challenges to schools and teachers.

Assessment of students who have neurological disabilities

No specific measures are used to assess students with neurological disabilities. During an assessment, however, testers may use various adaptations—support adaptations, prosthetic adaptations, and general adaptations.

Intervention with students who have neurological disabilities

These disabilities are primarily medical and therapeutic conditions, and intervention is broad. Intellectual disability is not a concomitant condition.

Medical intervention

Medical intervention may include preventing problems such as **contractures**, a shortening of muscles, tendons, and ligaments that results in postural distortion.
Drug therapy is effective for seizure control, either eliminating or reducing the frequency of seizures. The type of drug used is related to the type of seizure pattern and the presence of drug side effects.

Therapy

Occupational and physical therapy are important for children with physical and neurological disabilities. Therapists work on motor development, positioning, and the use of adaptive equipment.

Technical aids

Technical aids are often necessary for mobility, daily living, and speech. Students need adaptive (assistive) equipment, which includes prosthetic, orthotic, and adaptive devices.

Prosthetic devices

Prosthetic devices replace lost body function and/or provide support. Many are used for mobility.

Orthotic devices

Orthotic devices are instruments that assist the action of a relatively nonfunctional part of the body.

Adaptive devices

Adaptive equipment includes prostheses and orthoses as well as computer technology and communication aids.

Educational intervention

Progress in medical science, improved technology, and changing attitudes have dramatically altered service delivery for these students.

Service delivery models

The educational setting for students with physical and neurological disabilities depends on the type and severity of the condition, the related services available, and the prognosis of the disability. Physical disability in itself is no reason for special class placement, and most children can be successfully educated in the regular classroom.

Curriculum

There is no special curriculum for students with physical and neurological disabilities. Children learn the same things as their peers.

Conductive education

Conductive education aims to promote personal development and educational and social fulfillment for children with motor difficulties related to brain and spinal problems.

Key Terms

adaptive equipment
contractures
flaccid paralysis
hydrocephalus
neurological impairments
orthotic devices
positioning
prosthetic devices
spina bifida
Traumatic Brain Injury

Practice Questions

Multiple-choice questions

1. Learning problems and abnormal development are most likely to be associated with
   a. Jacksonian seizures and ideopathic epilepsy.
   b. generalized seizures and symptomatic epilepsy.
   c. petit mal and partial seizures.
   d. grand mal and ideopathic epilepsy.
   e. all of the above

2. A child in your classroom has a grand mal seizure. You should
   a. place a spoon in the child's mouth so that she will not bite her tongue.
   b. call 911 immediately.
   c. call the child's parents and have them remove the child.
   d. wait out the seizure and then turn the child's head to drain any saliva.
   e. panic.

3. Children who have suffered damage to the motor cortex or the pyramidal tract of the brain suffer what type of cerebral palsy?
   a. spastic
   b. athetoid
   c. tremors
   d. rigidity
   e. ataxia

4. Epilepsy may be described by all of the following statements, except
   a. epilepsy is characterized by seizures.
   b. epileptic seizures are the result of functional disturbance of brain cells that causes an excessive discharge of electrical energy.
   c. epileptic seizures may last for less than a minute.
   d. epilepsy is caused solely by genetic factors.
   e. epilepsy is broadly categorized as symptomatic or ideopathic.

5. When assessing youngsters with physical disabilities, it is appropriate for the assessor to
   a. modify administration procedures.
   b. assist children in handling materials.
   c. position children for maximum performance.
   d. select only part of a measure or measures.
   e. all of the above

6. Petit mal seizures are likely to
   a. be seen in children more than adults.
   b. occur when the individual is in a conscious state.
   c. occur several times daily.
   d. occur when the child is sedentary.
   e. all of the above

7. Children with health and/or physical disabilities may meet problems in school because
   a. the disability means that they attend school later than their peers.
   b. illness or a disability means that they miss long periods of schooling.
   c. they have more limited vitality or energy than other children.
   d. they may have a lack of mobility or ambulation.
   e. all of the above

8. When it comes to teaching children with physical disabilities in the classroom, teaching procedures
   a. are the same as for other children.
   b. are quite different from those for other children.
   c. will require modifications because these children are usually also mentally retarded.
   d. can be accomplished only with the help of an aide.
   e. should be adapted, often quite dramatically.

9. It is true that
   a. brain injury is always accompanied by epilepsy.
   b. epilepsy is always a sign of brain injury.
   c. in ideopathic epilepsy, symptoms of brain injury are seen.
   d. in symptomatic epilepsy, symptoms of brain injury are seen.
   e. None of the above are true.

10. A congenital defect that is the result of incomplete closure of the spinal column during fetal development is
   a. arthritis.
   b. multiple sclerosis.
   c. quadriplegia.
   d. spina bifida.
   e. muscular dystrophy.

11. When we speak of hemispheric dominance, we say that
   a. neither hemisphere is dominant over the other.
   b. each hemisphere possesses specialized talents and brings different skills to a given task.
   c. neither hemisphere is competent to analyze data and program a response alone.
   d. the two hemispheres of the human brain are complementary.
   e. all of the above

12. For children with cerebral palsy, surgery serves to do all except
   a. cure the condition.
   b. ease contractures.
   c. correct dislocations.
   d. repair joints.
   e. reduce the risk of arthritis.

13. Jane has spina bifida. She is in a wheelchair and suffers incontinence and kidney problems. She has
    a. spina bifida occulta.
    b. spina bifida with meningocele.
    c. spina bifida with myelomeningocele.
    d. spina bifida and hydrocephalus.
    e. none of the above

14. The resource individual who will assist Jane with wheelchair mobility training is the
    a. physical therapist.
    b. orientation and mobility specialist.
    c. occupational therapist.
    d. classroom paraprofessional.
    e. peer.

15. Many individuals with epilepsy will have a warning in the form of a motor, visual, hearing, or olfactory process prior to their seizure. This warning is referred to as a(n)
    a. aura.
    b. psychomatic process.
    c. wait period.
    d. warning signal.
    e. tinnitus.

16. Match the lobes of the brain to their function
    a. occipital
    b. parietal
    c. frontal
    d. temporal
    e. fifth lobe

    ___ sexual and emotional functions
    ___ spatial orientation
    ___ anticipatory activity
    ___ vision
    ___ auditory activity

Recall questions

1. The most prevalent and serious additional problems associated with cerebral palsy are ________ disorders.

2. The most severe type of spina bifida is ________.

3. About 80 percent of children with spina bifida with myelomenigocele also suffer from ________.

4. The five classifications of cerebral palsy according to motor ability are ________, ________, ________, ________, and ________.

5. Epilepsy is a condition produced by ________.

6. ________ cerebral palsy is characterized by involuntary movements of the muscles.

7. The bundle of nerve fibres that join the two hemispheres of the brain is the ________.

8. ________ devices are used to replace lost body functions; ________ devices assist a limb's action.

9. An absence seizure is more correctly referred to as ______ epilepsy.

10. Joey is wearing equipment to support his back and spine. This is a ______ jacket.

True–false questions

1. As a general rule today, youngsters who are physically disabled are educated in special self-contained classrooms. T F

2. It is fairly common for a person with epilepsy to exhibit more than one type of seizure. T F

3. All types of spina bifida result in lower limb paralysis and incontinence. T F

4. A number of specific educational and psychological assessment measures have been developed especially for the population of students who have physical disabilities. T F

5. Hydrocephalus, combined with spina bifida, is likely to result in multiply disabling conditions. T F

6. At birth, a child has full neural growth. T F

7. Cerebral palsy is a progressive condition that worsens over time. T F

8. The corpus callosum joins the spinal cord to the brain. T F

9. Teachers do not need to learn about positioning and carrying a child with a physical disability as there will always be an aide present. T F

10. In Tourette syndrome, the involuntary muscular and cerebral tics tend to wane and change. T F

Short-answer questions

1. The developmental consequences of cerebral palsy vary in relation to many factors. List five factors.

2. Outline the distinct stages often seen in the progress of a grand mal seizure.

3. It is extremely important that teachers be aware of a child's epilepsy and the procedures to follow during a seizure. List five things that a teacher may do if a child has an epileptic seizure in the classroom.

4. List and briefly describe the three classifications of spina bifida. Include physical consequences.

5. List the developmental consequences of untreated hydrocephalus.

Applications

1. In the educational journals, find three articles relating to communication systems used with children who have severe disabilities. Present a report consisting of a description, comparison, and evaluation of the three articles. (See Application Question 1 in Chapter 1 of this study guide for report format.)

2. Sketch a physical plan of an elementary classroom. Show where you would seat a child in a wheelchair and one using crutches. Explain why.

3. Read the case study of Kent on p. 434 of the text and the IEP on p. 458. Kent has assistance from a physical therapist and a speech therapist. Outline the areas on which the therapist will focus. On which areas can the teacher and the therapists work co-operatively?

4. Using the research literature as a base, evaluate and discuss one type of medical intervention used with youngsters with exceptional conditions and/or learning difficulties. For example, drug therapy, surgery for cerebral palsy, or a cochlear implant for a deaf child.

Activities

1. Visit a classroom where a child with cerebral palsy is integrated. Observe the manner in which the teacher accommodates the child.

Portfolio item

Borrow a wheelchair and use it for a day in a shopping mall. Log all the places you visited and evaluate them in terms of mobility for a wheelchair user, access, ease of use, service, and so on. As well, keep a diary of your own feelings; be especially aware of how other people interact with you. Alternatively, follow the same procedures using a pair of crutches.

Chapter 13

Children with Pervasive Developmental Disorders

Learning outcomes

After reading this chapter, you should be able to:

- Differentiate between infantile autism and childhood schizophrenia;
- Understand the array of etiologies proposed to account for these conditions;
- Appreciate the developmental consequences of psychosis and infantile autism;
- Identify the range of service delivery models that are available;
- Identify tactics that will support these children in inclusive classrooms.

Introduction

Different types of conditions are found under the developmental disorder umbrella, including childhood psychoses, childhood schizophrenia, infantile autism, and severe and profound mental retardation. Childhood psychoses and infantile autism represent the most extreme forms of emotional and behavioural disorders.

Definitions of pervasive developmental disorders

Children with pervasive disorders have conditions that are chronic and lifelong. These individuals are developmentally disabled.

Prevalence

Childhood psychoses are low-incidence conditions. Infantile autism is less frequent than childhood schizophrenia. Boys outnumber girls in the autistic population and rates of additional disabilities are high.

Childhood schizophrenia

Childhood psychosis is a general term used to refer to any number of maladaptive behaviours or clusters of behaviours. Psychotic children demonstrate problematic and bizarre behaviour; they fail to recognize, understand, or respond appropriately to people in their environment. The major category of childhood psychosis discussed in the text is schizophrenia.

Childhood schizophrenia often occurs in early puberty. Onset follows a period of more or less adequate development. In childhood schizophrenia, ego development declines or is arrested.

Infantile autism

Youngsters who are autistic may generally be characterized as non-verbal and non-relating. There are degrees of autism and other children with disabilities may demonstrate patterns of autistic behaviour without the full syndrome. The onset of autism is before thirty months of age.

Classification of pervasive developmental disorders

In the text, the term *pervasive developmental disorder* is used to encompass both autistic and psychotic children because in affected children many basic areas of development are affected. Both groups demonstrate impairments in language use and interpersonal relationships and show bizarre and deviant behaviour.

Nevertheless, there are significant differences between childhood schizophrenia and infantile autism. These relate to etiology, age of onset, behavioural manifestations, and prognosis.

Asperger's syndrome

The profiles of individuals with Asperger's syndrome differ from classic autism although the same domains of communication, socialization, behaviour, and activities are affected.

Etiology of pervasive developmental disorders

Recent research leans toward biological factors as the major cause of childhood psychoses and infantile autism. However, etiological data should be regarded as inconclusive given the multiple determinants of these conditions.

Childhood schizophrenia

Accumulating evidence points toward biological causative factors in childhood schizophrenia. Investigators are studying fetal complications, neurological dysfunctions, and genetic factors.

Infantile autism

Although Eugene Bleuler used the term in 1906, the syndrome of autism in children was first identified by Leo Kanner in 1943. Kanner characterized these children as withdrawn and showing an obsessive desire for sameness. He found the parents to be highly intelligent, unusual achievers, emotionally cold, aloof, and reserved, which led later researchers to interpret children's autistic behaviour in terms of lack of adequate parenting.

As evidence mounted that home and family conditions could not account for autism, investigators turned to the examination of a range of biochemical, sensorimotor, neurological, and cognitive defects to account for the presence of the extreme behaviours manifested by children with autism. Evidence exists that genetics, fetal complications, biochemical disturbances, and central nervous system damage may be precursors of autism.

Developmental consequences of pervasive developmental disorders

Childhood psychoses and infantile autism affect nearly every area of development and seriously hinder all aspects of progress. Cognition, language, perception, and social and emotional development are all involved and affected by the conditions.

Children with autism or schizophrenia demonstrate maladaptive behaviours that fall largely within two classes. The first is aggressive behaviour, either self-directed (self-injurious behaviour) or directed toward others. The second class of maladaptive behaviour is **self-stimulation**, a persistent, stereotypic, repetitive mannerism.

Childhood schizophrenia

Childhood schizophrenia occurs later than infantile autism. After a period of more or less adequate development, children regress dramatically. Youngsters who are schizophrenic show disturbances in mood, thought, and behaviour; children are emotionally apathetic, indifferent, and withdrawn.

Physical and motor development

Children who are schizophrenic commonly lag in motor development.

Cognitive development

Some variability in intellectual functioning is found among children with schizophrenia.

Language development

As children regress, their speech becomes limited and may reveal incoherent thinking.

Social and emotional development

Children show a marked reduction in interests, attachments, and relationships. They show disturbed social relationships and impairments in their interactions with parents, family members, and others in the environment.

Infantile autism

Children who are autistic show extreme aloneness from infancy onward. They do not respond to other humans, do not begin to establish relationships, and may show aversion to physical contact. As they grow, autistic children indulge in repetitive and ritualistic play, self-stimulation, and, sometimes, self-destructive behaviour. They do not develop attachments to people but do become strongly attached to inanimate objects.

Physical and motor development

Children with autism tend to be healthier than other children with pervasive disorders. Motorically, children show grace and dexterity. Nevertheless, basic self-help skills and toilet training are often very difficult to develop in such children.

Cognitive development

Children who are autistic often score poorly in cognitive functioning. Indeed, researchers point out that a large proportion of this population falls into the range of intellectual disability.

Perceptual development and sensory response

Children with pervasive developmental disorders, especially those diagnosed as autistic, may display abnormal responses to visual stimuli. They seem to suffer from constraints in attending to relevant cues and may exhibit a generalized over- or under-responsiveness to incoming stimuli. Stimuli from all the senses may be interpreted differently by children who are autistic. Visual stimuli may induce hand fluttering, crossing eyes, side glancing, or fixating on lights.

Language development

The language of children with infantile autism is often non-existent or bizarre. Children may use echolalia, parroting, meaningless jargon, **neologistic speech**, or repeat questions and statements incessantly. Children who are autistic are almost invariably delayed in speech use and many never develop speech at all. Lack of language affects other functional areas: play, symbolic thought, and abstract reasoning.

Social and emotional development

Impairments in social relatedness are increasingly considered to constitute some of the core symptoms of autism. The prognosis for children with autism is dismal. At the moment only about one child in six makes an adequate social adjustment and is able to do some kind of regular work in adulthood.

Assessment of children who have pervasive developmental disorders

In the past, children who were psychotic were considered untestable by standardized intelligence tests. The use of a battery of measures, however, makes assessment both possible and a prerequisite to fruitful treatment. Diagnosticians assess language, behavioural, and social skills, as well as mental ability and academic functioning. Many of the measures used are designed as questionnaires for those close to the child.

Psycho-educational assessment

Psychologists administer both formal and informal assessment measures to students who are developmentally disabled. Specialized instruments are often needed to explore particular diagnostic and treatment questions. Specially designed measures are also used to accommodate the variation typical of the profiles of children who are autistic.

Functional assessment

Many assessors adopt a functional approach to testing that examines a child's performance within the context of naturalistic environments. Interviews with the parents and others who know the child is the functional assessment method most commonly used by practitioners.

Intervention with children who have pervasive developmental disorders

At present, no specific treatment exists to help children who are psychotic or autistic reduce their anxiety and cope more effectively with reality. No one treatment method has proven notably effective with these children, and the prognosis remains poor.

Medical intervention

Drug therapy, specifically stimulants and tranquilizers, show promising results with youngsters who are schizophrenic. On the other hand, drug therapy for the treatment of autism presents generally inconclusive and unpromising results.

Therapy

A wide variety of therapies have been used with children with psychoses and infantile autism. These include psychotherapy, family therapy, speech and language therapy, megavitamin therapy, play therapy, and music therapy.

Technical aids

For children who are not often interested in other people or comfortable with them, a computer may serve as a catalyst for social interaction.

Educational intervention

In the past, children with psychoses and autism were placed in institutions. Today, most children remain in their own homes. Residential programs are proposed only for seriously delayed children, for children on whom extensive observation and assessment is necessary, and when family relief is required.

Service delivery models

A growing number of parents and educators are calling for the inclusion of all students within the mainstream of regular education, including those with severe disabilities. Nevertheless, there is acute disagreement within the field as to whether students with intensive educational needs belong in general education classrooms.

Educational approaches

Three major approaches are employed in the education and training of children with pervasive developmental disorders.

Psychodynamic approaches

The psychodynamic approach is widely used. Treatment aims at reactivating stalled developmental processes.

Behavioural approaches

Psychotherapy has not been very effective with autistic children; behavioural programs appear to achieve better results. While there are no promises of normalization or intellectual improvement, behaviour therapy has been used to teach children with autism a range of behaviours that provide them with a more useful existence.

Curriculum

The major goals of intervention are to decrease inappropriate behaviours and increase appropriate functioning. Many children require teaching of social skills, skills for independent living, and pre-academic skills. Language training is essential.

Key Terms

childhood psychosis
childhood schizophrenia
neologistic speech
self-stimulation

Practice Questions

Multiple-choice questions

1. Intense research is directed toward childhood psychoses and infantile autism. This is because
   a. the conditions, although relatively rare, are showing a marked increase in prevalence.
   b. an understanding of the conditions will lead to clearer conceptions of how the brain, behaviour, and the environment relate.
   c. researchers are now sure that all psychoses have a genetic base and are searching for genetic and chromosomal causes.
   d. many more girls than boys are affected and understanding the conditions will provide a clearer conception of non-sex-linked disorders.
   e. all of the above

2. When the behavioural and thought processes of an individual become so disturbed that the person is out of touch with reality, the general description of the condition is
   a. psychosis.
   b. Heller's disease.
   c. neurological disability.
   d. Usher's syndrome.
   e. Little's disease.

3. Although children with schizophrenia and those with autism show many of the same behaviours, there are differences in
   a. age of onset.
   b. nature of the manifested behaviours.
   c. prognosis.
   d. etiology.
   e. all of the above

4. Current research on childhood schizophrenia and infantile autism indicates that the best way to look at the etiology of the conditions is through
   a. multiple determinants.
   b. genetic or chromosomal problems.
   c. prenatal complications.
   d. biochemical disturbances.
   e. environmental variables.

5. Etiologically, infantile autism has been specifically associated with
   a. fragile X syndrome.
   b. genetics.
   c. neurological dysfunction.
   d. maternal age.
   e. all of the above

6. In terms of timing, infantile autism is characterized by
   a. onset in early puberty.
   b. onset between three and five years of age.
   c. onset before thirty months of age.
   d. onset coinciding with the beginning of school.
   e. onset at any time during the developmental period.

7. Of the following behaviours, which is found in children with schizophrenia but not in children who are autistic?
   a. delusions and hallucinations
   b. odd movements and facial grimaces
   c. poor communication
   d. poor academic functioning
   e. withdrawal

8. The theories of Leo Kanner and Bruno Bettelheim regarding the causes of infantile autism can be broadly categorized as ________ theories.
   a. nature
   b. nurture
   c. genetic/chromosomal
   d. biochemical
   e. neurological

9. Twin studies on psychoses and autism indicate that
   a. if one monozygotic twin has childhood schizophrenia, the other is more prone to the condition.
   b. in fraternal twins, the likelihood of both twins being affected by schizophrenia is much less than in monozygotic twins.
   c. in autism, the prevalence is higher among family members of children with the disorder.
   d. the incidence of autism in the identical twin of an autistic child is higher than in the general population.
   e. all of the above

10. Which of the following would be most appropriate in the assessment of a child with infantile autism?
   a. self-report rating scales.
   b. standardized achievement tests.
   c. developmental checklists.
   d. curriculum-based assessment.
   e. All of the above are appropriate.

11. The approach to severe emotional disturbance and psychoses that aims to help children understand the inner forces that guide their behaviour is the ________ approach
   a. psychodynamic
   b. behavioural
   c. ecological
   d. holistic
   e. none of the above

12. All of the following describe the language of children with infantile autism except
   a. language is often delayed.
   b. language may contain much echolalia.
   c. children may use neologic speech.
   d. language, at whatever level, is used to communicate.
   e. unusual pronoun use and prosody is present.

13. A residential program for a child who is autistic may be proposed only when
   a. family relief is necessary.
   b. extensive observation and assessment are necessary.
   c. the child is delayed in toileting.
   d. the child is lagging in self-help skills.
   e. all of the above

14. From the research on intervention with children who are psychotic or autistic, the major conclusion about drug use is that
   a. drug therapy has practical utility for youngsters who are schizophrenic.
   b. drug therapy shows promising results with children who are autistic.
   c. anti-convulsive drugs are the most widely used.
   d. stimulant drugs are rarely employed.
   e. all of the above

15. Eleven-year-old Randy is diagnosed as autistic. He is just entering puberty. The research suggests that
   a. Randy's problems are likely to worsen.
   b. Randy will show a marked improvement in functioning.
   c. there will be a positive increase in Randy's speech and language behaviour.
   d. there will be no noticeable differences in Randy's functioning.
   e. peer interactions will improve.

16. Match the language term to the description.
   a. neologism
   b. echolalia
   c. aphasia
   d. aphonia
   e. apraxia
   ___ lack of voice
   ___ made-up words
   ___ imitation of another person's speech
   ___ the inability to program, position, and sequence the muscle movements involved in speech
   ___ the inability to communicate effectively with verbal language because of comprehension and/or production difficulties often due to brain damage

Recall questions

1. Of the developmental stages of preschool, childhood, and adolescence, schizophrenia is most common in ________.

2. Self-stimulation is defined as ________.

3. When the prognoses for children with schizophrenia and for those with autism are compared, the outcomes are worse for those with ________.

4. Three conditions considered to be pervasive developmental disorders are ________, ________, and ________.

5. The onset of infantile autism is typically before ________ of age.

6. Two proposed causes of infantile autism are _____ and ______.

7. The first person to use the term *autistic* was ______, in 1906.

8. Of childhood schizophrenia or infantile autism, _____ is the more common.

9. There are two main classes of maladaptive behaviour: self-injurious and self-______.

10. The made-up words used by some children with autism are referred to as ______.

True–false questions

1. Adult schizophrenia and childhood schizophrenia are the same types of conditions and, except for developmental variables, affect individuals in the same way. T F

2. Today's researchers generally agree that infantile autism is typically the result of prenatal complications, especially toxemias. T F

3. Drug therapy using stimulants significantly improves the functioning of individuals with infantile autism. T F

4. General agreement exists concerning the terminology and classification systems used with youngsters who are severely and profoundly disordered. T F

5. Currently, almost all children with infantile autism are institutionalized. T F

6. Childhood schizophrenia is more common than infantile autism. T F

7. Standardized achievement tests are generally appropriate in the assessment of a child with severe infantile autism. T F

8. Facilitated communication has been conclusively shown to be effective for all persons with autism. T F

9. The early development of speech is a good predictor of the future speech and language progress of a child who is autistic. T F

10. Asperger's syndrome is a relatively new addition to the catalogue of psychiatric disorders in DSM-IV. T F

Short-answer questions

1. When Leo Kanner first identified the autistic syndrome in 1943, he focused upon certain characteristics of the children and their parents. List these.

2. Children who are autistic often show minor physical anomalies. List three of these.

3. List and briefly explain five possible biological causes proposed for infantile autism and childhood schizophrenia.

4. List five self-stimulating behaviours that may be observed in a child who is autistic.

5. Children who are autistic show many problems in speech and language development. List ten unusual speech patterns noticed in children who are autistic.

Applications

1. In the educational journals, find three articles relating to one of the following topics:
   - the etiology of infantile autism;
   - educational approaches used with schizophrenic children;
   - facilitated communication

   Present a report consisting of a description, comparison, and evaluation of the three articles. (See Application Question 1 in Chapter 1 of this study guide for report format.)

2. Read the IEP for David on p. 483 of the text. The objectives listed in this extract relate to David's participation in an art class with his normally developing peers. Another objective for David is to use simple speech when it is modelled for him. Expand David's art class objectives by noting objectives in oral speech. Include both peer and teacher modelling.

Activities

1. Behavioural approaches have been used to teach children who are autistic a variety of skills. List ten skills that the text notes as being established through behavioural techniques. From the list, select one self-help skill. Break the skill down into its smallest components. Describe how a behavioural approach may be used to establish this skill in an autistic child.

2. What facilities are available for children with pervasive developmental disorders in your community? What approaches are taken in the training and education of these children?

3. Attend a meeting of the local parents' association for autistic children.

Portfolio item

Locate a children's book that has a major character with a disability or has as its purpose to teach children about differences and disabilities. Explain briefly the theme and then explain how you would use this book to influence and instruct children about disabilities. Note the grade level for which the book is suitable, how you would introduce the topic, and some of the discussion questions. Add a lesson plan for the initial lesson.

Chapter 14

Children with Severe and Multiple Disabilities

Learning outcomes

After reading this chapter, you should be able to:

- Recognize the various ways in which multiple disabilities are described;
- Relate the etiology of multiple disabilities to other etiologies described in the text;
- Understand the developmental consequences of dual or multiple disabilities;
- Discuss educational intervention for students with multiple disabilities;
- Identify various types of augmentative communication.

Introduction

Children with multiple disabilities show evidence of independent and interdependent deficits in two or more areas of functioning. Innumerable combinations of impairments are possible, although some appear more often than others and some are more difficult to cope with. Individuals may suffer multisensory impairments such as deaf-blindness, or they may have conditions that combine sensory disorders with physical, neurological, or mental disabilities.

Students with multiple disabilities present a range of special educational and psychological needs. To an even greater degree than for children with single disabilities, each child must be considered individually.

Definitions of severe and multiple disabilities

In the area of multiple disabilities, both generic and specific definitions exist. Generic definitions tend to be comprehensive and general, with broad parameters. Because of their broadness, generic definitions have some disadvantages.

Given the disadvantages of generic definitions, many educators prefer definitions that are more categorical and specific. Educators define children as multisensory impaired, multiple dependent handicapped, deaf-blind, and so on. Such specific definitions serve to focus on individual problems and allow access to specialized services.

Prevalence of severe and multiple disabilities

It is extremely difficult to obtain accurate figures for students with multiple disabilities because Canada does not have a national registry of disabled children; the interpretations of the definitions of certain populations, such as deaf-blind, have recently changed dramatically; and children are often counted in terms of their **primary disability** (other conditions that arise are known as **secondary disabilities**). As well, figures are affected by changes in technology and demographic trends, and social factors affect prevalence estimates.

Classification of severe and multiple disabilities

In Canada, individuals with multiple disabilities are classified according to the primary disability, the agency providing services, and the type of educational program.

Etiology of severe and multiple disabilities

A wide variety of etiologies are responsible for multiple disabilities. Many of the causes are also the villains in other childhood disabilities existing alone, such as deafness, blindness, and intellectual disabilities.

Genetics, maternal rubella, birth traumas, and childhood infections such as meningitis and encephalitis are major factors in multiple disabilities. On the whole, chromosomal disorders account for the least number of multiple disabilities. Maternal rubella is most dangerous if contracted by the mother during the first trimester, the time when the organs are developing. Meningitis can cause cerebral palsy, convulsive disorders, and hearing and visual handicaps. Further causes of multiple disabilities include hydrocephalus, central nervous system damage, and complications associated with prematurity.

Syndromes

Usher's syndrome is a genetically determined condition in which a hearing disability is combined with progressive visual impairment resulting from pigment degeneration of the retina.

Developmental consequences of severe and multiple disabilities

The variety of disabilities and combinations of disabilities make generalizations about consequences almost impossible. Each combination of disabilities forms a completely unique child.

Physical development

Children with severe or multiple disabilities often show uneven development and lags in reaching developmental milestones. They are very often late in reaching developmental milestones. Walking, using first words, and toilet training may be quite delayed. In some children, they never emerge.

Cognitive development

Multiple disabilities do not necessarily correlate with intellectual dysfunctions. However, the conditions tend to distort, delay, and interfere with children's perceptions of incoming stimuli. Children find the world irregular and unpredictable.

Communication

Children with severe and multiple disabilities have enormous difficulties with speech and language development. Children may be at prelinguistic or minimally linguistic levels.

Academic achievement

Learning and educational attainments depend upon the age of onset of the conditions, their nature, the time of intervention, and the quality of educational services provided.

Social and emotional development

Social interactions are severely restricted by severe and multiple disabilities. Co-occurring disabilities, including motor dysfunction, convulsive disorders, and delayed speech development, contribute to the lack of social behaviour observed among children who are multiply disabled.

The behaviour of these children is frequently characterized by self-abusiveness, intense self-stimulation, and repetitive and stereotyped movements and behaviours.

Assessment of children with severe and multiple disabilities

The diagnosis and assessment of multiple disabilities require a multi-disciplinary approach employing a battery of measures. It often begins with a medical assessment that includes medical history, psychological and psychiatric assessment, laboratory tests and cytogenetic studies, neurophysiological investigation, and neuroradiology. Psycho-educational assessment includes a range of tools and measures.

Assessment of hearing

It is very difficult to assess the auditory acuity and functioning of multiply disabled children, and special techniques have been devised. Hearing acuity may be tested through electrophysiological or behavioural methods. Electrodiagnostic procedures provide information regarding responses to auditory stimuli; behavioural measures give further comparative results that may be used for prognostic purposes.

Assessment of vision

It is also hard to determine whether multiply disabled children have usable vision. In order to assess the electrical activity of the visual pathway and occipital cortex of the brain, electrophysiological techniques are used. In addition to electro-diagnostic techniques, children should receive thorough eye examinations.

Psycho-educational assessment

Children with severe and multiple disabilities challenge the ingenuity of even the most experienced assessors. Assessment focuses on intellectual function and other domains, especially language, and explores the child's impairments and abilities. Methods include psychometric tests, learning tests, direct observation, and informal interviews. Psycho-educational assessments are most successful when they focus on functional areas of competence, are made over a period of time, are taken at regular intervals, are done in surroundings familiar to the child, incorporate tasks and materials familiar to the child, and include observational data and interviews. Informal interviews may be conducted with parents, teachers, and other important persons in the child's life. **Arena testing** is an observational assessment approach in which people from several disciplines focus on their particular domains within the context of play.

Intervention with children who have severe and multiple disabilities

Services provided to individuals who are multiply disabled cover a broad range, and include medical, therapeutic, and educational personnel. Generally, treatment hinges on etiology and the specific combination of the disabling conditions.

Medical intervention

A variety of medical procedures are used. Teachers should be aware of these procedures and should keep an emergency protocol for each child. (See Chapter 11.)

Therapy

Children need speech and language therapy, as well as occupational and physical therapy. Physical and occupational therapists work on gross motor development, muscle relaxation, and fine motor control. Speech and language therapists assist in speech and language development and feeding problems.

Technical aids

Students will use a range of adaptive equipment and computer technology.

Educational intervention

Education for students with multiple disabilities extends schooling beyond its traditional parameters.

Service delivery models

School-age students with multiple disabilities may be served in a range of settings—the regular classroom with support, a self-contained classroom, a residential school, and the hospital-based day school.

Increasingly, children who are deaf-blind or who have other severe or multiple disabilities are being educated in general classes. Defensible reasons for placing children with severe and profound disabilities in general classrooms are access to social relationships with peers and access to normalized learning environments. However, there is still disagreement within the field as to whether students with intensive educational needs belong in general education classrooms.

Educational approaches

Approaches include early intervention, team models, systematic procedures, appropriate curricula, program modifications, and support services.

Team approaches

In the training and education of students with severe and multiple disabilities, **team approaches** have developed in order to eliminate traditional professional boundaries while encouraging communication and information sharing.

Curricula

Curricula must reflect all areas of development.

Educational needs include language development, visual and auditory training, mobility training, and self-care skills. Psychosocial needs include adaptive behaviour, group activities, life skills, and a range of socialization experiences.

Functional skills

Taught skills should be **functional skills**, and include language development, visual and auditory training, mobility training, and self-care skills.

Communication training

Specialized language training for children who are prelinguistic or minimally linguistic uses two methods—presymbolic training and communication-first methods.

Alternative methods of communication

Anything that augments speech or accomplishes communicative function is **augmentative communication**. Augmentative communication may be aided or unaided. An alternative communication system is called a **communication mode**.

Unaided approaches

Unaided approaches use signals, codes, gestures, and signs. Signal and code communications include yes–no signals, audio signalling, Morse code, Amerind, and American Sign Language.

Aided approaches

Aided approaches often use communication boards with Blissymbolics. Both Blissymbolics and other picture systems are displayed on communication boards. Some current boards are sophisticated; they may have voice outputs that provide prerecorded or programmed speech in the form of words, phrases, or sentences.

Orientation and mobility training

Orientation and mobility specialists help the visually impaired child to develop a knowledge of the environment and enhance the ability to find specific locations.

Program modifications

A school may elect one person, often a special education teacher, to act as a support facilitator. This person not only works with the students who are severely or multiply disabled but also helps regular classroom teachers adapt instruction and aids in facilitating peer acceptance.

Key Terms

arena testing
augmentative communication
communication mode
functional skills
primary disability
secondary disabilities
transdisciplinary model
Usher's syndrome

Practice Questions

Multiple-choice questions

1. Definitions of children who are multiply and severely disabled include those who are
   a. deaf-blind and deaf mentally retarded.
   b. blind mentally retarded.
   c. severely emotionally disturbed.
   d. profoundly mentally retarded.
   e. all of the above

2. In the area of multiple disabilities, the one statement that is true is
   a. the differences among students are greater than the similarities.
   b. the similarities among students are greater than the differences.
   c. the population is extremely homogeneous.
   d. all children with multiple disabilities are also mentally retarded.
   e. children can be reliably grouped into specific disability classifications.

3. The best description of developmental consequences of multiple disabilities is that multiple disabilities
   a. are so varied that it is impossible to make generalizations.
   b. depend largely on the etiology of the condition.
   c. are closely related to the type and depth of the combination of conditions.
   d. show varied consequences.
   e. all of the above

4. Only one conclusion can be drawn about educational intervention for students with severe and multiple disabilities. That is,
   a. the goals of education tend to be the same as those for children with mild disabilities.
   b. all educators agree that the general classroom is the best place to achieve these goals.
   c. all educators agree that the special school is the most appropriate setting to reach educational goals.
   d. education must extend beyond its traditional goals.
   e. all children with severe and multiple disabilities can be efficiently served in general classrooms with support.

5. The learning and educational attainments of children who are deaf-blind depend upon the
   a. quality of education.
   b. age of onset of the disabling conditions.
   c. time when intervention was initiated.
   d. nature and severity of the dual conditions.
   e. all of the above

6. The syndrome in which familial nerve deafness is associated with pigment degeneration of the retina is known as
   a. Turner's syndrome.
   b. Down syndrome.
   c. Usher's syndrome.
   d. Little's disease.
   e. Klinefelter's syndrome.

7. Blissymbolics has been used successfully with children with
   a. mild intellectual disabilities.
   b. language delays.
   c. profound hearing losses.
   d. severe motor disabilities.
   e. profound hearing losses.

8. Thorough eye examinations of children who are multiply disabled are used to determine
   a. the existence of ocular pathology.
   b. ocular motor function.
   c. tracking ability.
   d. pupillary light reflexes.
   e. all of the above

9. The best indicators of the level of skills and awareness in a child with multiple disabilities are
   a. observational data and IQ tests.
   b. IQ tests and curriculum-based assessment.
   c. observational data and parent interviews.
   d. observational data and achievement tests.
   e. curriculum-based assessment.

10. For a sixteen-year-old student who is multiply disabled, which of the following skills is the most functional?
   a. placing pegs in a pegboard
   b. putting coins in a vending machine
   c. winding a toy
   d. making papier mâché puppets
   e. all are equally functional skills

11. On a school-based team, the coordination role is usually assumed by the
   a. parent.
   b. principal.
   c. physician.
   d. teacher.
   e. aide.

12. The most appropriate travel aid for a child who is deaf-blind is a
   a. guide dog.
   b. Mowat sensor.
   c. white cane.
   d. human guide.
   e. all are appropriate

13. Children with multiple disabilities have special problems with communication because
   a. they often have no modality through which to communicate.
   b. there is not enough sensory input on which to form a symbol system.
   c. they do not have the actions that act as functional units of communication.
   d. they often do not have the purposive gaze or hearing acuity needed to acquire language.
   e. all of the above

14. Children lacking communication are often divided into two broad groups of
    a. dyssymbolic and dysphasic.
    b. prelinguistic and minimally linguistic.
    c. language delayed and language disordered.
    d. speech delayed and speech disordered.
    e. mute and language disordered.

15. When generic definitions of multiple disabilities are used, they tend to
    a. gloss over the effects of visual and hearing handicaps.
    b. make interpretations of the needs of individual children more difficult.
    c. preclude children's access to specialized services.
    d. preclude specialized programming.
    e. all of the above

16. Match the person to the event.
    a. Eugen Blueler
    b. Leo Kanner
    c. Rosemary Crossley
    d. Bruno Bettelheim
    e. Douglas Biklen

    ___ defined the category of autism in 1943
    ___ first to use the word *autism*
    ___ brought facilitated communication to North America
    ___ devised facilitated communication
    ___ wrote about parents and causes of autism

Recall questions

1. Most often, children who are multiply disabled are classified according to their ________.

2. Familial nerve deafness associated with pigment degeneration of the retina is known as ________.

3. For children who cannot talk, augmentative communication is developed by a ________ therapist.

4. Of increasing or decreasing, the number of children with multiple disabilities attending residential schools in Canada is ________.

5. The goals on an IEP for a child with multiple disabilities are usually written for ________ year(s).

6. On a school-based team for a child with multiple disabilities, it is the _______ who usually assumes the role of service provider.

7. The traditional instructional model used in teaching students with multiple disabilities is the ________ approach.

8. When teaching skills to a child with multiple disabilities, the most critical element is that the skills be ________.

9. Children lacking communication are often divided into two groups: minimally linguistic and ________.

10. Treatment for children with multiple disabilities usually hinges on two factors: the combination of conditions and the ________.

True–false questions

1. Blissymbolics were originally designed for use as a universal language. T F

2. The development of communication strategies is the least of the problems of youngsters who are multiply disabled. T F

3. When a battery of tests are used, the discrepancies and inconsistencies in the profiles of individual children with multiple disabilities become clear. T F

4. A child who is deaf-blind cannot be included in a regular school program because of the child's severe communication and behavioural problems. T F

5. Most children who are deaf-blind are profoundly deaf and totally blind. T F

6. Psycho-educational assessment of children with multiple disabilities is carried out so as to obtain an IQ score. T F

7. The best place to teach language skills to a child with multiple disabilities is in a clinical setting. T F

8. Amerind is just a simpler version of American Sign Language. T F

9. John communicates using gestures. This is referred to as unaided augmentative communication. T F

10. It is estimated that severe handicaps account for about one percent of the school-aged population. T F

Short-answer questions

1. Explain and compare the terms *multiply disabled, multisensory impaired,* and *multiple dependent handicapped.*

2. In Canada, individuals who are multiply disabled are classified in three ways. List and explain these.

3. List five causes of multiple disabilities.

4. List and briefly explain the areas that may be included in the medical assessment of a child with multiple disabilities.

5. List five types of unaided augmentative communication.

Applications

1. In the educational journals, find three articles relating to:
   - teaching deaf-blind children;
   - administrative arrangements in Canada for multiply disabled children.

   Present a report consisting of a description, comparison, and evaluation of the three journal articles. (See Application Question 1 in Chapter 1 of this study guide for report format.)

Activities

1. In your district, what provisions are made for children with multiple disabilities? List educational and therapeutic options.

2. Research the life and contributions of Helen Keller. Present this in chronological order.

3. Prepare a basic teaching tool for a deaf-blind child. The tool must be very simple and use both touch and sound.

Portfolio item

Obtain works relating to Laura Bridgman and Helen Keller and their early education. Illustrate for the class the ways in which Howe and Sullivan stimulated language and concept learning.

End Test 5

1. The approach to severe emotional disturbance and psychoses that aims to help children understand the inner forces that guide their behaviour is the ________ approach.
   a. psychodynamic
   b. behavioural
   c. ecological
   d. holistic
   e. metacognitive

2. Generally, the area of least concern for educators intervening with children with chronic health conditions is
   a. intellectual functioning.
   b. emotional development.
   c. adaptive behaviour.
   d. social development.
   e. interpersonal relationships.

3. Rather typically, children with special health care needs who are in special education are receiving help because
   a. they are unable to handle the stresses of the regular classroom.
   b. the health problems impinge on intellectual functioning.
   c. they have missed much school because of the conditions.
   d. the teacher cannot handle them in the regular classroom.
   e. they do not interact with peers appropriately.

4. When there is damage of dysfunction to the brain and/or spinal cord, conditions are categorized as
   a. health disabilities.
   b. neurological impairments.
   c. musculoskeletal impairments.
   d. chromosomal aberrations.
   e. hereditary conditions.

5. Severe qualitative subnormalities that are not normal for any stage of development are generically categorized as
   a. health disorders.
   b. pervasive developmental disorders.
   c. mild mental retardation.
   d. learning disabilities.
   e. behavioural disorders.

6. The one behaviour that is seen in children with schizophrenia but not in those with autism is
   a. delusions and hallucinations.
   b. withdrawal.
   c. temper tantrums.
   d. lack of language ability.
   e. failure to interact with people in the environment.

7. _____ is a leading cause of deaf blindness.
   a. Joubert syndrome
   b. Down syndrome
   c. Heller's syndrome
   d. Usher's syndrome
   e. Little's disease

8. Slow degeneration of muscle fibres is a symptom of
   a. muscular dystrophy.
   b. spina bifida.
   c. epilepsy.
   d. child abuse.
   e. autism.

9. The type of cerebral palsy characterized by poor coordination, poor posture, and poor balance is
   a. spastic.
   b. athetoid.
   c. tremors.
   d. ataxia.
   e. rigidity.

10. Focal seizures are categorized as
   a. grand mal seizures.
   b. petit mal seizures.
   c. motor seizures.
   d. partial seizures.
   e. recurrent seizures.

11. *Neologisms* are
   a. prolonged repetition of other people's words and phrases.
   b. made-up language often used by children with autism.
   c. syntactic differences.
   d. difficulties in articulation seen in children with cerebral palsy.
   e. visual problems seen in children with Down syndrome.

12. Efficient behaviour therapy can
    a. cure autism.
    b. bring a child to normal or near-normal functioning.
    c. provide a child with adequate speech skills.
    d. modify deficits and excesses in behaviour.
    e. eliminate self-stimulating behaviour.

13. The play of children with infantile autism
    a. tends to be bizarre and disordered.
    b. where possible, involves other children in the environment.
    c. is similar to that of other children with exceptionalities.
    d. is at appropriate developmental levels for the child's age.
    e. follows normal stages, but lags behind that of normally developing children.

14. Which of the following health disorders is most clearly associated with deficits in intellectual function?
    a. diabetes mellitus
    b. cystic fibrosis
    c. asthma
    d. allergies
    e. none of the above

15. In educational terms, children with cystic fibrosis require
    a. intense academic interventions.
    b. special class placement.
    c. special school placement.
    d. major adjustments to curriculum content.
    e. none of the above

16. Gastrointestinal allergies are reactions to
    a. inhalants.
    b. contactants.
    c. ingestants.
    d. injectants.
    e. dust.

17. Among the following conditions, the highest prevalence rate is for
    a. infantile autism.
    b. childhood schizophrenia.
    c. mild intellectual disabilities.
    d. learning disabilities.
    e. cerebral palsy.

18. Which of these classifications of cerebral palsy is the most common?
    a. spasticity
    b. ataxia
    c. rigidity
    d. athetosis
    e. tremors

19. Epilepsy is best described as
    a. a disease.
    b. a symptom of gross brain damage.
    c. a condition inevitably associated with retardation.
    d. a condition unamenable to amelioration through drug therapy.
    e. an electrical storm in the brain.

20. Automatic, involuntary motor patterns that are triggered by specific stimuli are known as
    a. reflexes.
    b. neonatal behavioural schema.
    c. survival tools.
    d. primitive reactions.
    e. none of the above

21. Spina bifida refers to
    a. a cleft in the bony arch of the vertebrae.
    b. a cleft of varying degrees of seriousness.
    c. a midline defect.
    d. a neural tube anomaly.
    e. all of the above

22. An inability to move muscles because of damage to the motor cells of the spinal cord is known as
    a. cerebral palsy.
    b. ataxia.
    c. dysnomia.
    d. flaccid paralysis.
    e. pyramidal impairment.

23. In some cases, the effects of a disease or condition can be modified or ameliorated by a special diet. Diet affects the course and amelioration of the condition in the case of
    a. PKU.
    b. cystic fibrosis.
    c. galactosemia.
    d. diabetes.
    e. petit mal epilepsy.

24. All of the following statements describe asthma, except
    a. attacks are characterized by wheezing and shortness of breath.
    b. physicians can pinpoint the factors that trigger an individual's attacks.
    c. various medications are used for treatment.
    d. many medications have side effects.
    e. in some cases, asthma is a fatal condition.

25. Among individuals with autism who are verbal, the most frequently seen language characteristic is
    a. unusual pronoun usage.
    b. peculiar prosody.
    c. restricted vocabulary.
    d. neologisms.
    e. echolalia.

26. Each of the following terms is relevant to a disabling condition. Match the term to the condition.

a. otitis media
b. athetosis
c. subaverage intellectual functioning
d. antisocial behaviour
e. stuttering

___ cerebral palsy
___ behavioural disorders
___ mental retardation
___ hearing impairment
___ speech disorder (5 x 1)

27. Many groups of children with special needs require alternative modes of communication. Although there is much overlap, match the mode to the group with whom it is most commonly used.

a. braille
b. Blissymbolics
c. large print
d. sign language
e. Amerind

___ blind
___ visually impaired
___ cerebral palsied
___ deaf
___ minimally linguistic (5 x 1)

28. Match the researcher to the area of interest.

a. Eugen Bleuler
b. Sante de Sanctus
c. Lewis Terman
d. Heinz Werner
e. James Hinshelwood

___ reading disabilities
___ children with brain damage
___ giftedness
___ schizophrenia
___ autism (5 x 1)

Total /50

Section 7

Intervention with Infants, Preschoolers, and Young Adults

Intervention refers to various types of care and education. Early identification and early intervention with high-risk children and children with disabilities serves to ameliorate the developmental consequences on the child and assist the family in acceptance and treatment of the condition.

In the past, the needs of adolescents with disabilities have tended to be ignored in the schools. Even today, there continues to be a limited emphasis on vocational goals or the transition to post-secondary settings.

A body of research literature indicates that young people with disabilities are not faring well in early adulthood, both in terms of occupations and in independent living. Because of this, educators of secondary students are stressing transition services and programming that includes functional academics, social and personal adjustment, and occupations.

Chapter 15

Early Intervention

Learning outcomes

After reading this chapter, you should be able to:

- Differentiate among the models used to look at family functioning;
- Understand the concepts and processes of early identification and early intervention;
- Understand the link between early childhood education and education in the regular school system.

Introduction

Learning is a lifelong experience of which an enormous amount takes place before children even reach school. By the time children are six years old, almost two-thirds of their ultimate cognitive ability is formed. After the age of six, a child's potential for further intellectual growth is slowed.

Families may differ greatly in structure, cultural values, and economic status, but most families with a child who is disabled have to cope with additional emotional adjustments and caregiving demands.

Early childhood special education (ECSE) is a new discipline designed to ameliorate the effects of a disability in a very young child and to assist the parents and family in dealing with the associated stress. Early identification and early intervention are essential elements of ECSE.

Parents and families

Parents of a child who is exceptional face the same types of dilemmas and crises that are common to all families. However, the advent of a special youngster brings its own unique trials. An exceptional child makes a major impact on the family climate, and modifications in roles and family structure become necessary. Professional support and intervention are vital to help the family cope with the stress created by a child with special needs.

Looking at families

A number of models have evolved that look at family functioning. These models are important because they largely determine intervention practices and processes.

Stage theories

Stage theories are the most traditional way of looking at parents and families. Stage theorists hold that the birth of a child with an exceptional condition shatters parental aspirations and expectations and brings a symbolic death of hopes and dreams. Although parents and their reactions are distinctly individual, most parents appear to pass through similar stages before they can accept the reality of the situation.

The initial reaction is shock, usually accompanied by denial and disbelief. This period is usually brief, as parents must confront the reality of providing daily care, therapy, and transportation. Denial may serve as a protective device, giving parents time to come to grips with the situation. Denial becomes maladaptive when it results in withholding necessary treatment from the child.

Anger may be directed at the child as a source of frustration, or inward to become fear, shame, and guilt.

Fear arises when parents hold unfounded suspicions and incorrect information regarding the condition and its implications. Guilt occurs when parents search for a cause of the problem and blame themselves. Guilt can be projected onto others in the form of resentment and hostility.

Shame and loss of self-esteem appear when the parent sees the child as a threat to the family's prestige. They may dread a stigma attached to the condition and fear social rejection.

Withdrawal, isolation, and depression are a result of mourning and grief. Ambivalence occurs as parents accept the child but harbour resentment that results in ambivalent feelings and added guilt. Overprotection, self-sacrifice, and defensiveness result when parents invest so much of themselves in the child that the dependence becomes reciprocal.

Although the timing is different for each family, many parents grow to accept the child and the condition. At the same time, they realize that the presence of an exceptional child will affect the family structure but believe that the family will survive.

Life-cycle approach

The life-cycle or lifespan approach sees a family moving through time and experiencing a series of events, tasks, and transitions as it does so. Various events may be stress provoking.

Systems approach

A systems theory sees the family as part of a social system where actions in one part of the system affect every other part.

Social support approach

Very similar to the systems approach, a social support approach stresses family functioning and the informal supports on which a family can rely.

Status of disability

When a child's condition is considered, this is not a theoretical model as others are. However, the type and degree of disability impacts on family functioning and the amount of parental stress. The amount of stress appears to be related to factors both within and outside the child. Dimensions of stress depend upon the diagnostic category, the age and sex of the child, the degree and severity of the condition, and child characteristics. A child may be fussy, more difficult to console, or have feeding problems.

Specific conditions

A diagnosis of intellectual disability is extremely difficult and disheartening. Children who are learning disabled represent a source of inconsistency and confusion within the family climate. Parents report higher rates of stress and tend to respond negatively to their child's academic experiences and to hold lower expectations of success.

For parents with normal hearing, the discovery that a child has a hearing loss is traumatic. Hearing parents tend to have little knowledge of hearing impairments, the effects of hearing loss, and communication modes. Similarly, the diagnosis of severe visual impairment is difficult for parents.

Behavioural problems can cause disruption in the home and embarrassment in public. Parents of children with infantile autism and schizophrenia may meet enormous stress. Caregivers must contend with the bizarre, withdrawn behaviours and the **gaze aversion** of the child who is autistic or the constant clinging of the child who is schizophrenic.

For parents, the gifted child may be both a blessing and a burden. Many parents become bewildered and frustrated; they feel inadequate in their child-management techniques, uncertain about appropriate schooling and unsure about how to stimulate and challenge their child. Sibling rivalry may develop when extra time and financial resources are directed to the child who is gifted.

Siblings

Siblings of children who are exceptional have different experiences than do children in other families. They may meet differing parental discipline and differing expectations. Resentment against the child with a disability may mount when siblings must spend time with the child, miss time with parents, and when restricted financial resources are directed to the special family member.

The extended family

The advent of a child with an exceptionality can have a considerable impact on the extended family. Grandparents suffer the same reactions as do parents upon diagnosis of the condition. This leaves the grandparents with a diminished capacity to offer support to the parents.

Early childhood special education

We use the phrase early childhood special education (ECSE) to encompass two major processes: **early identification** and **early intervention**. Both processes are directed toward the needs of young children at risk or children with exceptionalities and their families. It includes early identification.

Early identification

A major change in special education is the increasing emphasis on early identification and early intervention. There are significant advantages in the early identification of potential learning disorders. Academically or socially at-risk children can be identified, referred for more in-depth diagnostic treatment, and provided with intervention programs that maximize strengths and aid in overcoming deficits.

Infant identification

Some infants will be identified right in the delivery room. Others will be assessed using infant scales of mental ability, developmental scales, and observations.

Preschool assessment

Measures used with preschoolers include screening, observation, informal and standardized measures, and medical assessment.

Kindergarten assessment

Kindergarten screening and assessment often stress readiness for school tasks.

Family needs assessment

The term *family needs* refers to a family's desire for services. A *needs assessment* looks at areas such as current conditions, needs, parent goals, and parent involvement.

Early intervention

Early intervention occurs at much the same time as early identification. There are many types of intervention provided by different people in different settings.

A strong research base supports early intervention. For example:

- Research in child development clearly demonstrates that the early years are a time of rapid learning.
- Early intervention can help ensure that all young children reach their full developmental potential.
- Early services can maximize skill development and reduce or alleviate the need for special services when a child enters school.
- Intervention sustains growth.
- Early intervention serves as a support that enhances family functioning, provides crucial information for parents, and makes parents the primary players in their child's developmental progress.
- For the school-aged child, the prime time for intervention is before the end of grade three.

Infant programs

Infants and preschoolers with disabilities may be served in the home, in clinic settings, in separate specialized programs, or within the regular complex of child care facilities. Those in the five to eight years of age range will be in regular schools and classrooms.

Home-based programs are often referred to as **home visiting**. Infant development personnel work with infants and toddlers in their own natural environments.

Preschool programs

Early childhood education is directed toward the special needs of young children. Across Canada, a variety of facilities exist to serve exceptional preschoolers. However, the stress is on natural settings. Early childhood programs focus on stimulating and sustaining growth in areas of development where a child demonstrates a lag.

Parent involvement

A wide range of professionals and paraprofessionals are available to support the parents and to help the child through various stages of development. Families will interact in some way with professionals from the disciplines of education, psychology, medicine, therapy, counselling, and allied public health and social work.

Parents as intervenors

For the infant and toddler, educational programming revolves around the family; it focuses on parent counselling and training. Parents play a crucial role in facilitating and maintaining developmental gains in their child. Many early intervention programs share the common goal of enhancing the child's development by helping parents to become effective intervenors. Parents may be involved in educational or therapeutic interventions in home-based programs, classrooms, or other settings.

For example, the parents of a child with a hearing impairment require instruction in the nature of hearing impairment, the stages of language development, the use of amplification, communication modes, and methods to stimulate and maintain language and speech. Parents of children with severe visual impairments require accurate information regarding the condition and support in their efforts to stimulate and interact with the visually impaired child. Intervention with children who have intellectual disabilities can accelerate development and encourage healthy parent–child relationships.

Transition

In educational terms, **transition** refers to the movement from one program to another. Transitions may cause stress to parents and child and careful planning and follow-up is necessary. It is important that parents receive information and be actively involved in the transition process.

Service delivery models

One of the most difficult choices for many parents is the location of the child's schooling. In concert with educators, many parents opt for inclusive classrooms; others are more cautious. Often, parents of children with significant disabilities are concerned with social integration, while parents of students with mild problems are more concerned with curricula and remediation.

Parent support

Professionals offer information, guidance, and support to parents and early intervention to the exceptional child.

Counselling

During counselling sessions, parents can be helped to openly express and confront their feelings about the exceptional child. They can be aided in understanding the diagnosis and guided in developing realistic expectations for the child.

Parent self-help groups

Support offered by community self-help groups supplements and complements counselling. These groups link parents encountering similar problems; they provide a forum for parents to discuss concerns and exchange ideas.

Key Terms

early identification
early intervention
gaze aversion
home visiting
transition

Practice Questions

Multiple-choice questions

1. The advent of a child who is exceptional within a family usually
   a. creates unique feelings and new pressures.
   b. has little effect on family functioning.
   c. deeply affects the parents but not the siblings.
   d. affects the siblings, but not the parents.
   e. all of the above

2. Dr. L., a researcher on families with children with special needs, looks at families in terms of how the entire family handles different events and transitions. This is referred to as a(n) ________ approach.
   a. systems
   b. stage theory
   c. social support
   d. life-cycle
   e. none of the above

3. In a stage theory model, researchers state that many parents pass through a stage where they deny the existence of a disability in a child. This period of denial may be described by all of the following statements except
   a. denial in parents may be quite protracted.
   b. denial may be stronger if the condition is not readily obvious to the parents.
   c. denial may serve as a protective device.
   d. denial is always maladaptive.
   e. eventually, denial may lead to "doctor shopping."

4. Current research and work on families with a member who is disabled stress that
   a. a systems approach is the most appropriate way to view families.
   b. approaches should be family centred, not just child focused.
   c. the entire family, including the siblings, must be included.
   d. the extended family should be seen as an operational part of the family.
   e. all of the above

5. Of the following factors, which appears to be most directly related to the stress experienced by parents of exceptional children?
   a. the sex and age of the child who is exceptional
   b. the exceptional child's ordinal position in the family
   c. the number of siblings
   d. the father's occupation
   e. the support given to the mother

6. Of the models used to look at families, embeddedness is a feature of the ________ model.
   a. systems
   b. stage theory
   c. life-cycle
   d. social support
   e. all of the above

7. Counselling with the parents of a child with a disability
   a. is necessary in only a few cases.
   b. is an important aspect of intervention programs.
   c. is not as important as psychotherapy with the child.
   d. is not generally successful because most parents are unwilling to participate.
   e. functions solely to provide information about the condition.

8. Mothers of children with disabilities are likely to obtain the greatest amount of support from the child's
   a. paternal grandfather.
   b. maternal grandmother.
   c. maternal grandfather.
   d. paternal grandmother.
   e. all of the above

9. PL 99-457 (1986) in the United States is
   a. an amendment to Public Law 94-142.
   b. an amendment that extends services to young children with disabilities and their families.
   c. a federal U.S. law.
   d. a law that is prescriptive about the obligations of service providers.
   e. all of the above

10. Research finds that the stress level in families of a child with a disability is directly related to the
   a. characteristics of the child.
   b. time when the diagnosis is made.
   c. severity of the child's condition.
   d. sex of the child.
   e. all of the above

11. Early identification would typically not include
   a. developmental checklists.
   b. rating scales.
   c. achievement tests.
   d. readiness measures.
   e. basic concept inventories.

12. The current emphasis on early identification and intervention is founded on
  a. research evidence from child development.
  b. models of successful performance.
  c. general observations.
  d. the need to ameliorate problems as early as possible.
  e. all of the above

13. The counselling of parents of children with disabilities is most clearly associated with initiatives in
  a. psychology.
  b. behaviour modification.
  c. psychoanalysis.
  d. social work.
  e. transactional therapy.

14. A major advantage of home-based programs for young children who are exceptional and their families is that
  a. they are cost-efficient.
  b. parents are provided with information about the condition.
  c. they give parents access to a variety of agencies.
  d. they are particularly well suited to the needs of families with infants.
  e. all of the above

15. To help children who are disabled make the transition from preschool to public school, preschool teachers should stress
  a. social skills.
  b. basic numeracy.
  c. printing.
  d. reading readiness.
  e. all of the above

16. Match the model to the description.
  a. stage theory
  b. systems approach
  c. social support approach
  d. status of disability perspective
  e. life-cycle approach
  ___ the family is a unit moving through time and experiencing a series of events, tasks, and transitions
  ___ parents pass through discrete stages before they can fully accept the child's condition
  ___ actions in any part of the family or system affect the other parts
  ___ families can help themselves through informal supports
  ___ the nature of a child's disability can have a substantial impact on parental stress and levels of acceptance

Recall questions

1. Parents suffer a ________ of their dreams and expectations upon the diagnosis of their child's disabling condition.

2. Families with children with disabilities seem to be particularly vulnerable to ___________.

3. The United States Public Law ________ amended PL 94-142 to provide services for preschool handicapped children and their families.

4. By definition, it is not really possible to identify children with learning disabilities in the preschool years because ________.

5. A teacher who works with infants in their own homes is a ________ teacher.

6. James has a profound hearing loss that was diagnosed when he was eleven months old. His mother is extremely depressed and has withdrawn from friends and neighbours. A stage theorist would say that as she confronts the reality of James' problems, she is passing through the stage termed ________.

7. Of very high, statistically significant, or low, the correlation between infant test results and later academic achievement is ________.

8. The movement from one service delivery system to another is referred to as ______.

9. A family's expressed desire for services to be obtained or outcomes to be achieved is referred to as ______.

10. Diagnosticians involved in early identification may use developmental checklists, ______, and ______.

True–false questions

1. In models that look at families, the systems approach and the social support approach are very alike. They differ in that the systems perspective sees the family as part of a wider social system and the social support approach looks at families as they pass through events and transitions. T F

2. Families differ widely in their response to the child who is exceptional. T F

3. The attachment process for infants who are disabled and their parents may be disrupted from birth. T F

4. Because learning disabilities are often so subtle and have no physical anomalies, the impact on the family climate is relatively mild and unimportant. T F

5. Nearly all siblings of children who are disabled report negative experiences. T F

6. In recent decades we have witnessed a dramatic increase in programming for preschool children who are learning disabled. T F

7. There is no profile of siblings of children with disabilities. In general, sibling reactions to a child who is disabled vary in type and intensity. T F

8. Generally, parents accept a diagnosis of disabling condition with equanimity. T F

9. Although early intervention is important, children who are exceptional generally make acceptable progress if left alone. T F

10. All the Canadian provinces and territories have mandatory special education legislation that includes preschoolers in special schooling. T F

Short-answer questions

1. Families of exceptional children are particularly vulnerable to stress. List five factors within the special child that may contribute to familial stress.

2. Resentment often develops among siblings in families with exceptional children. List five factors that may contribute to sibling resentment.

3. Parent counselling serves many purposes for the parents of a child with a disability. List five of the aims of parent counselling.

4. List ten factors that may contribute to the stress felt by parents of children with disabilities.

5. List the major points of each of the models used to look at families with a member with a disability.

Applications

1. In the educational journals, find three articles relating to the efficacy of early intervention as currently practised. Present a report consisting of a description, comparison, and evaluation of the three articles. (See Application Question 1 in Chapter 1 of this study guide for report format.)

2. Identify and list all the services existing for infant and preschool exceptional children in your area.

3. Invite the parents of an exceptional child to visit the class. Ask them to speak about the child and the child's condition, their experience upon diagnosis, and the later experiences with the family, neighbours, intervenors, school staff, and other personnel. Ask the parents to give suggestions that will help prospective teachers to work more effectively with parents in the future.

Activities

1. Visit a preschool, home, or any location where you can obtain a tape recording of adults interacting with very young children. Tape about half an hour of the interactions. Transcribe the tape and evaluate it in terms of the types of speech patterns referred to as *motherese*.

2. Many items in the home can serve as "teaching toys" for exceptional preschoolers. For example, a coffee can and a wooden spoon make a wonderful drum; the can filled with sugar cubes becomes a rattle. Prepare a toy from items in the home and explain how you would use it.

Portfolio item

Imagine that you are the parent of a newly diagnosed severely disabled infant. Write a letter to a close friend explaining your initial reactions to the diagnosis and the steps that you took to ensure the child's welfare.

Chapter 16

Adolescents and Young Adults

Learning outcomes

After reading this chapter, you should be able to:

- Understand the special needs of adolescents with disabilities;
- Relate the material in this chapter to earlier categorical chapters;
- Discuss models of inclusive schooling and their validity for adolescents with special needs;
- Appreciate the need for transition services and understand the transition process and its major components.

Introduction

Students with disabilities experience a wide variety of post-secondary outcomes. Young people with disabilities may enroll in university or community college; they may enter competitive employment or military service; or they may be supported in more restrictive employment and sheltered workshops.

Various means of assisting young adults are being implemented. Three main areas are stressed: academic achievement, social and personal adjustment, and post-school adjustment. These are grouped under the rubric of transition services.

Adolescents

The differences between children and adolescents are significant and exist across physical, emotional, mental, and social areas. Biologically, adolescents attain puberty with its accompanying physical changes. Psychologically, adolescence is a period of self-discovery and developing self-reliance. During the adolescent years, students develop their own unique identities. Socially, the peer group becomes more important than the family.

When a student has an exceptional condition, many of the problems faced by every adolescent are magnified. Not only may these students have difficulty in meeting the demands of the environment generally, but also they may feel inadequate in the classroom and have personal and social problems.

Teachers of secondary students must appreciate the changing nature of a student's needs that accompany adolescence. Teachers will also meet apathy and lack of motivation among students who have met, and continue to meet, school failure.

Students do not outgrow learning disabilities, hyperactivity, or reading problems. The difficulties remain with them into adolescence; many persist into adulthood. At both stages the problems may become more pronounced.

Concepts of transition

As used in relation to the needs of adolescents with disabilities, **transition** has a number of meaning and foci:

- Transition as an ongoing experience.
- Transition as a movement.
- Transition as a school program focus.

The school's responsibilities in transition

At the school level, transition involves the provision of school experiences that will assist in location and maintaining employment together with training in skills for successful adulthood. The school should also identify community resources to assist students and involve students and parents.

Preparation for transition

Schools must provide preparation for transitions. This preparation should include systematic and planned opportunities for students' interactions with normal peers and should start much earlier than high school.

Formal transition plan

For secondary students with mild disabilities, there are three essential components in senior programming: work preparation skills, functional academics, and life-skills training (which includes counselling and sex education).

For students with severe disabilities, curriculum should expose them to job options in the community in which they live; teach specific work skills such as using tools and equipment; and teach work-related skills, such as transportation and personal hygiene.

Preparation should include an individual transition plan as part of a student's IEP. The plan will include goals and objectives, timelines, and designations of responsible persons or agencies.

Service delivery

Integration at the secondary levels is harder to implement than it is for young children because of interwoven factors—student characteristics, the traditional secondary curriculum, and the future needs of students with disabilities.

Student characteristics

Adolescents do not outgrow their learning difficulties, nor is simple maturation matched with an increase in motivation and achievement. Factors correlated with students with mild disabilities include physiological and neurological problems, deficits in cognitive processes such as memory and metacognitive awareness, disorders of attention, social behaviour problems, communication problems, and perceptual problems.

Curriculum

Adolescents with disabilities who spend the majority of their school day in general education classes are expected to meet the same demands as their non-disabled peers. For many, this may be an arduous or impossible task.

Future needs

The overall secondary curriculum is not congruent with the present needs of many senior students with disabilities; some of the necessary curricular elements are simply not present in the educational mainstream. Traditional secondary-school subjects are generally not related to the future needs of students; preparation for independent living requires much more than academic goals for adolescents who are disabled. As well, students may not have either the interest or the reading ability required for academic credit courses.

Counselling

Both guidance and vocational/career counselling are important for adolescents with disabilities and for those who are gifted.

Guidance counselling

Guidance counselling provides students with an awareness of their disability and its implications as well as positive aspects of functioning. For example, adolescents who are visually impaired may experience confusion, uncertainty, and anxiety during their teen years. Many may be caught up in their disability, unable to establish relationships, and unaware of the mores of their peer group. Visually impaired students need help in developing realistic attitudes and expectations regarding career choice. They must be aided in determining their own interests and abilities. Efforts must be made to facilitate interaction between students who are visually impaired and their sighted peers. For students who are hearing-impaired, counselling should also encourage peer relations and extra-curricular activities.

Vocational/career counselling

To establish students' levels of readiness and suitability for particular occupations, educators use **vocational evaluations**. For gifted students, school counselling at the secondary level is crucial. Effective counselling can be a component of career choices and decisions for gifted adolescents.

Sex education

The sexual and social needs of exceptional persons do not differ significantly from those of the general population. Sex education is a major concern for those dealing with adolescent students with intellectual disabilities. If normalization is to become a reality, this issue must be fully addressed.

Functional academics

Secondary students with disabilities require the skills to meet the demands of their present and future environments. **Functional academics** are those areas of the curriculum that have meaning to learners and are relevant to their after-school lives. Functional academics may be taught as part of intensive remedial programming.

Vocational education and work experiences

Full- or part-time work-study programs provide students with the opportunity to learn vocational skills in both vocational school programs and on-the-job training.

Social skills instruction

Social skill deficits are characteristic of students with disabilities such as learning disabilities, behaviour disorders, and intellectual disabilities. Specific training in social skills can be a factor in job success.

Self-management

Students also need assistance to develop the skills needed for independent living. These may include skills such as hygiene and grooming, money handling and budgeting, housekeeping, and leisure and vocational skills.

Futures planning

Transition should ensure access to community support and continuity of services.

Parent involvement

Parent involvement continues to be a major gap in successful transition services. The available evidence and collective experience of families suggest that current transition efforts are far from optimal.

Post-school experiences

Despite difficulties, many young people with disabilities move into post-secondary education or competitive employment with their non-disabled peers.

Dropouts

Many students who continually meet school failure simply drop out of school. While it is difficult to predict who will be a **dropout**, poor reading performance and retention at the third-grade level do correlate with later dropping out.

Life after school is difficult for all dropouts. Problems are compounded when the young person also has a disability.

Competitive employment

Many students with disabilities face difficulties in job finding and job retention. Various reasons account for this. Some students lack the basic skills needed for employment; others show low motivation and negative attitudes.

Supported employment

Supported employment, referred to in the past as sheltered workshops, offers more structure for persons with disabilities.

Post-secondary education

Of all groups with disabilities, those with learning disabilities represent the greatest number in post-secondary education. However, those who have suffered traumatic brain injuries represent the fastest-growing segment of the disabled population entering post-secondary institutions.

Key Terms

dropout
functional academics
guidance counselling
transition
vocational evaluation

Practice Questions

Multiple-choice questions

1. The major difference between elementary and secondary special education programs is that
   a. students in secondary programs are provided with more remedial instruction in core areas, especially reading, than they are in elementary programs.
   b. elementary programs tend to be developmental in nature; secondary programs tend to be compensatory in nature.
   c. elementary programs stress the development of basic skills but secondary programs do not.
   d. secondary programs stress functionality; elementary programs do not.
   e. There are no differences.

2. The text states that secondary-school students with disabilities have not, in the past, received their fair share of special education services. Although no specific reasons are given for this, we could assume that all of the following statements except ________ account for inadequate services.
   a. Some teachers feel that students are so near the end of their school careers that remedial and special programming is of little value.
   b. Students who have received special education at the elementary levels do not need special programming in secondary school.
   c. The scheduling of the day in many secondary schools makes special programming more difficult than it is at elementary levels.
   d. Some teachers hold that if a student received special education throughout elementary school, then it is not much use trying any longer.
   e. None of the above.

3. Secondary teachers of students with disabilities must be concerned with students'
   a. possible negative attitudes toward school.
   b. emerging sexuality.
   c. independent living skills.
   d. vocational interests.
   e. all of the above

4. Research on adolescent students with ADHD finds that
   a. almost all outgrow ADHD.
   b. about 50 percent outgrow ADHD.
   c. ADHD persists in almost all students.
   d. only 20 percent outgrow ADHD.
   e. none of the above

5. The area(s) that the educational system should stress for adolescents with disabilities is/are
   a. functional academics.
   b. vocational counselling.
   c. guidance counselling.
   d. social skills training.
   e. all of the above

6. Adolescents with behavioural disorders are
   a. among the students most likely to drop out of school.
   b. among the most difficult to train in transition programs.
   c. in need of intensive guidance and vocational programming.
   d. lacking in the basic skills needed for employment.
   e. all of the above

7. When the sexual needs of persons with disabilities are considered, we can say that
   a. individuals with physical disabilities do not have sexual needs.
   b. many persons who are intellectually disabled are asexual.
   c. sexual development and cognitive development proceed at the same pace in persons with intellectual disabilities.
   d. most people with physical and intellectual disabilities have little need for physical contact.
   e. the sexual needs of persons with disabilities differ from those of non-disabled persons.

8. Collaborative planning for transition should include
   a. parents.
   b. community agencies.
   c. special educators and vocational educators.
   d. regular educators.
   e. all of the above

9. Eighteen-year-old Claire is a talented pianist. As a talented student, her career plans
   a. were probably fixed prior to adolescence.
   b. will change between 16 and 18 years of age.
   c. are unsettled, since giftedness means multipotential.
   d. will probably change when she reaches 21 years of age.
   e. none of the above

10. A vocational evaluation is used to
   a. help clients identify their capacities and limitations.
   b. formulate realistic vocational goals.
   c. determine needs for rehabilitation planning.
   d. suggest whether the student's goals are realistic.
   e. all of the above

11. Studies of the work experiences of young adults with disabilities show that
   a. they have little difficulty in obtaining employment but trouble in maintaining jobs.
   b. youths in virtually every disability group are employed at a lower rate than the general population.
   c. students with behaviour disorders do better at obtaining and retaining employment than do those with learning disabilities or mild intellectual disabilities.
   d. while students with disabilities have difficulty in obtaining employment, they are good at keeping jobs once found.
   e. job retention tends to be best among students with behaviour disorders as compared to others with mild disabilities.

12. The three major reasons that students themselves give for dropping out of school are:
    a. alienation, irrelevant courses, frustration.
    b. low self-concept, frustration, pregnancy.
    c. drug use, delinquency, incarceration.
    d. marriage, pregnancy, having a job.
    e. poor health, poor self-concept, self-development.

13. For adolescents with disabilities, ________ correlates most highly with increases in employability.
    a. real paid work experiences before graduation
    b. enrolment in vocational classes
    c. training in work personality and social skills
    d. training in work competencies
    e. reading and writing ability

14. For adolescent students with mild disabilities, studies indicate that
    a. most, if not all, students outgrow their disabilities.
    b. the gap between these students and their non-disabled peers narrows in secondary school.
    c. consistent and systematic special education in elementary school remediates almost all learning problems.
    d. as students mature, they show increases in both achievement and motivation.
    e. social and academic problems often worsen as students mature.

15. Mr. Counsellor is working with Jamie, an adolescent identified as having quite severe behavioural disorders. The major goals of counselling are to
    a. deal with Jamie's affect.
    b. help Jamie to understand why he acts in the way he does.
    c. explore with Jamie the possibility of change.
    d. offer alternative ways of behaving and responding.
    e. all of the above

Recall questions

1. The WISC-III is to IQ as ________ is to vocational evaluation.

2. When thirteen-year-olds are compared to eighteen-year-olds, ________-year-olds tend to have higher self-esteem.

3. Within the educational system, transition is defined as ________.

4. Functional academics are defined as academics ________.

5. Of high or low, adults who are disabled tend to experience ________ rates of unemployment.

6. When educators undertake an assessment of an adolescent's readiness for adult work settings and potential for different types of occupations, the process is known as ________.

7. A school dropout is defined as ________.

8. An adolescent student's transition plan should be part of his or her ________.

9. According to studies undertaken by Robert Slavin and his colleagues among grade-three children, two predictors of later dropping out of school are ________ and ________.

10. The movement from preschool to school and from school to the workforce is known as ________.

True–false questions

1. Counselling is of little value to adolescents who are exceptional. T F

2. In the past, a great deal of attention has been paid to programs for adolescents with disabilities. T F

3. Rapid physiological change is characteristic of the period of adolescence. T F

4. Sex education is of little use to students who are physically disabled. T F

5. Of all disabled learners, those with behaviour disorders seem to be best at attaining and retaining employment. T F

6. People with intellectual disabilities are unlikely to develop the same sex drives as their normally developing peers. T F

7. Secondary special education programs are more compensatory in nature than are elementary programs. T F

8. Students who have been in work experience programs tend to respond better to occupational demands on the job than do students who have not been in such programs. T F

9. In general, as students with disabilities get older they show an increase in motivation and achievement. T F

10. While job finding and job retention are difficult for persons with intellectual disabilities, young adults who are learning disabled are able to both find and retain employment. T F

Short-answer questions

1. Outline the major problems that adolescents with disabilities meet in the workforce.

2. List the personnel who need to be involved in successful transition programs.

3. Explain the value of school counselling for gifted adolescents.

4. List five reasons why students drop out of school.

5. The IDEA (1999) mandates that transition activities for adolescents should promote the movement from school to post-school activities. Seven alternatives are listed. List these.

Applications

1. In the educational journals, find three articles relating to:
   - occupational status of young adults with learning disabilities;
   - post-school outcomes for young adults who are behaviourally disordered.

   Present a report consisting of a description, comparison, and evaluation of the three journal articles. (See Application Question 1 in Chapter 1 of this study guide for report format.)

Activities

1. Interview a disabled adult in the workforce. Focus on the problems and the triumphs this person has had.

2. Relate sex education for persons with intellectual disabilities to normalization.

3. You are a school counsellor working with students with mild intellectual disabilities. Discuss two areas of concern for these students; for example, vocational evaluation and sex education.

Portfolio item

Reread the case study of Chris in Chapter 16. Now relate it to the material on the deaf community in Chapter 9. Finally, view the film *Children of a Lesser God.* Present a paper on the deaf community and the needs and wants of deaf people based on the text and the film. Undertake background research if necessary.

End Test 6

1. The percentage of Canadian school-aged students who will require special education at some time in their school careers is ____ percent.
   a. 12
   b. 1
   c. 24
   d. 15.5
   e. 30

2. When discussing ways to include students in general classrooms, the author differentiates between adaptations, accommodations, and modifications. Of the following, the adaptation is
   a. an FM system.
   b. special seating.
   c. co-operative learning.
   d. increased lighting.
   e. wheelchair access.

3. The AAMR classification approach to mental retardation focuses on
   a. symptom severity.
   b. symptom etiology.
   c. developmental consequences.
   d. behavioural manifestations.
   e. symptom timing (whether congenital or postnatal).

4. For a child with a mild intellectual disability, success in the regular classroom depends upon
   a. the availability of support services.
   b. adaptations to environment, assignments, pace of instruction, and so on.
   c. curriculum modifications.
   d. individualized planning.
   e. all of the above

5. Studies show that the fastest-growing segment of the population of persons with disabilities entering post-secondary institutions is those with
   a. traumatic brain injuries.
   b. learning disabilities.
   c. deafness.
   d. visual disabilities.
   e. mild hearing impairments.

6. Canadian studies indicate that among adolescent students with disabilities, those most likely to graduate from high school are those in the categories of
   a. gifted and physically disabled.
   b. gifted and learning disabled.
   c. learning disabled and mildly intellectually disabled.
   d. hearing impaired (deaf) and gifted.
   e. deaf and learning disabled.

7. A home-visiting teacher would work with parents on
   a. providing information about other agencies.
   b. demonstrating techniques to use with the child.
   c. discussing parent–child relationships.
   d. showing how to mould and reinforce appropriate behaviour.
   e. all of the above

8. Home-based programs are founded on the supposition that
   a. centre-based programs are rarely effective.
   b. very few parents can afford the time to go to centre-based programs.
   c. the home is the natural environment for very young children.
   d. parent involvement is not possible in clinic settings, although it is in the home.
   e. parents will not attend clinic programs.

9. Pradi is wearing a Boston jacket. This supports the
   a. back and spine.
   b. upper thighs and spine.
   c. calves and ankles.
   d. neck.
   e. Jackets can be made to support any body part.

10. A surgically implanted shunt is used to treat
   a. hydrocephalus.
   b. cerebral palsy.
   c. microcephaly.
   d. brain injuries.
   e. cystic fibrosis.

11. It is harder to implement inclusion at secondary levels because
   a. the gap between students with disabilities and their peers widens with age.
   b. the instructional emphasis is different in secondary school than in elementary programs.
   c. older students with disabilities often do not have the academic skills for regular classroom work.
   d. the skills needed for success in the workplace may not be taught in regular settings.
   e. all of the above

12. PL 99-457 in the United States is prescriptive in nature in that
   a. it mandates the full inclusion of parents in decision making.
   b. all intervenors must comply with an IFSP.
   c. it extends the legal rights afforded children under PL 94-142.
   d. it includes specific provisions for infants and preschoolers with disabilities.
   e. all of the above

13. Which of these can be arrested surgically if there is early diagnosis?
   a. muscular dystrophy
   b. multiple sclerosis
   c. cystic fibrosis
   d. hydrocephalus
   e. juvenile diabetes

14. Work-study programs for secondary-school pupils with disabilities are primarily concerned with
   a. the vocational destination of pupils.
   b. the academic proficiency of students.
   c. social skill development.
   d. the development of abstract reasoning.
   e. reading and literacy skills.

15. For young children with disabilities, the transition process is best described as
   a. the movement from one service delivery system to another.
   b. the movement from high school to the adult workforce.
   c. the movement between the regular classroom and special programming.
   d. the movement into work experience programs.
   e. changes in lifestyle and needs.

16. Of the following, which statement is descriptive of individuals who are severely intellectually disabled?
   a. They form a homogenous population.
   b. The prevalence of additional disabilities is equal to that seen in children with mild intellectual disabilities.
   c. They demonstrate poor speech and inadequate social skills.
   d. Educational programming focuses on academics.
   e. All of the above are descriptive.

17. It is particularly difficult for parents to understand and cope with schizophrenia because psychotic disorders affect
   a. various aspects of adaptive behaviour.
   b. the perception and ordering of experience.
   c. the assessment of reality.
   d. the success of interpersonal relations.
   e. all of the above

18. Although psychopharmacology is an increasingly common medical intervention for students with ADHD, the whole area of drug therapy is contentious. At the moment, we can say that
    a. drug therapy with children is an exact science.
    b. drug use has been shown to produce permanent effects in most children.
    c. drug therapy is more successful when combined with the K.P. Diet.
    d. drugs are generally successful in the short term only.
    e. the use of drugs is decreasing.

19. According to the research literature, the causes of juvenile delinquency are
    a. unfortunate family relationships.
    b. low self-confidence in the youngster.
    c. the youngster's fear of failure.
    d. poor self-concept.
    e. All of the above are proposed causes of delinquency.

20. Parent education for children with chronic health disabilities focuses on
    a. showing parents how to promote their child's independence.
    b. helping parents reach an acceptance of the disability.
    c. drawing parents into the intervention process.
    d. helping parents to recognize the child's strengths and abilities.
    e. all of the above

21. The most important aspect in metacognition for students is their increasing ability to
    a. monitor their own learning strategies.
    b. discriminate by listening.
    c. comprehend non-verbal communication.
    d. design webbing for independent study.
    e. use social skills appropriately.

22. In order for children to be considered retarded under the AAMR definition, they must exhibit
    a. subnormal intellectual functioning.
    b. deficits in adaptive behaviour.
    c. manifestation during the developmental period.
    d. all of the above
    e. any two of the above

23. The terms *gifted, creative,* and *talented* are often used interchangeably although the meanings are slightly different. The difference in meanings occurs because
    a. children who are gifted are not necessarily talented.
    b. not all children who are gifted are highly creative.
    c. giftedness is a prerequisite to talent.
    d. a person may be talented only in one area, and not be academically gifted.
    e. all of the above

24. According to the text, the two best predictors of delinquency are
    a. measures of parental family management techniques and child problem behaviour.
    b. a lack of entrenched societal norms and values and lack of a coherent set of values.
    c. poor self-regulation of behaviour and an innate criminal personality.
    d. learning disabilities and academic difficulties.
    e. grade retention and reading difficulties.

25. Figures on the prevalence of behavioural disorders in the school-aged population show that
    a. girls outnumber boys in every category.
    b. lack of teacher tolerance may be inflating prevalence estimates.
    c. the great proportion of students fall into the severe category of behaviour disorders.
    d. prevalence is highest during the secondary-school years.
    e. numbers are actually on the decrease.

26. The most important criterion that allows a person membership in the deaf community is
    a. having a severe to profound hearing loss.
    b. using ASL as the primary mode of communication.
    c. attending, or having attended, a residential school.
    d. having a congenital hearing loss.
    e. all of the above

27. The braille cell contains
    a. nine dots, three high and three wide.
    b. six dots, three high and two wide.
    c. raised print and dots.
    d. raised dots and dashes.
    e. twelve dots, three high and four wide.

28. Functional skills can also be referred to as ________ skills.
    a. self-help
    b. adaptive
    c. independent living
    d. life
    e. all of the above

29. In the field of intellectual disabilities, we can say generally that
    a. the field has expanded dramatically in recent years.
    b. an increasing interest in the field is currently being witnessed.
    c. children with mild intellectual disabilities can nearly always be identified before they reach school.
    d. with formal schooling, the prevalence of mental retardation tends to decrease.
    e. none of the above

30. An observational assessment approach in which people from different disciplines focus on various domains of a child's functioning is referred to as
    a. arena testing.
    b. dynamic assessment.
    c. developmental assessment.
    d. readiness measures.
    e. multiple viewpoint testing.

31. The instructional program for students with moderate levels of intellectual disabilities should focus on the development of
    a. functional skills.
    b. abstract thinking abilities.
    c. advanced communication.
    d. academic skills.
    e. metacognitive strategies.

32. By the time that they reach their sixth decade, people with Down syndrome very often suffer from
    a. Alzheimer's disease.
    b. leukemia.
    c. cancer.
    d. heart disease.
    e. all of the above

33. The "six-hour retarded child" is the youngster who
    a. is a habitual truant.
    b. fails to meet the demands of the school but functions adequately elsewhere.
    c. is a perpetual behavioural problem in school.
    d. spends most of the school day in the resource room.
    e. all of the above

34. What do each of these acronyms or short forms stand for?
    a. AAMR
    b. CACL
    c. CNIB
    d. ACLD
    e. DSM-IV
    f. LRE
    g. dB

35. In North America, bilingual education for students who are deaf uses two languages. These are ______ and ______.

36. The most common screening procedure for hearing impairment is the _____ test.

37. Of functional causes, underlying organic causes, or educational functioning and achievement, educational researchers assess differences in children with exceptional conditions in terms of ______.

38. When gifted and non-gifted adolescents and young adults are compared, it is the ________ group that is likely to show more changes in career plans.

39. When teaching skills to a child with multiple disabilities, the most critical element is that the skills be ________.

40. Kate, a child with multiple disabilities, requires special positioning and handling. The teacher would learn the techniques from a(n) ________ therapist.

41. Reading with the Optacon and with braille are much the same process. T F

42. For students with special needs, the most fundamental social change of recent decades has been a recognition of educational equity together with the provision of equal access to an education in the manner most appropriate to their needs. T F

43. Type II diabetics produce quantities of insulin but they do not use it efficiently. T F

44. There are both philosophical and pragmatic differences between mainstreaming and inclusive schooling. On a pragmatic basis, the major difference that defines inclusive schooling is that the stress is on social interaction, not academics. T F

Total /50

Appendix: Answer Key

Chapter 1: Introduction to Children Who Are Exceptional

Multiple-choice questions

1. d	6. e	11. b	16. d a c b e
2. e	7. c	12. e	
3. c	8. c	13. a	
4. c	9. e	14. b	
5. a	10. b	15. a	

Recall questions

1. special education
2. mild intellectual disabilities, learning disabilities, mild behaviour disorders, mild hearing impairment, mild visual impairment; infantile autism, schizophrenia, severe and profound disabilities, deafness, blindness
3. low
4. advocate
5. Leo
6. adaptive behaviour
7. epidemiology
8. 2 001 400
9. support
10. habilitation

True–false questions

1. F	4. F	7. F	10. F
2. T	5. F	8. F	
3. T	6. F	9. F	

Chapter 2: Issues and Trends in Canadian Special Education

Multiple-choice questions

1. b	6. a	11. c
2. a	7. b	12. b
3. c	8. c	13. e
4. a	9. e	14. a
5. e	10. d	15. e

16. a. Council for Exceptional Children
    b. least restrictive environment
    c. Regular Education Initiative
    d. Individual Education Plan
    e. Wechsler Intelligence Scale for Children, III

Recall questions

1. WISC-III, WISC-R, Stanford-Binet
2. intervention
3. assessment
4. place the child before the disability
5. PL 94-142
6. infant, preschool
7. curriculum-based assessment
8. all, except Nova Scotia and PEI
9. objectives
10. Elwood, Eaton

True–false questions

1. F	4. T	7. F	10. F
2. T	5. F	8. T	
3. T	6. F	9. F	

Chapter 3: Risk Factors and Children at Risk

Multiple-choice questions

1. b	6. a	11. b	16. a b d c e
2. e	7. d	12. e	
3. a	8. a	13. e	
4. a	9. c	14. e	
5. b	10. d	15. b	

Recall questions

1. PKU, galactosemia
2. cystic fibrosis
3. encephalitis
4. cytogenetics
5. intrinsic, extrinsic
6. genetic defects
7. 21
8. lack of oxygen
9. primary or secondary
10. amniocentesis

True–false questions

1. T	4. F	7. T	10.T
2. F	5. F	8. T	
3. F	6. F	9. F	

End Test 1

Multiple-choice questions

1. e	6. b	11. a
2. c	7. d	12. a
3. c	8. e	13. c
4. d	9. e	14. b
5. a	10. a	15. e

Matching questions

16. a b d e c
17. a e d b c
18. b e d c a
19. a e b d c

True–false questions

20. T	25. F	30. T
21. F	26. F	31. F
22. T	27. F	32. F
23. F	28. F	33. F
24. T	29. T	34. T

Chapter 4: Children with Speech and Language Differences

Multiple-choice questions

1. a	6. a	11. a	16. b a d e c
2. e	7. d	12. b	
3. b	8. a	13. b	
4. e	9. c	14. a	
5. b	10. c	15. a	

Recall questions

1. echolalia
2. structural inadequacies, neurological problems, hearing impairments
3. holophrasic, telegraphic
4. stuttering, dysfluency
5. pragmatics
6. grammatical, naturalistic
7. voice
8. articulation or phonological
9. respiration, eating
10. Limited English proficient

True–false questions

1. T	4. T	7. F	10. T
2. T	5. T	8. F	
3. F	6. T	9. F	

Chapter 5: Children with Learning Disabilities

Multiple-choice questions

1. c	6. b	11. d	16. e c b d a
2 e	7. c	12. c	
3. a	8. e	13. d	
4. a	9. e	14. a	
5. e	10. e	15. c	

Recall questions

1. impulsivity, distractibility, hyperemotionalism, hyperactivity
2. directionality, laterality
3. learned helplessness or outward locus of control
4. task analysis
5. discrimination
6. mixed symbols
7. Feingold
8. dysgraphia
9. "poor teaching"
10. metacognition

True–false questions

1. T	4. F	7. F	10. F
2. F	5. T	8. F	
3. F	6. F	9. F	

Chapter 6: Children with Intellectual Disabilities

Multiple-choice questions

1. a	6. b	11. e	16. e d a c b
2. b	7. a	12. b	
3. a	8. e	13. e	
4. e	9. c	14. a	
5. a	10. d	15. a	

Recall questions

1. Wechsler Intelligence Scale for Children III
2. IQ, adaptive behaviour
3. mild
4. learning disabled, emotionally disturbed, behaviourally disordered
5. locus of control
6. profound
7. decrease dependence on others, increase awareness of the environment, teach self-help skills, push achievement higher
8. self-stimulating, self-mutilation, or self-injurious
9. non-organic
10. genetic counselling, primary prevention

True–false questions

1. T	4. F	7. F	10. T
2. T	5. F	8. T	
3. T	6. F	9. F	

End Test 2

Multiple-choice questions

1. e	6. a	11. c	16. a	21. d
2. b	7. e	12. b	17. d	22. e
3. b	8. e	13. e	18. d	23. b
4. b	9. b	14. c	19. d	24. e
5. b	10. d	15. b	20. b	25. c

Matching questions

26. a d b c e
27. a c b d
28. e a d c b

True–false questions

29. F	33. F	37. F
30. T	34. T	38. F
31. T	35. F	39. T
32. T	36. F	

Chapter 7: Children and Youth with Behavioural Disorders

Multiple-choice questions

1. a	6. a	11. d	16. f a b d e c
2. b	7. a	12. a	
3. a	8. a	13. b	
4. d	9. b	14. d	
5. d	10. a	15. b	

Recall questions

1. socialized aggression, immaturity, motor excess, anxiety and withdrawal, psychoses
2. holistic
3. behavioural
4. conduct disordered
5. aggression
6. Diagnostic and Statistical Manual; American Psychiatric Association
7. psychothereupetic or psycho-educational
8. play therapy
9. reinforcement
10. bed wetting

True–false questions

1. T	4. F	7. T	10. F
2. F	5. F	8. T	
3. F	6. F	9. F	

Chapter 8: Children Who Are Gifted, Talented, and Creative

Multiple-choice questions

1. a	6. c	11. b	16. a b c d
2. e	7. a	12. c	
3. b	8. e	13. a	
4. d	9. a	14. b	
5. a	10. b	15. c	

Recall questions

1. Lewis Terman
2. 120, operations, contents, products
3. good ability, creativity, high task commitment
4. precocity
5. uneven development
6. they require special education to reach their potential
7. Guilford, Gardner
8. talent
9. literature, science, maths, arts; handwriting and mechanical areas
10. WISC-III

True–false questions

1. T	4. F	7. F	10. T
2. T	5. F	8. T	
3. F	6. T	9. F	

End Test 3

Multiple-choice questions

1. a	8. e	15. e	23. b
2. e	9. b	16. a	24. b
3. a	10. b	17. e	25. e
4. a	11. b	18. e	26. c
5. e	12. a	19. e	27. c
6. b	13. b	20. a	28. a
7. e	14. e	21. b	29. a
		22. b	30. c

Matching questions

31. a b e d c
32. a e b c d
33. a d b e c

True–false questions

34. T	36. T	38. T
35. F	37. T	

Chapter 9: Children with Hearing Impairments

Multiple-choice questions

1. c	6. c	11. b	16. e a d c b
2. a	7. b	12. d	
3. b	8. b	13. a	
4. d	9. b	14. b	
5. b	10. e	15. e	

Recall questions

1. ASL, English
2. decibels, hertz
3. communication mode
4. auditory atresia
5. middle
6. impedence
7. FM
8. profound
9. total communication
10. cochlea

True–false questions

1. F	4. F	7. F	10. F
2. F	5. F	8. F	
3. F	6. F	9. F	

Chapter 10: Children with Visual Impairments

Multiple-choice questions

1. d	6. c	11. a	16. c a d b e
2. b	7. a	12. d	
3. d	8. a	13. b	
4. c	9. d	14. a	
5. a	10. c	15. c	

Recall questions

1. oculomotor
2. myopia, hyperopia, astigmatism, presbyopia
3. hyperopia
4. lacrimal
5. visual field
6. Snellen
7. albinism
8. retinitis pigmentosa
9. white cane
10. de l'Épée; braille

True–false questions

1. F	4. F	7. T	10. F
2. F	5. T	8. F	
3. F	6. F	9. F	

End Test 4

Multiple-choice questions

1. e	7. c	13. e	19. a
2. d	8. c	14. d	20. a
3. e	9. a	15. d	21. b
4. e	10. e	16. a	22. c
5. e	11. d	17. b	23. c
6. e	12. a	18. d	24. a
			25. d

Matching questions

26. e a b c d
27. c e d b a
28. b d a e c
29. a e d b c
30. e a d b c

Chapter 11: Children with Special Health Care Needs

Multiple-choice questions

1. b	6. a	11. b	16. e a d b c
2. d	7. b	12. a	
3. a	8. a	13. d	
4. a	9. e	14. c	
5. a	10. c	15. a	

Recall questions

1. contactants, ingestants, injectants
2. atrophy, dystrophy
3. musculoskeletal impairments
4. physical abuse, neglect, emotional abuse
5. general classrooms
6. cystic fibrosis
7. red blood cells
8. muscles
9. Type II
10. asthma

True–false questions

1. T	4. F	7. T	10. F
2. F	5. F	8. F	
3. T	6. F	9. T	

Chapter 12: Children with Neurological Disabilities

Multiple-choice questions

1. b	6. e	11. e	16. e b c a d
2. d	7. e	12. a	
3. a	8. a	13. c	
4. d	9. d	14. a	
5. e	10. d	15. a	

Recall questions

1. speech
2. with myelomeningocele
3. hydrocephalus
4. spastic, athetoid, ataxia, tremor, rigidity
5. an electrical discharge in the brain
6. athetoid
7. corpus callosum
8. prosthetic; orthotic
9. petit mal
10. Boston

True–false questions

1. F	4. F	7. F	10. T
2. T	5. T	8. F	
3. F	6. F	9. F	

Chapter 13: Children with Pervasive Developmental Disorders

Multiple-choice questions

1. b	6. c	11. a	16. d a b e c
2. a	7. a	12. d	
3. e	8. b	13. e	
4. a	9. e	14. a	
5. e	10. c	15. a	

Recall questions

1. adolescence
2. a persistent, stereotypic, repetitive mannerism
3. autism
4. profound mental retardation, psychoses, autism, multiple disabilities
5. 30 months
6. genetics, toxemias, birth complications
7. Eugen Bleuler
8. schizophrenia
9. stimulating
10. neologisms

True–false questions

1. F	4. F	7. F	10. T
2. F	5. F	8. F	
3. F	6. T	9. T	

Chapter 14: Children with Severe and Multiple Disabilities

Multiple-choice questions

1. e	6. c	11. d	16. b a e c d
2. a	7. d	12. c	
3. a	8. e	13. e	
4. d	9. c	14. b	
5. e	10. b	15. e	

Recall questions

1. primary disability
2. Usher's syndrome
3. speech/language
4. decreasing
5. five
6. teacher
7. developmental
8. functional
9. prelinguistic
10. etiology

True–false questions

1. T	4. F	7. F	10. F
2. F	5. F	8. F	
3. T	6. F	9. T	

End Test 5

Multiple-choice questions

1. a	7. d	13. a	19. e	25. e
2. a	8. a	14. e	20. a	
3. c	9. d	15. e	21. e	
4. b	10. d	16. c	22. d	
5. b	11. b	17. d	23. a	
6. a	12. d	18. d	24. b	

Matching questions

26. b d c a e
27. a c b d e
28. e d c b a

Chapter 15: Early Intervention

Multiple-choice questions

1. a	6. d	11. c	16. e a b c d
2. d	7. b	12. e	
3. d	8. b	13. d	
4. e	9. e	14. e	
5. a	10. e	15. a	

Recall questions

1. death
2. stress
3. PL 99-457
4. they have not yet faced academic tasks
5. home visiting
6. shock
7. low
8. transition
9. family needs
10. rating scales, readiness measures, basic skills inventories

True–false questions

1. F	4. F	7. T	10. F
2. T	5. F	8. F	
3. T	6. F	9. F	

Chapter 16: Adolescents and Young Adults

Multiple-choice questions

1. b	6. e	11. b
2. b	7. c	12. a
3. e	8. e	13. a
4. b	9. a	14. e
5. e	10. e	15. e

Recall questions

1. Becker's Vocational Interest Inventory, Transition Competence Battery
2. eighteen
3. the movement from one service delivery system to another
4. that have meaning and relevance to the learner
5. low
6. vocational evaluation
7. any person who leaves secondary school for any reason prior to graduation
8. IEP
9. retention in grade, poor reading
10. transition

True–false questions

1. F	4. F	7. T	10. F
2. F	5. F	8. T	
3. T	6. F	9. F	

End Test 6

Multiple-choice questions

1. a	9. a	17. e	25. b	33. b
2. c	10. a	18. d	26. b	
3. a	11. e	19. e	27. b	
4. e	12. e	20. e	28. e	
5. a	13. d	21. a	29. e	
6. a	14. a	22. d	30. a	
7. e	15. a	23. e	31. a	
8. c	16. c	24. a	32. a	

34. a. American Association on Mental Retardation
    b. Canadian Association for Community Living
    c. Canadian National Institute for the Blind
    d. Association for Children with Learning Disabilities
    e. Diagnostic and Statistical Manual, 4th edition
    f. Least restrictive environment
    g. decibel

Recall questions

35. English, ASL
36. sweep
37. functioning and achievement
38. gifted
39. functional

True–false questions

40. F	42. T
41. T	43. F